Music Online For

MW00909633

Top Sites for Music Online

Site name	URL	Description
MP3.com	www.mp3.com	News, information, and MP3 files
Classical.Net	www.classical.net	Classical music
Hyperreal	www.hyperreal.org	Electronica music
Jazz Online	www.jazzonline.com	Hangout for jazz lovers
SonicNet	www.sonicnet.com	News, radio, chats, and cybercast events
Support Online Hip-Hop	www.sohh.com	Hip-hop music and culture
iMusic	www.imusic.com	Music information and community
Ticketmaster.com	www.Ticketmaster.com	Concert tickets

Top Sites for Live Music

Site name	URL	Description
House of Blues	www.hob.com	Rock, pop, blues, and R&B
L.A. Live	www.lalive.com	Alternative rock from Los Angeles
Rolling Stone Webcasts	www.rollingstone.com	Rock and pop shows
KCRW	www.kcrw.com	Eclectic radio performances
MTV	www.mtv.com	Video performances
Real Concert Guide	http://realguide.real.com/music/?s=concertseries	Big guide to live happenings

For Dummies®: Bestselling Book Series for Beginners

Music Online For Dummies®

Cheat Sheet

Tips for Buying Music Online

- Search the Federal Trade Commission's site (`www.ftc.gov`) for info about fraudulent dealers.
- Never disclose personal passwords or credit card numbers to unknown parties.
- Use a secure server for transactions.
- Always pay with credit cards.
- When buying or selling on an auction site, take advantage of escrow services.
- Avoid promotions that seem too good to be true; they usually are.

Top Music Magazines Online

Site name	URL	Description
Rolling Stone.com	`www.rollingstone.com`	General music news and information
Spin	`www.spin.com`	General music news and information
Musician	`www.musicianmag.com`	For serious musicians
Alternative Press	`www.ap.com`	Alternative, hip-hop, and electronica
Circus	`www.circusmagazine.com`	Heavy metal
Q	`www.qonline.co.uk`	Pop music culture from England
Relix	`www.relix.com`	Acid rock from San Francisco
Vibe	`www.vibe.com`	Urban and hip-hop music and culture
Billboard	`www.billboard.com`	Music business magazine

For Dummies®: Bestselling Book Series for Beginners

Music Online

FOR

DUMMIES®

Music Online FOR DUMMIES®

by David Kushner

IDG Books Worldwide, Inc.
An International Data Group Company

Foster City, CA ◆ Chicago, IL ◆ Indianapolis, IN ◆ New York, NY

Music Online For Dummies®

Published by
IDG Books Worldwide, Inc.
An International Data Group Company
919 E. Hillsdale Blvd.
Suite 400
Foster City, CA 94404
www.idgbooks.com (IDG Books Worldwide Web site)
www.dummies.com (Dummies Press Web site)

Library of Congress Control Number: 00-101845

ISBN: 0-7645-0705-2

Printed in the United States of America

10 9 8 7 6 5 4 3 2 1

1O/RS/QX/QQ/IN

Distributed in the United States by IDG Books Worldwide, Inc.

Distributed by CDG Books Canada Inc. for Canada; by Transworld Publishers Limited in the United Kingdom; by IDG Norge Books for Norway; by IDG Sweden Books for Sweden; by IDG Books Australia Publishing Corporation Pty. Ltd. for Australia and New Zealand; by TransQuest Publishers Pte Ltd. for Singapore, Malaysia, Thailand, Indonesia, and Hong Kong; by Gotop Information Inc. for Taiwan; by ICG Muse, Inc. for Japan; by Intersoft for South Africa; by Eyrolles for France; by International Thomson Publishing for Germany, Austria and Switzerland; by Distribuidora Cuspide for Argentina; by LR International for Brazil; by Galileo Libros for Chile; by Ediciones ZETA S.C.R. Ltda. for Peru; by WS Computer Publishing Corporation, Inc., for the Philippines; by Contemporanea de Ediciones for Venezuela; by Express Computer Distributors for the Caribbean and West Indies; by Micronesia Media Distributor, Inc. for Micronesia; by Chips Computadoras S.A. de C.V. for Mexico; by Editorial Norma de Panama S.A. for Panama; by American Bookshops for Finland.

For general information on IDG Books Worldwide's books in the U.S., please call our Consumer Customer Service department at 800-762-2974. For reseller information, including discounts and premium sales, please call our Reseller Customer Service department at 800-434-3422.

For information on where to purchase IDG Books Worldwide's books outside the U.S., please contact our International Sales department at 317-596-5530 or fax 317-572-4002.

For consumer information on foreign language translations, please contact our Customer Service department at 1-800-434-3422, fax 317-572-4002, or e-mail rights@idgbooks.com.

For information on licensing foreign or domestic rights, please phone +1-650-653-7098.

For sales inquiries and special prices for bulk quantities, please contact our Order Services department at 800-434-3422 or write to the address above.

For information on using IDG Books Worldwide's books in the classroom or for ordering examination copies, please contact our Educational Sales department at 800-434-2086 or fax 317-572-4005.

For press review copies, author interviews, or other publicity information, please contact our Public Relations department at 650-653-7000 or fax 650-653-7500.

For authorization to photocopy items for corporate, personal, or educational use, please contact Copyright Clearance Center, 222 Rosewood Drive, Danvers, MA 01923, or fax 978-750-4470.

is a registered trademark under exclusive license to IDG Books Worldwide, Inc. from International Data Group, Inc.

About the Author

David Kushner writes frequently about digital and popular culture. He is a contributing editor for *Spin* magazine and a frequent contributor to *The New York Times, Rolling Stone, Yahoo! Internet Life, Salon, Feed, The Village Voice,* and *Entertainment Weekly*. His column on digital music appears regularly on RollingStone.com. Prior to becoming a full-time journalist, Kushner was a senior producer and writer for SonicNet, the award-winning music Web site. Kushner lives in Brooklyn, New York, where he is working on a book about computer gamers.

ABOUT IDG BOOKS WORLDWIDE

Welcome to the world of IDG Books Worldwide.

IDG Books Worldwide, Inc., is a subsidiary of International Data Group, the world's largest publisher of computer-related information and the leading global provider of information services on information technology. IDG was founded more than 30 years ago by Patrick J. McGovern and now employs more than 9,000 people worldwide. IDG publishes more than 290 computer publications in over 75 countries. More than 90 million people read one or more IDG publications each month.

Launched in 1990, IDG Books Worldwide is today the #1 publisher of best-selling computer books in the United States. We are proud to have received eight awards from the Computer Press Association in recognition of editorial excellence and three from Computer Currents' First Annual Readers' Choice Awards. Our best-selling ...For Dummies® series has more than 50 million copies in print with translations in 31 languages. IDG Books Worldwide, through a joint venture with IDG's Hi-Tech Beijing, became the first U.S. publisher to publish a computer book in the People's Republic of China. In record time, IDG Books Worldwide has become the first choice for millions of readers around the world who want to learn how to better manage their businesses.

Our mission is simple: Every one of our books is designed to bring extra value and skill-building instructions to the reader. Our books are written by experts who understand and care about our readers. The knowledge base of our editorial staff comes from years of experience in publishing, education, and journalism — experience we use to produce books to carry us into the new millennium. In short, we care about books, so we attract the best people. We devote special attention to details such as audience, interior design, use of icons, and illustrations. And because we use an efficient process of authoring, editing, and desktop publishing our books electronically, we can spend more time ensuring superior content and less time on the technicalities of making books.

You can count on our commitment to deliver high-quality books at competitive prices on topics you want to read about. At IDG Books Worldwide, we continue in the IDG tradition of delivering quality for more than 30 years. You'll find no better book on a subject than one from IDG Books Worldwide.

John Kilcullen
Chairman and CEO
IDG Books Worldwide, Inc.

Eighth Annual Computer Press Awards ➢1992

Ninth Annual Computer Press Awards ➢1993

Tenth Annual Computer Press Awards ➢1994

Eleventh Annual Computer Press Awards ➢1995

IDG is the world's leading IT media, research and exposition company. Founded in 1964, IDG had 1997 revenues of $2.05 billion and has more than 9,000 employees worldwide. IDG offers the widest range of media options that reach IT buyers in 75 countries representing 95% of worldwide IT spending. IDG's diverse product and services portfolio spans six key areas including print publishing, online publishing, expositions and conferences, market research, education and training, and global marketing services. More than 90 million people read one or more of IDG's 290 magazines and newspapers, including IDG's leading global brands — Computerworld, PC World, Network World, Macworld and the Channel World family of publications. IDG Books Worldwide is one of the fastest-growing computer book publishers in the world, with more than 700 titles in 36 languages. The "...For Dummies®" series alone has more than 50 million copies in print. IDG offers online users the largest network of technology-specific Web sites around the world through IDG.net (http://www.idg.net), which comprises more than 225 targeted Web sites in 55 countries worldwide. International Data Corporation (IDC) is the world's largest provider of information technology data, analysis and consulting, with research centers in over 41 countries and more than 400 research analysts worldwide. IDG World Expo is a leading producer of more than 168 globally branded conferences and expositions in 35 countries including E3 (Electronic Entertainment Expo), Macworld Expo, ComNet, Windows World Expo, ICE (Internet Commerce Expo), Agenda, DEMO, and Spotlight. IDG's training subsidiary, ExecuTrain, is the world's largest computer training company, with more than 230 locations worldwide and 785 training courses. IDG Marketing Services helps industry-leading IT companies build international brand recognition by developing global integrated marketing programs via IDG's print, online and exposition products worldwide. Further information about the company can be found at www.idg.com. 1/26/00

Dedication

To Sue, for keeping me plugged in.

Author's Acknowledgments

Thanks to my friends, my family, my editors, and Shin Fat — the best band that never was.

Publisher's Acknowledgments

We're proud of this book; please register your comments through our IDG Books Worldwide Online Registration Form located at `http://my2cents.dummies.com`.

Some of the people who helped bring this book to market include the following:

Acquisitions, Editorial, and Media Development

Senior Project Editor: Jeanne S. Criswell

Acquisitions Editor: Steven H. Hayes

Senior Copy Editor: Ted Cains

Proof Editors: Teresa Artman, Dwight Ramsey

Technical Editor: Derek Sivers

Permissions Editor: Carmen Krikorian

Associate Media Development Specialist: Megan Decraene

Editorial Manager: Rev Mengle

Media Development Manager: Heather Heath Dismore

Editorial Assistant: Candace Nicholson

Production

Project Coordinator: Maridee Ennis

Layout and Graphics: Gabriele McCann, Brent Savage, Julie Trippetti, Erin Zeltner

Proofreaders: Corey Bowen, Susan Moritz, Marianne Santy, York Production Services, Inc.

Indexer: York Production Services, Inc.

Special Help: Ed Adams, Timothy J. Borek, Rebekah Mancilla, Rev Mengle

---

General and Administrative

IDG Books Worldwide, Inc.: John Kilcullen, CEO

IDG Books Technology Publishing Group: Richard Swadley, Senior Vice President and Publisher; Walter R. Bruce III, Vice President and Publisher; Joseph Wikert, Vice President and Publisher; Mary Bednarek, Vice President and Director, Product Development; Andy Cummings, Publishing Director, General User Group; Mary C. Corder, Editorial Director; Barry Pruett, Publishing Director

IDG Books Consumer Publishing Group: Roland Elgey, Senior Vice President and Publisher; Kathleen A. Welton, Vice President and Publisher; Kevin Thornton, Acquisitions Manager; Kristin A. Cocks, Editorial Director

IDG Books Internet Publishing Group: Brenda McLaughlin, Senior Vice President and Publisher; Sofia Marchant, Online Marketing Manager

IDG Books Production for Branded Press: Debbie Stailey, Director of Production; Cindy L. Phipps, Manager of Project Coordination, Production Proofreading, and Indexing; Tony Augsburger, Manager of Prepress, Reprints, and Systems; Laura Carpenter, Production Control Manager; Shelley Lea, Supervisor of Graphics and Design; Debbie J. Gates, Production Systems Specialist; Robert Springer, Supervisor of Proofreading; Trudy Coler, Page Layout Manager; Troy Barnes, Page Layout Supervisor, Kathie Schutte, Senior Page Layout Supervisor; Michael Sullivan, Production Supervisor

Packaging and Book Design: Patty Page, Manager, Promotions Marketing

◆

The publisher would like to give special thanks to Patrick J. McGovern, without whom this book would not have been possible.

◆

Contents at a Glance

Cartoons at a Glance

By Rich Tennant

"Guess who found a Kiss merchandise site on the Web while you were gone?"

page 71

"Would it ruin the online concert experience if I vacuumed the mosh pit between songs?"

page 197

INTENSE BUT UNINFORMED AUDIOPHILE BILLY WIGGINS ENJOYS HIS CUSTOM BURNED CD COLLECTION OF DIAL UP MODEM WARBLES

page 145

"I hope you're doing something online. An indie band like yours shouldn't just be playing street corners."

page 247

"It's bad enough he fell asleep waiting for a huge music file to download into his music folder, but wait until he finds out he hit the 'SEND' button instead of selecting 'DOWNLOAD'."

page 9

Fax: 978-546-7747
E-mail: richtennant@the5thwave.com
World Wide Web: www.the5thwave.com

Table of Contents

Introduction

The Internet Killed the Radio Star

Being a music fan used to be easy.

Millions of years ago, you'd just bang a couple of rocks together, smack some bones on your head, and — voilà! — you'd have an instant symphony.

In this millennium, you may feel like you need to be a rocket scientist to know how to navigate the burgeoning worlds of music — online and offline.

Of course, you can easily enjoy your favorite albums and artists the old-fashioned way:

- You can slide a CD, a tape, or even a dusty old piece of vinyl onto your stereo.
- You can head down to the mall to buy a concert ticket or a T-shirt.
- You can flip on the stereo and tune in to your favorite radio station.

But, these days, that's like listening out of only one speaker.

To get the most out of the music world, to stay on the cutting edge, to find the freshest information and the newest music, and to participate in the coolest communities, you have to go online.

The Internet won't ever replace the experience of listening to your favorite artist in concert, but for fans and musicians alike, the Net is sure to enhance the musical experience. All you need to know is how to access the online music world.

That's where this book comes in.

Cyberspace Oddity: The Rise of Music Online

Over the past few years, music online has become a way of life for fans and artists across the world. And, contrary to popular belief, it's not just a techie thing.

Yes, you can find newfangled formats like MP3 that enable you to listen to near CD-quality music straight off the Net. And, yes, to exploit MP3, you need a certain amount of technical know-how. But that's just one slice of the pie.

More than anything else, music online is about community. After all, the Net isn't just a bunch of chips and wires, to paraphrase Charlton Heston in the movie *Soylent Green*, "The Net is people!"

The rise of music online — whether you're talking about a Sonic Youth news-group or a Hank Williams, Jr., Web ring — is all about people who want to share either their love for a specific band or musical genre, or even a bit of their own music. And, of course, you can find plenty of people who want to sell you stuff.

When you enter the world of music online, you're not just tuning into soft-ware; you're entering a community.

The Great Promises

When most people hear that I wrote a book about music online, they often say something like, "I hear you can download any album you want online for free."

This assumption is understandable. After all, the Net has long been about freedom — freedom of expression and information. And, for quite a long time, the Net has been about freedom of music. From the beginning, intrepid indie bands have uploaded their music tracks for equally intrepid fans to peruse.

These days, with the rise of MP3, the assumptions have gone a bit haywire. You've no doubt seen the hype about the so-called revolution of music online — about how record stores, record labels, and any of the familiar stuff you find offline will disappear.

That's what the hype says, but it couldn't be further from the truth.

The Reality Check

The good news is that the online world offers a bunch of cool stuff — but it doesn't offer *everything*. Artists still need to make money, as do record labels, record stores, concert halls, T-shirt makers, and . . . you get the idea. So if *everything* was online, then a lot of people would be out of business.

Maybe a better way to think about the Net is that it gives us *access* to music. And the access is pretty unbelievable. Here are just a few things you can do:

- Find out the date of the next Smashing Pumpkins concert.
- Buy tickets.
- Talk with other fans.
- Trade music.
- Read interviews.
- Listen to new songs.

You can do absolutely everything *except* download albums for free. Doing so would be illegal (see Chapter 5 for more information on copyright). And if you're the Smashing Pumpkins — a nice enough band from Chicago who wants to keep making a living through their music — such copyright violations pretty much stink.

Sometimes, even online, you just gotta pay.

But most of the time — yes! — you don't.

Who Are You? Who? Who? Who? Who?

If you're reading this book, then you're one of three types of people: a music fan, a musician, or both. Fortunately, you don't have to go to graduate school to be any of these (although, if you're still trying to master sandpaper blocks, it might not be a bad idea).

The last thing you are when it comes to music is a dummy. You know what you like, what you don't like, what makes you shimmy your shins, what makes you shed a tear. Hey, if you find yourself reaching for a box of tissues every time you hear "I'm Too Sexy for My Shirt," who am I to argue?

I'm betting that if you shelled out the cash for this book, then you're a certifiable genius of your own musical likes and dislikes:

- Hip-hop
- Rock
- Jazz
- Pop
- Techno
- Country
- Blues
- Heavy metal speed polka???
- Whatever

If you dig it, that's all that matters. However, you may need a little help in navigating the vastness of the music online world.

In this book, I take you on a tour of music online without casting aspersions on any particular form of music (assuming, of course, that you're not a fan of my former band, Shin Fat). The nice thing is that no matter what kind of music you like, you can find a way to access it online.

I also assume that you have at least a basic knowledge of online life: You know how to connect and access the Web. You know the basics of searching online for information. You know about e-mail. That's about all you need at this point. With your musical smarts and eagerness to explore the electronic frontiers, you're set to go.

With this book, you can do the following:

- Find sites on your favorite artists.
- Buy CDs, concert tickets, t-shirts, and other merchandise.
- Find, listen to, and record MP3s.
- Tune in to Net concerts and radio stations.
- Be your own online DJ.
- Join or run your own online music community.

Sound good?

Let's rock! Or, um, if you prefer, let's polka!

How This Book Is Organized

Up until now, you've probably read this introduction straight through. Though you can surely proceed through the rest of the book that way, don't feel obliged to do so. I won't be offended if you skip around, scan, and peruse as need be.

In fact, I wrote this book so that you can splatter it with pizza stains as you feverishly flip for the specific chapter you need. That's what I would do.

I arrange topics in a categorical, somewhat systematic way so that you can jump to the section that pertains to your musical whim of the hour. Perhaps one night you need to hunt down some front-row Korn tickets or a Miles Davis T-shirt; maybe the next you need to find that elusive Backstreet Boys Net radio show.

I divide this book into five main parts to help you find your way. I also throw in a big, fat directory to music online sites, which includes all kinds of totally groovy artist sites, label sites, merchandise sites, music news sites, and anything else you can and can't think of right now. Here's how it all breaks down.

Part I: The Sound of Music Online

This part gets you prepped for the wild world of music online. You discover the range of experiences awaiting you on the Net. You also hotwire your PC with the right hardware and software so that it sounds kind of like that other listening device — the stereo.

Part II: Surfing Safari — Finding Music (and Music Stuff)

This part looks at how you can find all kinds of cool music and music stuff (read: merchandise) online. You learn the tricks of successful song-hunting. Plus, you get acquainted with the burgeoning world of e-shopping. And you discover how you can find one of the most fulfilling and helpful parts of the listening experience: other fans.

Part III: MmmmmmP3 Bop

This part talks about the art and science of listening to and creating MP3s. You get all the down and dirty details of using players, storing songs, and taking tunes on the road. You also dive into the domain of CD burners — the increasingly affordable hardware that lets you make your own CDs and CD-ROMs.

Part IV: Becoming a Net Radiohead

In this part, you find out what you need to do to enjoy the wide world of instant — or streaming — audio (and video) music: from radio stations in Berlin to hip hop concerts in Detroit.

Part V: The Part of Tens

This part explores the big questions that affect your present and future enjoyment of music online, from sharpening your focus as a song surfer to staying on top of important trends and issues.

Part VI: Music Online Directory

A handy, dandy directory of artist, label, record, news, and other music-related sites.

Conventions Used in This Book

This book may bend your ear, but I do my best to not bend your brain, too. To alert your cranium to new and potentially unwieldy information, I use the following conventions throughout the book:

- ✔ URLs and other online addresses are indicated like this:

    `www.dave.com`

- ✔ Hypertext links are underlined just as they appear in your Web browser.

- ✔ Words that you type, such as keywords and search terms, appear in **bold**, so that they're easy to distinguish. (For example, you may want to search for the rock group R.E.M. at your favorite search engine, so you'd type **R.E.M.** in the search field.)

- ✔ New terms are *italicized* the first time they appear. Usually, you find the term defined soon afterward.

Icons Used in This Book

While you're perusing this book, you'll come across some icons to help you find your way. When you see these symbols, you know you're getting the following info:

No, this icon doesn't mean that I'd like the check. The Remember icon tells you to pay close attention to a particularly meaty bit of information that can save you time and hassles down the line.

Argggh! The dreaded Technical Stuff icon! Head for the hills when you see this icon; it means that you're about to run into some nasty technical stuff that's sure to induce snoring. Read only if you have aspirations to be a computer geek.

This icon means that I've taken a break from writing to go shoot arrows in my personal archery range. Okay, not really. Actually, this icon signals a hot tip from me to you. Take note.

This little bomb means to watch out: The information that follows may have unexpected or thoroughly frustrating results. Proceed with caution.

Warnings, Foolish Assumptions, and Static

Don't forget this is music *online*, not offline. One of the biggest mistakes you can make is to expect the online world to emulate the offline world. As you may have already experienced, the offline and online worlds are entirely different planets. Though you can pop a CD into your stereo and play it in about five seconds, you can spend minutes — maybe even hours — getting your computer prepared for the online musical experience. Take a breather. After you get over the hurdle of figuring things out, they get easier.

Also, because of the evolving nature of music online, some of the software you download will be in *beta*, which means they're not quite ready for prime time. Programmers release programs before they're finished in order to get feedback from potential users.

Make sure you look closely at the version of a program before you start using it.

Can Get There From Here

Man, I could use a break, how about you? Think I'll boot up that new live song from the Radiohead concert site before I dive into the rest of the book. Feel free to jump in anywhere.

Part I
The Sound of Music Online

The 5th Wave

By Rich Tennant

"It's bad enough he fell asleep waiting for a huge music file to download into his music folder, but wait until he finds out he hit the 'SEND' button instead of selecting 'DOWNLOAD'."

In this part . . .

This part explores music on the Internet and looks at the necessary wares you need to get started.

You find out how to turn your PC into a stereo by adding the necessary sound cards and peripheral hardware. Then, you look at the necessary software — the players that bring the audio and video to life.

Chapter 1

The World Wide Stereo

In This Chapter

▶ Getting in touch with your inner music fan

▶ Exploring the seven wonders of the music online world

▶ Getting acquainted with the basics and background of music online

To understand the world of music online, you may want to think of it in terms of the growth of the World Wide Web. Before the Web, the Internet was just a bunch of scattered text and images that only academics, hardcore techies, and dogged research scientists really knew how to navigate.

Then along came a snazzy little program called a *Web browser,* which provided a user-friendly, magazine-style way to travel across the Internet. Instead of looking at messy lines of disorganized text, *Web surfers* can zoom through a multimedia landscape of images, pictures, and, yes, sounds. The Net was no longer just a place to do research; it could entertain you. It was ready for music.

In this chapter, I give you the basics of understanding the world of music online. I assume you already have Internet access and are savvy enough to get around on the Web. But if you need to brush up on your basic Internet skills, check out any of the Internet-related *For Dummies* books that you can find at your local bookstore.

The Art of Being a Music Fan

The best way to begin exploring music online is to think about how you operate offline. Whether you're aware of it or not, you probably have a pretty ritualized way of being a music fan. Almost everyone does. The better you understand your likes, dislikes, needs, and wants as a music fan offline, the better prepared you are to tackle the online world of music.

Take me, for example. I'm a typical music fan for a guy in his early 30s. Like most guys, I had a fairly intense obsession with my chosen rock gods, Rush. Yes, I'm a little embarrassed to admit it, but back then my bedroom was plastered with, at highest count, 13 posters of the power sci-fi rock trio. I had Rush t-shirts, Rush birthday cakes, and even my own stylish black Velcro Rush wallet.

By high school, I had gone from rabid fan to obsessive collector. I had to have everything Rush: magazine articles, backstage passes, and every album, single, and obscure recording. I had to have sweatshirts and programs, songbooks and baseball caps. If it had the name *Rush* on it, I had to have it.

Now, if I were a teenager in the year 2000, being an obsessive music fan would be much easier. Instead of schlepping out to the magazine store to rifle through the racks of rock magazines, I could just search for "Rush" on any Internet *search engine*, such as Yahoo! (www.yahoo.com) or AltaVista (www.altavista.com). Figure 1-1 shows the Yahoo! home page with **Rush** typed in the search field.

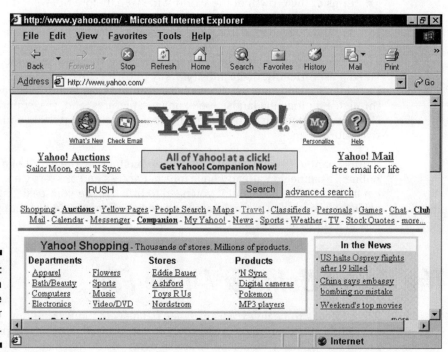

Figure 1-1:
Yahoo! is a good place to start your search.

Instead of biking from record store to record store, I could surf shopping sites like CDNOW (`www.cdnow.com`) or Tower Records (`www.towerrecords.com`) for available Rush recordings. Figure 1-2 shows what a search of CDNOW returned.

Instead of rummaging through flea markets and music stores for the complete *Moving Pictures* songbook, I could just call up a site like the On-line Guitar Archive (`www.olga.net`), as shown in Figure 1-3, and find all kinds of files to show me how to play just like Rush guitarist extraordinaire, Alex Lifeson. Well, almost like him anyway.

You can also find tablature for other instruments as well, such as drums, keyboard, and bass guitar. Just type in the kind of tablature you're looking for in Yahoo! to see a list of tablature sites. By the way, in case you don't already know, *tablature* is simply a transcription of a certain instrument's part in a song. For example, a guitar tablature of a song tells which chords to play and when to play them. Think sheet music.

Truth is, I'm not as obsessed with my childhood favorite band today as I used to be. But like any fan or musician, I'm still passionate about the music I enjoy.

If you can tap into the passion that got you into music in the first place, you can have all the more success and fulfillment when you venture out onto the Net.

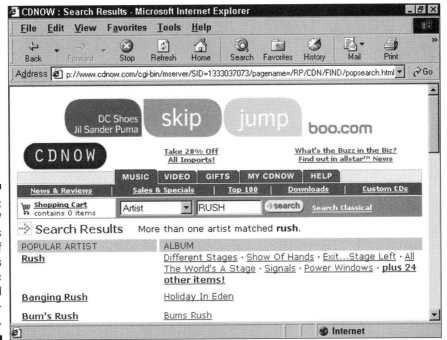

Figure 1-2: CDNOW sells hundreds of thousands of music CDs and merchandise.

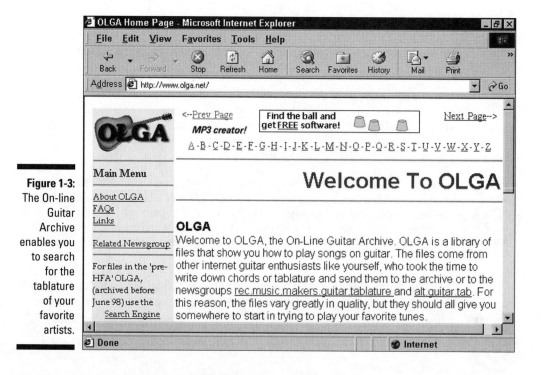

Figure 1-3:
The On-line
Guitar
Archive
enables you
to search
for the
tablature
of your
favorite
artists.

The Seven Wonders of the Music Online World

For the sake of your day-to-day explorations, you're most likely to deal in one of these seven areas:

- ✔ Audio
- ✔ Video
- ✔ Merchandise
- ✔ News and information
- ✔ Radio
- ✔ Concerts
- ✔ Community

Sounds kind of like the stuff you play around with offline, right? It is, plus more.

Audio

Music isn't much without audio. It's like the sky without air, the sea without water, the . . . um, help me out here, will you? Despite all the trimmings that go along with music — shirts, posters, magazines, and so on — the most important thing is the sound.

To exist online, music audio — or any audio for that matter — must be in a form that you can access and listen to on your computer. And that form would be . . . digital, baby!

If you really want to know, *digital music* is nothing much more than *binary code*, which essentially means strings of ones and zeros. When strung together in their own unique ways, the numbers can be decoded into, say, the love theme from *Titanic* or "Number of the Beast" by Iron Maiden — though, fortunately, never an accidental mix of the two.

For almost as long as people have been using computers, they've been coming up with different software programs that let you record and listen to music through these machines. You may have heard of *MIDI* or *WAV* files. These were among the first ways that musicians could convert their music into digital formats.

These days, music online takes one of two audio formats:

- ✔ streaming audio
- ✔ nonstreaming audio

Streaming audio

Streaming audio does exactly that — it streams fluidly, and almost instantly, onto your computer. Click a button and the music flows — that is, as soon as it can make its way over the often-congested Net wires and into your machine.

But you pay a price for the instant access. Streaming audio is not stored on your hard drive; instead, music plays from the *hosting site* — the Web site that stores the music file — and stops when the music's done. Basically, streaming audio is like a radio broadcast. You tune in and listen, and then the music fades away.

To listen to streaming audio — or any online audio, for that matter — you need to use special programs. Currently, the most popular program for streaming audio is RealPlayer from RealNetworks (www.real.com), which is available for both PC and Macintosh. Microsoft Windows and the Mac OS also come with their own audio players that can handle streaming audio: Windows Media Player and QuickTime Player, respectively.

Nonstreaming audio

Nonstreaming audio does not play instantly on your computer, as streaming audio does. Instead, you must download the music file to your hard drive and play the file later. The bad news is that you have to wait to hear the music. And how long you wait depends on how fast your Internet connection happens to be and how big the music file is. The good news is that after you download the music file, it's yours to play again and again.

The most popular form of nonstreaming audio today is *MP3*, a convenient acronym for a format with the unseemly name, *Mpeg Audio Layer 3*. To enjoy MP3, you simply download your chosen MP3 file and play it using an *MP3 player*. If you already have RealPlayer, Windows Media Player, or QuickTime Player (as mentioned previously for playing streaming audio), then you're set. You can also find dozens of other MP3 players on the Internet. See Chapters 9, 10, and 11 for more on MP3.

Video

Long before the Internet killed the radio star, music video was already digging the grave. Ever since MTV came on to the culture scene back in the early 1980s, you'd be hard-pressed to imagine a new pop song without an accompanying video.

You can find plenty of music video online, ranging from digital versions of the same fare you catch on MTV or VH1 to *indie* (or independent) footage these networks would never air. The Internet is truly the most democratic medium around these days, which means that anyone with the time and the will can participate.

This situation means that bands, even small garage ones like my former outfit, Shin Fat, can use their camcorder to shoot a video and just put it online (though I'm not so sure that anyone would want to see the lost footage for Shin Fat's epic track, "Whitefish").

Most online music video comes in the streaming variety, which means you need a special player, such as RealPlayer, Windows Media Player, or QuickTime Player. Also, with streaming video, just like with streaming audio, you can't save the video file to your hard drive for later viewing. To view the video again, you have to re-stream it to your computer.

Merchandise

Stuff. As any music fan knows, there's nothing like some good stuff to go along with the tunes. Here's just a smattering of the kinds of stuff you can get on the Internet:

- ✔ T-shirts
- ✔ Wallets
- ✔ Posters
- ✔ Figurines
- ✔ Computer games
- ✔ Banners
- ✔ Instruments
- ✔ Songbooks
- ✔ Magazines
- ✔ Books

You name it — the stuff is out there.

And, of course, you can find plenty of people who want to sell you the stuff. Electronic commerce sites — a.k.a. *e-commerce sites* — are filled with all kinds of music-related merchandise. Instead of having to wait for the next local concert to buy that latest Shania Twain jersey, you can just boot up a country music Web store.

Even better for some are the many sites offering concert tickets. Major ticket companies, such as Ticketmaster (www.ticketmaster.com) and Bass Tickets (www.basstickets.com), offer the option of purchasing concert tickets over the Net (see Figure 1-4). Buying tickets online is a fast way to get good seats while avoiding those annoying busy signals and long lines.

Radio

Music wouldn't be much without radio. Radio is how we tune in to the latest artists, pass the time while we jog, and stay sane during endless morning commutes.

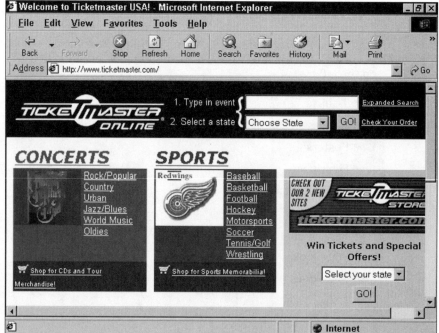

Figure 1-4:
You can
search
for and
purchase
concert
tickets at
Ticket-
master's
Web site.

Though not nearly as portable as its offline counterpart, *Net radio* has a lot to offer. Unlike offline radio, Net radio isn't limited by any broadcasting range. With literally thousands of radio stations broadcasting their shows over the Internet, you can tune in to a pop music show from Korea while sitting on the Florida coast.

Plus, all kinds of Net-only radio shows are made exclusively for broadcast over the Internet. These programs, such as those developed by Pseudo.com (www.pseudo.com) in New York, often offer more experimental or cutting-edge content than you find on your local FM station (see Figure 1-5).

Sometimes, these programs throw in a live video feed so that radio seems a lot more like television. You may find interviews with your favorite bands or even impromptu studio performances.

Net radio usually comes in streaming format, because it emulates the offline listening experience. So to tune in, you can use the same software you use for any other streaming audio (see "Streaming audio" earlier in this chapter).

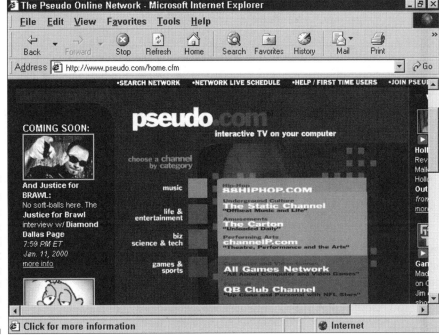

Figure 1-5: Pseudo.com is a site in New York City that offers Net-only radio shows.

Concerts

The crowds. The sweat. The butane lighters waving precipitously in the air. Nothing quite captures the group hug that is a live concert, not even the Internet. But it comes close. These days, artists from the Rolling Stones to Tori Amos have *netcasted* their concerts to the online audience.

Because the events are live, the audio and, occasionally, the video are generally streamed over the Net, which means that you tune in with your preferred streaming audio player, kick back, and enjoy the show.

Bear in mind: Netcasts are sometimes hard to receive because of overly busy servers and net congestion.

Sites like SonicNet (www.sonicnet.com) and LiveConcerts.com (www.liveconcerts.com) — see Figure 1-6 — regularly netcast a variety of live musical performances, including gargantuan events like the Tibetan Freedom Festival.

To add that all-powerful human element, some sites offer live chat simultaneously with the netcast, so that you can commune with other like-minded fans. Waving a lighter at your desktop, however, can be dangerous.

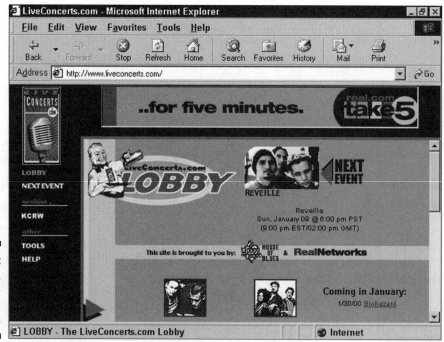

Figure 1-6:
LiveConcerts.
com broad-
casts music
events daily.

News and information

Every music fan has to stay informed. The Net, of course, is perfectly catered to keeping you pumped with news and information. If you want to know something about your favorite band or style of music, you can find something out there to keep you clued in. Just explore the following sources:

- ✔ **Newsgroups** are sprawling, usually unedited message boards where surfers write (or *post* in Netspeak) their views and rants about their favorite bands. The alt.music.rush newsgroup is for old diehards like me.

- ✔ **Mailing lists** — sometimes called *listservs* — are e-mail discussion and information services that you must subscribe to. You can join, for example, a Tom Waits mailing list to get all the latest updates and info on his whereabouts and recordings.

- ✔ **Music news sites** are the music equivalents of CNN. Sites like Addicted to Noise (www.addictedtonoise.com) and MTV (www.mtv.com) feature daily updates of news and information. Figure 1-7 shows the Addicted to Noise Web site.

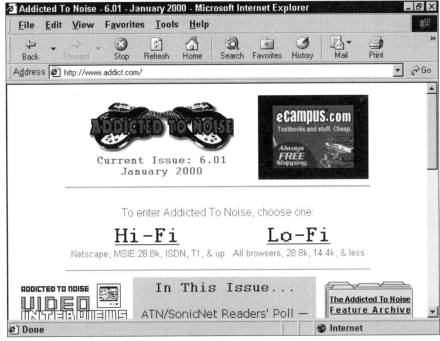

Figure 1-7:
Addicted to
Noise
presents
daily music
news
information.

And don't forget about the bevy of personal homepages devoted to bands for the latest gossip and information. Like all homespun products, though, the reliability of the info may be a little suspect.

Community

It's one thing to be, say, a Busta Rhymes fan, but it's a whole different experience to be among a group of people who share your passion. The community for music online is sprawling and seemingly endless. And it's no surprise. After all, music fans, particularly fans of the Grateful Dead, were among the first pioneers on the Net.

Today, fans mingle in newsgroups, mailing lists, or live *chats*. They run their own Web sites, events, and even offline gatherings. Some sites such as iMusic (`www.imusic.com`), as shown in Figure 1-8, are run by companies that are empowering fans with the tools to create their own special interest groups.

For a more detailed look at the wild and wacky world of music online communities, see Chapter 8.

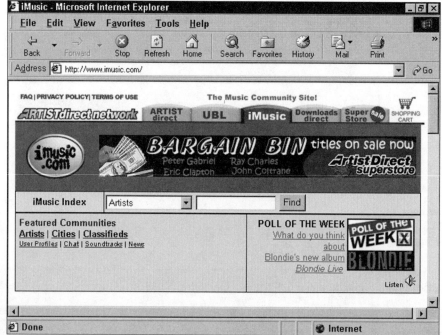

Figure 1-8:
iMusic is a
community
site for a
variety of
music fans.

The Background of Music Online

Like intrepid explorers, people looking for music and music-related stuff online have to be armed with the right knowledge. Throughout your journeys, you're sure to run across some references to original manifestations of music online. Most are still around in some form or another. So if you're going to venture out on the wires, you'd better be prepared to know what's around the corner.

Here's a little primer in the background of music online. If you know about these basics of Net surfing, feel free to skip ahead.

BBS blues

Long before college students were burning up their Net connections looking for the latest MP3s, they were hanging out in *bulletin board services (BBS)*.

Launched extensively in the late 1980s and early 1990s, BBSes are text-based, online community centers where people with special interests gather to leave messages for each other, trade software, or chat in real-time. These sites, which still exist today, were the foundation for music community online — places where fans and musicians could stay in touch and share information even if they lived across the country from each other.

Unsurprisingly, music fans were some of the first to stake their flags in these new electronic frontiers. Acid rock legends The Grateful Dead inspired one of the most dedicated legions of music fans.

As one of the oldest BBSes, The Well (www.thewell.com) remains a buzzing hive for Deadheads. Figure 1-9 shows The Well's home page.

SonicNet (www.sonicnet.com) began as a BBS. Now, it's one of the most comprehensive music information sites on the Web.

Tommy, can you FTP me?

For a while, the Internet wasn't as easy as *point 'n' click*. It was more like *fetch 'n' get*. Finding information took a lot more work and effort than it does today.

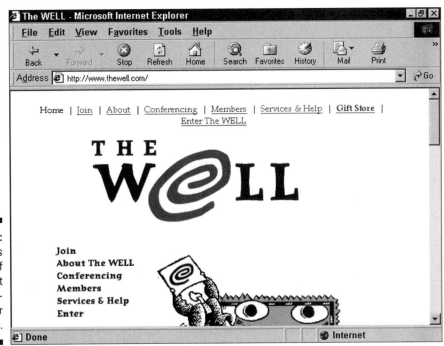

Figure 1-9: The Well is one of the oldest online communities for music fans.

Dedicated music online surfers still trade files the old way by using *file transfer protocol* (FTP). Simply put, FTP means that you essentially can put a file on to or get a file off of someone else's computer. But instead of using a disk to transfer a file, your computer dials up the other person's computer and transfers the file over a phone line. Because the owner of the other computer probably doesn't want every Joe or Jill Shmoe rummaging through his or her stuff, he or she probably gives you a secret password that lets you get in.

Today, FTPing is most commonly used with MP3s. CuteFTP (`www.cuteftp.com`) is among the more popular FTP programs. As I discuss in more detail in Chapters 3, 9, 10, and 11, many MP3 files are distributed by private individuals from their own homes.

To get these songs, the owners may require you to access the files from their computer *servers* — the hardware that stores files for Internet access. If they say, "Hey, dude or dudette, you gotta FTP my server," you'll know what they mean.

E-zines

Way back when, someone got the bright idea that people may be compelled not only to search for information online but also to actually take the time to read. Electronic magazines, or *e-zines,* quickly began filling the demand.

Zines have a long and important history in popular music. Offline, so-called *fan zines* date back to the birth of rock 'n' roll, when intrepid kiddies literally cut and pasted together their own fan papers and distributed them at concerts. With the advent of photocopying technologies, fan zines became more accessible. Anyone could type out his or her own fan zine, devoted to a favorite band, and copy it for others to buy, hopefully.

Electronic zines are made very much in the same spirit. You can find three basic types of e-zines on the Web:

- ✔ *Fan e-zines* are created by and for other fans. People who make sites such as DeepFried BugVision (`www.bugvision.com`), an e-zine dedicated to the Seattle fringe rock scene (see Figure 1-10), are made for the love of the music, not the prospect of money.

- ✔ *Professional e-zines* (available only on the Net), such as Addicted to Noise, look to entertain, inform, *and* make a buck. The quality may be better, but you have to endure the advertising.

- ✔ *Cross-media e-zines* appear in both print and electronic formats. Many of these, such as Spin (`www.spin.com`) or Rolling Stone (`www.rollingstone.com`), combine articles and information that appear in the regular newsstand version with new features made specifically for the Web site.

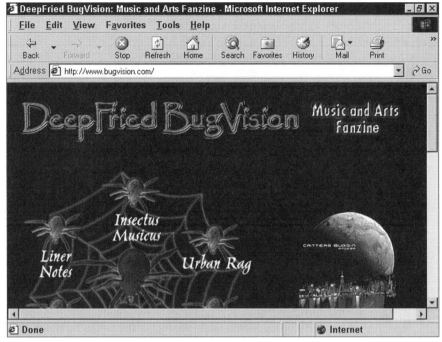

Figure 1-10:
The
DeepFried
BugVision
Web site.

Chat scratch fever

Okay, here's a topic: Garth Brooks versus Mick Jagger. Who's the more talented musician? Discuss.

Music fans have strong opinions, and no better bastion of strong opinions exists than on the Internet. Since the beginning of BBSes, fans have been chatting with each other about the wonders and perils of the music world.

Here's a look at the two types of chat environments out there:

- ✔ *Moderated chats* usually have hosts who try, often unsuccessfully, to make the conversation linear. These types of chats, found regularly on online services such as America Online (www.aol.com), are the electronic equivalent of classic radio shows like Rockline. These chats give you the chance to ask some questions of your favorite bands in the hope that they'll write back.

- ✔ *Unmoderated chats* are the free-for-all gabfests found all over the Web. Some software, such as ICQ (www.icq.com), enables users to chat across the Net (see Figure 1-11). ICQ is an anything-goes hangout where enthusiasts can congregate to talk about last night's Dixie Chicks concert or the new Mariah Carey video.

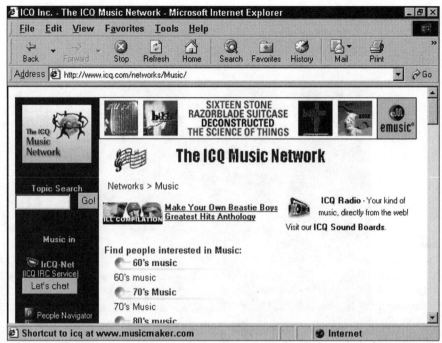

Figure 1-11:
ICQ chat
rooms for
music fans.

Netcasts

Netcasts. Cybercasts. Webcasts. All of these terms mean basically the same thing — live or previously recorded events that are broadcast over the Internet. Concerts are obviously perfect for netcasts, as are interviews and special events like the MTV Video Music Awards.

Some of the earliest netcasts were done with early software like M-Bone. Back in 1993, an independent band called Severe Tire Damage (`http://chocolate.research.digital.com/std/control.html`) netcast its own concert using M-Bone. The next year, though, the Rolling Stones claimed that *they*, in fact, would be the first band to broadcast a show online. To protest this misinformation, STD decided to interrupt the Stones' broadcast with its own 20-minute set.

How's that for taking charge?

Revolution #MP3

Of all the breakthroughs in online music, none has rocked the world quite like MP3. Virtually every major magazine has published extensive articles on the subject. Record companies have held emergency summits. Unsigned bands, who could only dream about people around the world listening to their music, suddenly had hope.

So what's the fuss all about? Here's the lowdown on MP3:

- ✔ MP3 is fast.
- ✔ MP3 is (usually) free.
- ✔ MP3 sounds almost as good as a CD.
- ✔ MP3s can be collected and saved.
- ✔ MP3s are easy to exchange over the Internet.

Look, Ma, no discs!

MP3 came along just when online music fans needed it. Prior to MP3's boom, music online was mainly the streaming sort — meaning that you couldn't save a song and listen to it again after you accessed it on a Web site.

The cool thing about MP3 is that after you download an MP3 file to your computer, you can play it whenever you want — kind of like a compact disc.

Some people like to imagine a day when you won't have to go into a record store anymore. Instead, you may wander up to a kiosk in a shopping mall, punch a few buttons, download your selected MP3 or other digitally formatted songs onto a disc, and then wander on your way.

Others imagine an even freer way to get music. You won't have to go to a mall. You just sit down at your computer, tap a few buttons, and download (for a fee) the latest album by your favorite artist. This is already happening, in fact, on a smaller scale.

Indies as pop stars

Say you're in an indie band, meaning you either have a record on a small, independent record label or you're just out there trying to make it on your own. In the past, you had to work pretty hard to get noticed. Maybe you made your own tape and tried to sell it at live shows. Maybe you put up fliers for your gigs. You hustled, scraped, saved, and did anything to let people know you exist.

With MP3 and Internet access, you suddenly have a platform for reaching not only your community, but also someone way across the world. With MP3, you can accomplish the following:

- ✔ Record digital versions of all your songs
- ✔ Post the music on the Internet
- ✔ Refer people to your Web site to check out your music
- ✔ Use e-mail and Web marketing to reach new fans
- ✔ Charge people to download your songs

Yes, you may still find that letting people know you exist is a challenge; nothing compares to the marketing forces of a major record label. And having an MP3 song on the Net sure isn't like having a video on MTV. But it's a start. With enough creativity and energy, an indie band with its own MP3 Web site can act like pop stars.

Pop stars as indies

Even big name music stars can get empowered by digital music delivery options such as MP3. In the past, major recording stars were pretty much limited to the machinations of corporate business. An artist had to release a new album according to someone else's rules. Certain songs had to be singles. Certain tours had to take place. Certain videos had to be made. The MP3 revolution has changed all that for the good. Artists like hip-hop star Chuck D of Public Enemy, David Bowie, Alanis Morissette, Tori Amos, and Prince have all experimented with taking back control of their music on the digital frontier.

Pop stars can now do the following:

- ✔ Post unreleased songs on the Internet
- ✔ Distribute live audio interviews
- ✔ Post special bonus concert excerpts
- ✔ Listen to music created by their fans

In effect, MP3 and the Internet allow artists to do something that they never really could do efficiently in the past — communicate directly with their fans.

What It All Means

Now that you have an overview of the World Wide Stereo, you may be asking yourself some obvious questions:

- ✔ What does this all mean?
- ✔ What good is it anyway?
- ✔ What's wrong with the old way?
- ✔ Will I ever listen to music the same way again?

The answers:

- ✔ A lot
- ✔ Plenty
- ✔ Nothing
- ✔ Nope

Music online comes down to one basic thing: power. The power to be entertained, informed, and connected in ways you never could before. It's never been easier to access so much stuff so quickly.

Still, rest assured that all these wonders are no replacement for the real thing. Ultimately, you can have all the community, radio, merchandise, and MP3s in the world, but nothing replaces the experience of listening to your favorite music on a pair of headphones and just disappearing into the sounds.

Music online doesn't replace music offline. It just makes it better.

Chapter 2

Desktop Rock: Turning Your Computer into a Music Machine

In This Chapter

▶ Listening to CDs on your computer

▶ Maximizing your computer for playing music

▶ Hooking up your stereo

▶ Adding cool extras

Computers weren't made for music. They were made, more or less, for word processing, calculations, spreadsheets, and a bunch of other stuff that you'd look really silly dancing to.

For anyone who wants to explore the world of music online, this challenge of turning a computer into a music machine is considerable. Though most new computers can play back music, they're not meant to be stereos.

So whether you listen to Bette Midler or Nine Inch Nails, you want to get the full oomph of the music experience through an awesome sounding machine — not some lame background music squeezing through your computer speakers. So roll up your sleeves, whip out that credit card, and prepare to turn your computer into a lean, mean music machine. In this chapter, you find out how to transform your hardware into rockware.

Listening to CDs on Your Computer

If you're like me, you enjoy playing music in the background while you work. (In case you're wondering, I'm listening to Nirvana's *In Utero* right now). You may not know this, but odds are, your computer can play music CDs!

What you need

In order to play music CDs on your computer, make sure you have the following stuff:

- ✔ A *computer*. Duh.
- ✔ A *CD-ROM drive*.
- ✔ External computer speakers that plug into your machine.
- ✔ If you have a Windows PC, a *sound card*, which is a piece of computer hardware that lets your computer play sounds. It probably came with your machine.

  If you have a Macintosh, you don't have to worry about a sound card. All Macs come equipped with built-in sound. Isn't that nice?
- ✔ A *CD player application*, which comes with either Windows or the Mac OS. Other programs can also play CDs on your computer. For more information, see Chapter 3.

Don't worry if you don't know what all this stuff is. You will know by the end of this chapter.

Play it, Sam

To fire up your favorite CD, follow these steps:

1. **Get a music CD.**

   Pick a CD, any CD. . .

2. **Press the Open/Close button of the CD-ROM drive, place the disc in the tray, and then press the Open/Close button again.**

3. **If your CD player application doesn't automatically start up, launch the program.**

   In Windows, choose Start➪Programs➪Accessories➪Multimedia➪ CD Player.

   In the Mac OS, choose the Apple menu and click AppleCD Audio Player.

   If you're using another program, go ahead and launch it.

4. **Click the Play button.**

   The buttons on the controller are similar to those you find on any car or home stereo. You can also stop, pause, move from track to track, and move forward or backward in a track. You can also adjust the volume.

How's that sound? Music to your ears, I hope.

Creating a Dream Music Machine

Think of a computer as a stereo. Audiophiles seldom go out and buy just one complete stereo. Instead, they carefully select each component separately — for example, a receiver, a tape deck, a CD player, speakers, equalizer, amplifier, and so on. If they listen to more albums than CDs, they invest more in a killer turntable.

If these audiophiles are into *DVDs* — short for *Digital Versatile Discs*, which can hold both audio and video — they may get a DVD player as well. More and more computers these days can play DVDs if they come with a DVD-ROM drive. Sites like DVD Express at `www.dvdexpress.com` (see Figure 2-1) carry many DVDs for music lovers.

You can modify and customize your computer in a similar fashion. You can start out with the basics — a monitor, a hard drive, a keyboard, and so on — and then add different *peripherals,* or additional hardware devices, as you see fit.

You can also customize your computer internally. You can add memory, different sound capabilities — whatever you desire. The following subsections show you how you can put together your dream machine.

Figure 2-1:
If you want high-quality concert videos, you can find many in DVD format at DVD Express.

Choosing a computer

Because any new desktop computer or laptop can play music, you don't need to worry too much about what you get. In general, like I always tell my friends, get the best one you can afford. However, keep in mind that with all the technological innovations happening, the computer you buy now may be out-of-date in just a few months. But that shouldn't stop you from constructing a killer computer system to satisfy your online music cravings.

Here are some things to consider if you are starting completely from scratch:

- ✔ **Macintosh or PC?** If that's the question, the answer is probably among the most personal in the high-tech world. Mac and PC users are equally dedicated to their wares. My sister-in-law bought a candy-colored Mac because it matched her sofa. My friend bought a PC because he likes playing all the latest computer games. For music purposes, you can find more goodies available for PC than Mac. Still, the average music online fan can be happy with either one. However, don't buy a computer *just* for music. Think about the other things you want to use it for, too.

- ✔ **Computing power.** A computer's strength is dictated by its *processor* — the device inside your computer that does all that complicated thinking. Processors are measured by the speed at which they make calculations; such measurements come in units called *megahertz*. If you're using a PC, I suggest getting at least a Pentium II processor. For a Macintosh, don't get anything less than a G3. For each platform, anything less than 300Mhz won't do you much good.

- ✔ **Monitor.** The bigger, the better. Though you're tweaking your computer for music, you're going to be viewing a lot of Web pages along the way. The more screen space you have to see what you're surfing, the more pleasurable the ride will be.

- ✔ **Keyboard.** An *ergonomic* keyboard can save your wrist from the dreaded wrist-crunch condition called *carpal tunnel syndrome.* (If you don't think carpal tunnel can happen to you, don't be so sure; for a while, I had to sleep with wrist splints.) Unlike normal keyboards, an ergonomic keyboard is split and angled in such a way to line up more comfortably with the natural position of your hands.

- ✔ **Mouse.** You can get by just fine with the mouse that comes with your computer, but you may want to invest in a mouse that has several buttons that you can program to do different things. Not bad for late nights of MP3 trolling.

Deciding on a sound card

Attention Mac users: You can skip this subsection. Your Mac comes with built-in sound capability that can knock your socks off.

For PC users, the *sound card* is the core of your computer's audio power. The sound card processes audio information and then sends it out through your speakers. Whether you know it or not, you most likely have a 16-bit sound card already inside your computer. The only reasons you may need to install a new sound card are as follows:

✔ You want a better, beefier card.

✔ You need to replace the card.

✔ You're adding a sound card to an older PC.

✔ You're building your own PC.

A basic sound card, like the popular series of SoundBlaster cards from Creative Labs (www.creativelabs.com) can do you fine. Figure 2-2 shows their home page.

Another company, Voyetra Turtle Beach (www.turtlebeach.com), as shown in Figure 2-3, also offers a variety of sound cards, with a price range usually between $50 and $200.

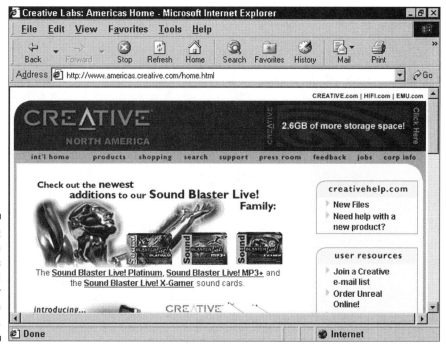

Figure 2-2:
Creative Labs offers good sound cards for souping up your system.

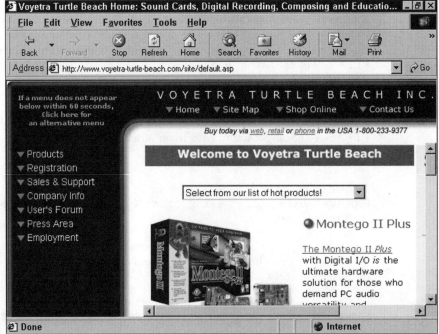

Figure 2-3:
Sound
cards from
Voyetra
Turtle
Beach.

Some companies offer *3D audio* sound cards; these sound cards are made especially for computer games. With them, you get all the magical sounds of flying bullets and whooshing phasers — obviously not the stuff of your favorite bands. But if you should choose a 3D sound card, it can handle your music as well.

Selecting speakers

Until recently, computer speakers were pretty much an afterthought. After all, who really needed to listen to those system startup tones in stereo? But with the increased popularity of computer games, DVDs, and music online, a good set of speakers is becoming essential.

You may be surprised at how good computer speakers can actually sound these days. Part of the reason is that some major stereo speaker manufacturers, such as Boston Acoustics, are now getting into the business as well.

The major speaker manufacturers understand that the future of the music listening experience will rely more and more on digital distribution, and consumers are going to demand better ways to enjoy the sounds.

Here are some features you can look for when selecting your computer speakers:

✔ **Price.** You can get a decent pair of speakers for about $100. Like anything else, you can spend more, depending on your passion. High-end speakers can cost as much as $400.

✔ **Subwoofer.** A *subwoofer* is an additional component to a computer speaker system that specifically handles the sound system's bass. Subwoofers usually sit on the floor, while the two stereo speakers are angled toward the listener from higher up. Using a subwoofer isn't necessary, but doing so gives you a richer, fuller bass sound — something especially nice when you use some tiny computer speakers for everything else.

✔ **Dolby Surround Sound.** *Dolby Surround Sound* is a feature you use mainly when listening to DVD concert movies that were shot with this special sound technology. For more on Dolby Surround Sound, check out Dolby's Web site at `www.dolby.com` (see Figure 2-4).

✔ **Rear speakers.** These speakers are for the true audiophiles; you place them behind you for that theater surround sound experience. You use these for listening mainly to DVD movie audio.

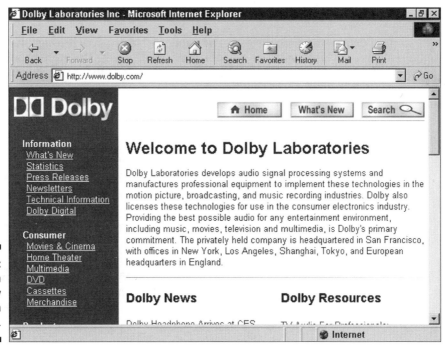

Figure 2-4:
You can enjoy Dolby sound on many DVDs.

Adding memory

Online, it's nice to be an elephant. In a nutshell, the more *random access memory,* or *RAM,* your computer has, the more programs your computer can run at a time. After you sink yourself in the playfield of music online, you may find yourself giving new meaning to the idea of *multitasking* — that is, doing a lot of things at once.

If you have 32 *megabytes* (MB) of RAM and use Windows 95 or Mac OS 8, you should be fine. But if you use Windows 98 or higher, or Mac OS 9 or higher, and you plan on watching DVDs and getting into MIDI or any kind of music production, you really need 64 or 128MB. And if you can afford even more, by all means, splurge.

Exploring bandwidth

Unlike the regular roads, speeding on the Information Superhighway is not only acceptable; it's the only way to ride.

Your onramp to the Superhighway is your *Internet service provider* (ISP) — the company that provides you online access — which is available for a variable monthly subscription.

Bandwidth, which measures how much data can flow through the telephone lines to and from your modem, is the golden ring. The more bandwidth, the faster the connection, the quicker you can download your favorite MP3s. Here's a look at the different options for playing with the bandwidth:

 ✔ *Dial-up* access means that your computer sends and receives data over the Internet through a modem. The speed of data through a modem is measured in *bits per second (bps).* When I downloaded my first song online, I was using a 2400 bps modem, which took about an hour to get one song. These days, most computers come with modems that can handle 56,000 bits per second (sometimes abbreviated 56K).

 Not bad, but not lightning-fast by any means. We're still in an era when we actually have time to kill during long downloads. And if you're using dial-up, you'd better get used to heading off for a snack while your MP3s download.

 ✔ *Integrated Services Digital Network (ISDN)* is basically a faster way to send and receive data over a telephone network. ISDN can be a couple of times faster than a 56K modem. Most major telephone companies offer the service for a monthly fee. Call them for the options.

- ✔ *Digital Subscriber Lines* (*DSL*) are being offered by a small number of providers and phone companies. DSL not only gives you high-speed access
  (30 times faster than a 56K modem), it gives you fast access for sending
  data upstream yourself — especially important for bands who want to post
  a lot of MP3s. Check with your ISP or local phone company for details.

- ✔ *Cable modems* are being enjoyed by a select, but happy, group of home
  surfers. Cable companies offer this service; if your neighborhood is wired
  for this, you can get it; if not, you have to wait. Right now, cable modems
  deliver data at about 500 times faster than a 56K modem. That's a noticeable difference. Contact your cable company for more information.

- ✔ *T1* connections, common in the workplace and some newfangled apart-
  ment buildings, offer high speed, *broadband* connections at around 1.5
  megabits per second (Mbps). That's cruising nice and fast. No wonder
  so many bosses are banning access to MP3 sites from the workplace.

Storing stuff

In a fairly classic scene from the film *Diner*, the 1950s coming-of-age film, one
guy chastises his girlfriend for messing up his meticulously organized record
collection. How dated, indeed. With music online, storing songs, sites, graphics, or whatever else suits your fancy is a nice, clean digital affair.

Your hard drive will probably suffice for most of your storage needs. My
motto, as always, is to get the biggest one you can afford. You can easily fill
up the space — especially if you get addicted to games. An 8-gigabyte (GB)
drive is pretty spacious.

Floppy disks are a problem. One MP3 song, for example, can weigh in at
about 4.5 *megabytes* (MB). A floppy can hold only about 1.4MB. That's a
squeeze. Though you may try to *compress* a song, floppies don't really make a
lot of sense for these kinds of things.

If you really start getting on a roll, you probably want to take your tunes on
the road. For more general, transportable storage needs, a portable storage
device like a *Zip drive* from Iomega (`www.iomega.com`) is a nice way to travel.
The Zip drive plugs right into the back of your computer and comes with its
own 100MB or 250MB discs. For more info on Zip drives, check out Iomega's
Web site, as shown in Figure 2-5.

The best medium for storing your MP3 and other computer sound files may
be the tried and true CD. You can get yourself a CD burner and, with the right
software, burn audio CDs that you can play in most conventional CD players.
You're limited to putting up to 80 minutes of audio on each disc. If you store
the MP3 files as data files, you can get tons of songs (up to 700MB worth) on
a single CD. However, if you go that route, you can't play the discs in your
normal CD player (though more and more CD and DVD players have the ability to play MP3 files). For more info on burning CDs, see Chapter 10.

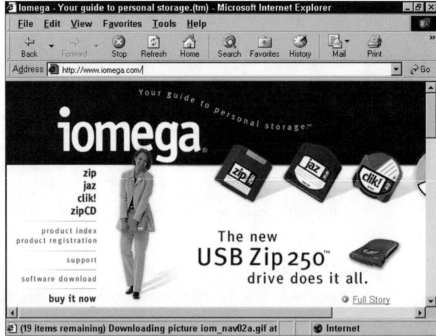

Figure 2-5:
Iomega's Zip drives are convenient devices for storing songs.

Hooking Up the Stereo

So if you're turning a computer into a music machine, why not just do the obvious: hook it up to the stereo? If you want to make audiotapes of your MP3s (or even streaming audio concerts) for your car's tape deck, this is probably a good idea. Also, if your band wants to convert a demo tape into MP3 format for posting on the Web, you can reverse the hookup — that is, run the sound out from your stereo into the microphone jack of your computer.

If you just want to listen to music you find on the Web, you may find it easier to just invest in some high-end computer speakers. A basic computer can do the essential functions of your stereo:

✔ Play compact discs.

✔ Play high-quality sound through high-end computer speakers.

The main reason most people seem to want to connect the two beasts is to crank their MP3s out of their stereo system. If you're set on doing that, the solution is actually pretty simple:

1. **Go to your local electronics or computer store and buy a stereo mini-plug that splits into two RCA plugs. (The clerk should know what this means.)**

2. **Plug the cord into the Line Out jack of your computer.**

3. **Plug the two RCA ends (just like your other stereo cables) into the back of your receiver. (You can usually find an extra input jack, possibly labeled AUX for *auxiliary*.) Prepare to rock.**

Stereo speakers are not magnetized in the same way as computer speakers. If you place your stereo speakers too close to your computer, they could damage your hard drive. Play it safe and keep at least a few feet of space between the two. Or, better yet, shell out some cash for a good set of computer speakers with a subwoofer.

Adding Groovy Extras

After you get started, you can easily get carried away with accessorizing your computer. Ultimately, a computer is a tool, and the more tools you have, the more stuff you can do. So if you want a breakdown of the possible extras (or *peripherals*) and how you can use them for music online, here's a nice birthday gift wish list.

Scanners

A *scanner* is like a digital copy machine. It connects to your computer and enables you to make digital images of any object that's scanned — photos, newspaper clippings, even the back of your hand.

For music fans, a scanner is definitely a plus. If, say, you end up running your own fan e-zine for your favorite band, you may want to scan all kinds of accumulated art for your site (watch out for copyright violations, of course). But even if you want to upload some photos of you and your buds outside the Marilyn Manson show, you can't beat a scanner. And with scanner prices falling as low as under $50, investing in a scanner is a sure thing.

You can get three types of scanners:

- ✔ *Flatbed* scanners are just that — flat. These make the most sense. You can lay out clippings nice and easy and get smooth clean copies.

- ✔ *Sheetfed* scanners are ideal if you're trying to save desk space. For these scanners, you manually feed whatever you want to be digitized into the machine. This is not ideal, though, for scanning little scraps of concert set lists or whatever else you may want to archive.

- ✔ *Handheld* scanners put the power of digitization in the palm of your hand. You swipe these scanners over a document to create a digital version. Perfect for scanning your old ticket stub collection.

Cameras

Digital cameras, which take digital pictures that you can post and trade on the Web, are becoming indispensable for the serious surfer. For musicians, a digital camera is the best way to snap shots of yourself — practicing, performing, posing — and spread them on the Net alongside your latest MP3s. For fans, digital cameras provide another cool way to let the world see you and all your obsessions.

Here are the kinds of digital cameras you may want to consider:

- **Web cams.** This nifty little eyeball plugs right into the back of your computer and beams an image of your pretty mug on-screen. If you have the gumption, you can hook up a live Web cam to your Internet home page and let people check you out 24/7 (24 hours a day, seven days a week). Plenty of bands are now doing this for a little DIY — Do-It-Yourself — promotion.

- **Digital cameras.** These devices take still images in digital form. Instead of using film, the pictures are stored on a disk. There's nothing to rewind, develop, or — oops! — accidentally expose to the light. Plus, you can zap the images right up on to a Web page — just the thing for showing pictures of you worshipping in your Courtney Love shrine.

- **Digital camcorders.** Like digital still cameras, these camcorders enable you to film images in digitized form. You can use a digital camcorder to film your band in performance or make your own music video, and then you can post the results on your Web site. Most of these camcorders come with optional accessories that make it pretty easy to plug the machine into the back of your computer and upload your goods.

CD burners

A *CD burner* is the common slang for a *CD-RW drive*, which enables you to record (and re-record) data — including audio — onto your own CDs. With these devices, you can do the following:

- Store about 80 minutes of audio per disc
- Store 700MB of computer data per disc
- Play audio CDs and CD-ROMs
- Use it as a portable CD player or storage device.

You can also find a few *DVD burners* on the market; these burners can store way more information. However, playback options for these discs are still very limited.

For more information about using CD burners with MP3, see Chapter 9.

Personal digital assistants

PDAs, or *personal digital assistants,* are handheld computers that let you access and process information. The PalmPilot (www.palmpilot.com) is one of the more popular PDAs on the market. For more on the PalmPilot, check out the Palm Web site, as shown in Figure 2-6.

Here are some of the things a music fan or musician can do with a PDA:

- ✔ Surf the latest music Web sites — however, you can't listen to music on a PDA. At least, not yet!

- ✔ Keep track of how much you're spending on music stuff.

- ✔ Keep set lists in the back of a concert hall.

- ✔ Write lyrics to your own songs when the urge strikes.

- ✔ Send e-mail to other fans. In fact, you can keep your friends up-to-date with e-mail and discussion group postings while you're at a concert!

- ✔ Store contact numbers of record labels, clubs, managers, and other music industry contacts.

- ✔ Transfer all your information to your desktop or laptop computer.

Figure 2-6:
The Palm
Web site,
home of the
PalmPilot.

Headphones

Take my advice: Invest in a good pair of headphones.

Unfortunately, a lot of computer speakers don't come with headphone jacks; instead, you have to plug your headphones directly into your computer. Most computers nowadays come with a standard headphone jack. In fact, iMacs come with two headphone jacks, so that both you and a friend can enjoy the music!

Also, a pair of headphones with its own separate volume control is nice, in case you want to adjust the volume while you're crashed out on the floor. Remote controls for computer audio are still fairly rare.

Playing digital music on portable wares

You can find all kinds of devices now that let you listen to digital audio on the go: walking, driving, flying, you name it. For more information, see Chapter 9.

Getting Away with the Minimum

Can you get away without all these goodies? Fortunately, you can. The minimum requirements are worth repeating:

- ✔ Computer
- ✔ External speakers
- ✔ Sound card
- ✔ Internet access

And if you're not sure about what else you need, you can always wait. Hang out a little bit online. Get a feel for what kind of music online fan you are. Then take it from there. As you do with a car, a house, or a stereo, you can always add some finishing touches and extra features later.

Chapter 3

Boom Box Software

In This Chapter
▶ Understanding the difference between shareware and freeware
▶ Getting to know the different digital audio software

*W*hen listening to music online, you need two things: hardware and software. The software required to play digital music is called — get this — *players*. How's that for logic?

Just the way, for example, a word processing program can open your text document, a digital music player can open a file of digital music.

Because the files are all in the same formats, you can use a variety of different players to listen to a song. You can also use other programs to record your own songs and make your own CDs.

In this chapter, I give you an overview of the major wares out there. You see which ones to use, when to use them, and just why you need so many different programs to begin with.

Just What Is a Player?

Simply put, a *player* is a piece of software that turns those digital ones and zeros into beautiful music. You're not limited to one player; you can have as many that will fit on your hard drive. And you can upgrade them, delete them, trade them — whatever makes you happy.

Unlike your stereo, players don't take up any shelf space.

Players, like many forms of software, are distributed over the Internet. And the people who make the players range from corporations, such as Microsoft, to the stereotypical hacker ensconced in a tiny attic room somewhere in Sweden. And you can't tell whose player is going to be better. You may as well, with a little caution, try them all.

Players are available in two forms online:

✔ *Freeware* means that a program is — you guessed it — available for free. Download it and enjoy it for nothing. Many companies and individuals make software available for free in the hope of selling advertising space to different participating businesses.

✔ *Shareware* is software that's available on a trial basis, after which you are requested to pay a certain price. Sometimes, a shareware program may expire after a given period of time unless you pay for it. Other times, the shareware is released on a kind of online honor code — technically, you can get away without paying the individual vendor, but then you can spend your lifetime feeling guilty that you didn't support this unique and diverse form of D-I-Y economics.

You can find a boatload of shareware at CNET's Shareware.com (`http://shareware.cnet.com`), as shown in Figure 3-1.

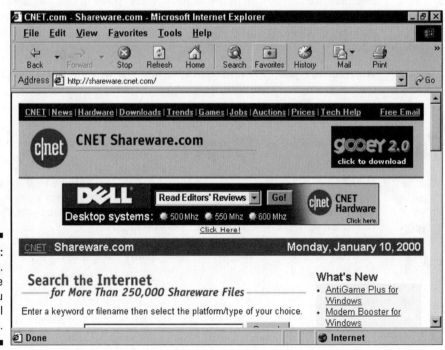

Figure 3-1: Shareware. com is a site where you can find trial software.

How to Practice Safe Surfing

When you download programs from the Internet, you need to keep your computer safe. Especially with music online, for which unknown individuals are making so many programs — you don't want your system infected by computer viruses. If you're downloading anything, a good idea is to invest in a virus protection program, such as Symantec's Norton AntiVirus (`www.norton.com`) or McAfee's VirusScan or Virex (`www.mcafee.com`). Figure 3-2 shows the Web site for Norton AntiVirus.

You can set up these virus protection programs to scan downloaded files to make sure that you don't get more than you bargained for.

Figure 3-2:
Check the
Web site for
Norton
AntiVirus for
the latest
news on
viruses.

Getting to Know the Software

Encoders. Rippers. Burners. Sounds like the stuff of a *Mission Impossible* movie.

These are some of the types of music software you will inevitably encounter on your journey. Here, I give you an overall look at the types of goods out there. In Chapter 4, you find out how to download and install the stuff.

Digital audio players

You can find basically two kinds of audio players:

- *MP3 players*, which are made specifically to handle MP3 files.
- *Streaming audio players*, which handle real-time audio, such as RealAudio or Windows Media.

Sometimes, the players can even do a little of both.

After you download and install them, these players appear on your desktop like a miniature version of your stereo interface. Most players share the following common features:

- **Standard operation buttons:** You find the typical operating buttons — Play, Stop, Pause, Rewind, Fast Forward, and so on — that you find on your offline CD player.
- **Volume controls:** This control does the same thing as your PC's regular volume control. You may also find a Mute function.
- **Playlists:** While most offline CD players have functions such as Random Play, Repeat, and so forth, your computer's audio player may also give you the ability to edit playlists — that is, choose the specific order you want to play the tracks in.
- **Display track or CD information:** MP3 files often come with embedded track info, such as the artist's name, the title, the name of the CD it's from, and perhaps even artwork. Many players can display this information for you. Also, because regular audio CDs don't store that kind of information on the disc, many players can download that information from an online database, such as CDDB (www.cddb.com).
- **Equalizer functions:** Many players come with equalizer functions that allow you to fine-tune your sound. For example, RealPlayer Basic comes with a three-channel equalizer that you can expand if you upgrade to RealPlayer Plus.
- **Compatibility with different sound formats:** Most players can play other sound formats — not just MP3 or streaming audio. Such formats include WAV, AIFF, MOV, and so on.

But my player does more than just play songs . . . what gives?

These days, you can hardly distinguish so-called streaming media players from players that handle digital audio, such as MP3. Many types of software, such as RealPlayer, Windows Media Player, and QuickTime Player, can handle MP3s, as well as streaming audio and a variety of other formats.

Actually, no standard for digital media online exists; in other words, the makers of all these different players haven't agreed on a single file type for online music. So, for the time being, you find music files in MP3 format or in other leading formats.

Eventually, you will probably be able to use just one program to handle all your music online needs. For now, in what is essentially the larval stage of this new technology, you should keep several players on hand for different types of audio files. That way, you're prepared to listen to any song you surf past online, no matter how it's encoded.

MP3 encoders

If you want to create your own MP3 files, you need to get an *MP3 encoder*. This software, often included in all-in-one programs like MusicMatch, let you convert a song from, say, a CD into an MP3 file that you can post on a Web site.

Most encoders have the following features:

- ✔ **Standard operation buttons:** These buttons mimic those on your cassette recorder — Record, Play, Pause, Stop, Eject, and so on.

- ✔ **Quality adjustments:** You can choose from a variety of different quality settings. The rule of thumb here: The lower the quality, the smaller the file size.

- ✔ **Input options:** You can choose from different inputs, such as microphone, line in, CD-ROM drive, and so on.

- ✔ **Drag-and-drop conversion:** You can drag a sound file onto an icon or an application window, and the MP3 conversion happens automatically. Nifty, huh?

Before you start converting your CDs to MP3, however, be sure to check out the legalities (and illegalities) of doing so in Chapter 5.

For more info on making your own MP3s, see Chapter 10.

CD-burning software

If you purchase a CD burner (see Chapter 2), which enables you to create your own CDs, you need some kind of tool that does the burning for you. These little jobs put the firepower in the burn, letting you transfer audio from your computer to a compact disc or CD-ROM. The audio CDs you make can be played in any regular CD player. Kiss your mix tapes good-bye!

Most CD-burning software share the following features:

- **Different formats:** CD-burning software can create CDs in a variety of formats, including audio CD, Mac-compatible and bootable, Windows-compatible and bootable, Mac-Windows hybrid, video CD, and so on.

- **Drag-and-drop burning:** You can just drag an existing audio or data CD onto the application window and all the tracks/data are burned onto a blank disc for you. This also works for individual music files.

- **Backup capabilities:** You can back up your entire computer hard drive onto data CDs. You can also back up that vast library of MP3s!

- **CD track information:** Most burners can access the CDDB database for CD artist and track information. Keep in mind, though, that if you're copying an audio CD onto another CD, that information is not stored on the disc.

- **Burn music from a variety of formats:** Not only can you burn a variety of sound files, but you can also record music from other sources, such as vinyl albums, cassette tapes, videotape, DVDs — any kind of external device that you can run a line out of and into your computer's line-in or microphone jack. Some software even comes with tools that enable you to digitally remove imperfections from recordings, such as tape hiss, vinyl burps, you name it.

Plug-ins

Plug-ins are nifty little add-ons that add functionality to your existing programs. Odds are, your Web browser has a folder of cool plug-ins that greatly enhance the way your browser works.

Plug-ins are generally small, free, and fast to download. For music programs, such as WinAmp, you can find these kinds of plug-ins:

- **Visualization:** These plug-ins add a vibrant visual element to the music, often in the form of light shows and animation.

- **Equalizers:** These plug-ins add advanced equalizer capabilities to your player for finer-tuning of your music.

- **Broadcasters:** You can get plug-ins that enable you to use your player to broadcast your music over the Internet.

- **Other added functionality:** Other plug-ins let you add DJ cross-faders and more input options, display your player in full-screen mode, enhance 3-D audio quality, change what language your player's interface appears in — just about anything you can imagine.

For Winamp plug-ins, check out the WinAmp Web site at `www.winamp.com`.

Making Sense of the Major Music Programs

In this section, I give you the very brief lowdown on the major music-related software programs out there. For space considerations, I can't cover all the programs — plus, new ones are arriving on the scene every day — but you can get a broad overview of the software you can choose from.

First, I give you a quick, at-a-glance guide to the major capabilities of the programs (see Table 3-1), then I list the software alphabetically, giving you a bit more detail on each.

Here's what each abbreviation in the table stands for:

- **PC:** Windows compatibility

- **Mac:** Macintosh compatibility

- **S/A:** Streaming audio

- **S/V:** Streaming video

- **MP3:** MP3 compatible

- **WAV:** WAV compatible

- **Rec:** Recording

- **CD:** CD burning

- **Enc:** MP3 encoding

Table 3-1				Music Programs at a Glance					
Program	PC	Mac	S/A	S/V	MP3	WAV	Rec	CD	Enc
A2B Player	✔	✔	✔						
Easy CD Creator Deluxe	✔				✔	✔	✔	✔	
Liquid Audio Player	✔	✔	✔		✔	✔		✔	
MusicMatch	✔				✔	✔	✔	✔	✔
QuickTime Player	✔	✔	✔	✔	✔	✔			
RealJukebox	✔		✔	✔	✔	✔	✔		
RealPlayer	✔	✔	✔	✔	✔	✔			
Sonique	✔				✔	✔			
SoundJam MP Plus		✔			✔	✔			✔
Toast Deluxe		✔			✔	✔	✔	✔	
WinAmp	✔				✔	✔			
Windows Media	✔	✔	✔	✔	✔	✔			

A2B Player

A2B (www.a2bmusic.com), as shown in Figure 3-3, is a proprietary music format that you need the freeware A2B Player to play. A2B features its own selection of artists for download from its Web site. You have to pay for the downloads, though.

Unlike other digital music formats, however, A2B songs can be played only on the computer that was used to download the music. If you're a road warrior with a handy laptop, for example, you have to download the songs again on that computer as well.

The A2B Player doesn't play regular MP3 or WAV files — only files coded in its own proprietary format.

Easy CD Creator Deluxe

Easy CD Creator Deluxe ($99) is a Windows-only program that enables you to burn your own CDs in a variety of formats. You can copy audio CDs onto other CDs for play in your offline CD player, and you can transfer your MP3 files to disc for easy storage.

Many new CD and DVD players have the ability to play discs full of MP3s. This is a handy way to get hours and hours of music onto one disc.

Easy CD Creator Deluxe also includes CD Spin Doctor, which allows you to record and clean up audio from other external sources, such as your turntable, cassette deck, VCR, and DVD player.

For more info on Easy CD Creator, check out www.adaptec.com.

Liquid Player

Established in 1996, Liquid Audio (www.liquidaudio.com) was one of the first companies to seriously embrace the digital audio format. Liquid Audio is its own proprietary music format, and you have to pay to download the featured artists on its Web site. You need the freeware Liquid Player (see Figure 3-4) — or the Liquid Audio plug-in for RealPlayer — to enjoy Liquid Audio files.

Liquid Audio has been somewhat eclipsed by the MP3 hype. Nevertheless, Liquid Audio is worth keeping tabs on simply because of its growing popularity and the variety of its musical offerings.

Liquid Audio can also play regular MP3 files and several other audio formats. It can also burn CDs in a limited number of CD burners.

MusicMatch Jukebox

The latest version of the freeware MusicMatch Jukebox (www.musicmatch. com), as shown in Figure 3-5, is an all-in-one affair. Not only does it let you play *and* create your own MP3s, but you can also use it to burn CDs, tune into Net radio, and download and play songs from its own music library. For more information on creating MP3s using MusicMatch, see Chapter 10.

To get more features, you can spend $29.99 to upgrade to MusicMatch Jukebox Plus, which gives you faster CD-burning and the ability to print your own CD jewel case inserts. Currently, MusicMatch Jukebox is Windows-only; however, a Macintosh version is in the works.

QuickTime Player

The QuickTime Player from Apple (www.quicktime.com), as shown in Figure 3-6, was originally exclusive to the Macintosh. However, Apple has recently released a Windows version of this popular software.

Figure 3-5:
The
MusicMatch
Jukebox
Web site.

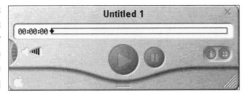

Figure 3-6:
Apple's
QuickTime is
a popular
way to
appreciate
streaming
media.

The QuickTime format is proprietary, and you need the player to enjoy it. While QuickTime is the standard for Mac users, Windows users may want to keep the QuickTime Player in their arsenals. QuickTime is currently the number two streaming media format behind RealMedia, and more and more streaming media events (both audio and video) are being broadcast in this format.

QuickTime supports most of the major digital audio formats. Be sure to check the QuickTime site for concert events to be broadcasted in the QuickTime format.

RealJukebox Plus

If you're looking for a program that handles RealMedia as well as MP3, A2B, and Liquid Audio, you can try RealJukebox ($29.99), as shown in Figure 3-7.

Currently available only for Windows, RealJukebox Plus is a nice, all-in-one program that not only plays music files, but also encodes MP3s, burns CDs (if you also have Easy CD Creator Deluxe), and downloads MP3 files to your portable MP3 player. Visit RealJukebox Central (www.real.com/rjcentral/) for tips on using the program and instructions on how to download new skins for the player.

RealPlayer

Founded in 1995, RealNetworks (www.real.com), the big daddy of streaming audio, is the leading developer of online streaming media products. You can download the freeware RealPlayer (see Figure 3-8) from www.real.com and upgrade to RealPlayer Plus for just $29.99.

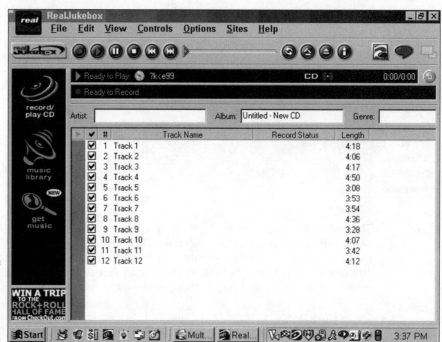

Figure 3-7: RealJukebox can also play MP3s.

RealPlayer's popularity is due to the fact that approximately 85 percent of all streaming media online — from concerts to sporting events — are encoded in RealAudio or RealVideo format. RealPlayer lets you listen to live concerts, Net radio shows, and other music files in a variety of formats, including MP3.

Sonique

The Windows-only Sonique Player (www.sonique.com) is for the more stylish crew in the MP3 crowd.

Like other programs, Sonique plays the standard formats, such as MP3, Windows Media, and plain old CDs on your computer. The latest version has its own built-in music search as well. Sonique also has its own equalizer and playlist controls, and it looks really, really sleek.

SoundJam MP Plus

SoundJam MP Plus (www.soundjam.com) for the Macintosh, whose Web site is shown in Figure 3-9, is an MP3 player and encoder that does the job just right. The software lets you convert CDs, QuickTime, or WAV formats into MP3. You

Figure 3-9:
SoundJam
is a nice
MP3 player
for Mac
users.

can get the freeware version, which is a typical MP3 player; this version lets you use the Plus features for 14 days. After the Plus features expire, you can still use it as a player, or you can purchase the full version for $39.95.

Toast Deluxe

From Adaptec, makers of Easy CD Creator Deluxe, comes Toast Deluxe, a Macintosh-only CD burner ($99). You can create your own audio and data CDs with just a few clicks of the mouse. You can also record audio from external sources, such as turntables, tape decks, VCRs, and DVD players, and you can clean up those awful hisses, clicks, and burps from your analog recordings. If you ever wanted to transfer all your albums and tapes to CD for easier portability and storage, Toast Deluxe is the tool for you.

Winamp

Winamp (www.winamp.com), as shown in Figure 3-10, has become one of the most popular MP3 players and for good reason: It's versatile enough to handle different kinds of digital audio, but thorough enough to give you the performance you need.

Figure 3-10:
Winamp is
one of the
more popu-
lar MP3
players.

In addition to handling your CDs, MP3s, MIDIs, WAVs, and Windows Media files, Winamp offers loads of plug-ins that can do everything from enhancing sound playback to turning Winamp into a desktop DJ system. For more info about MP3 DJ wares, see Chapter 9.

Windows Media Player

Not surprisingly, Bill Gates decided to get into the streaming media game. With the success of RealPlayer, Microsoft debuted its response: the Windows Media Player. The idea behind Windows Media Player, whose Web site appears in Figure 3-11, is to provide one program that can handle all your digital music needs — even if you're a Mac user. Windows Media Player also supports RealAudio and RealVideo formats.

If you have the version of Windows Media Player that came with Windows 95 or 98, you need to download the latest version if you want to play MP3s.

But what if I use Linux?

The choice of reliable MP3 players for Linux users is small, but growing. The best one right now is the Xaudio Player, which you can download from www.xaudio.com. But as Linux continues to take the computing world by storm, keep on the lookout for additional players at your favorite Linux hubs.

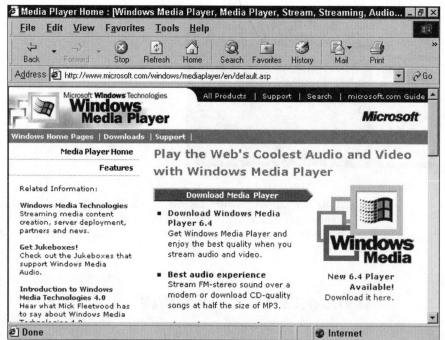

Figure 3-11:
The
Windows
Media
Player
Web site.

Chapter 4

Downloading and Installing Digital Audio Players

***

In This Chapter

▶ Downloading and installing digital music players

▶ Troubleshooting an installation

▶ Finding (human) help

***

*Y*ou say you want a revolution? No problem. Net music wares such as MP3 are here to change your life, your listening habits, and your music collection. But first, you have to get your hands — and your hard drive — dirty. Like all shareware on the Internet, the burgeoning crew of digital music players is a mixed blessing.

The good news is that, for the most part, digital music players are free and easy to find. This is also the bad news.

Because developers are so eager to make their latest, greatest wares available online, their programs are seldom without bugs.

Sometimes, you may have to swat a few little mosquitoes, but other times, you may run into kamikaze flying roaches. And, unfortunately, when things go wrong, you have no warranty to wield or 800 number to dial for technical support. What to do? Put on some mellow music and read on.

In this chapter, you get the skinny on how to install your digital audio players and what to do if something goes wrong.

How It's Supposed to Work

Here's the good news: Most of the time when you're surfing, downloading, and installing software, you won't have any problem at all. Most Web sites have clearly marked download links, and most installation programs ask you just the right questions and take care of placing the program files in the right place on your computer.

However, the three most deceptive words in digital culture may very well be *point and click*. Inherently, you're led to believe that the two separate steps of downloading and installing software are no-brainer tap dances. As a result, if something goes wrong, you figure it's your fault — or your computer's. Just remember, this line of thinking is a pipe dream . . . especially when the pipes on the Internet are congested.

The art of downloading

After you find the digital music player you desire, the first step is to download it. Methods for downloading software are as numerous and varied as the Web sites offering software. So here, in extremely general terms, are the hoops you may have to jump through to get your software:

1. **Go to the home page of the people who make the player.**

2. **Click a link that says something like <u>Download</u> or <u>Download Now</u>.**

   This link usually takes you to a special download page with a choice of servers. Though Webmasters usually recommend that you choose the server closest to you, don't be afraid to surf to another coast. Because the information is all traveling over a similar computer network, the difference is barely noticeable.

   You may also have to enter some information about yourself, such as your name and e-mail address. You may find a check box for indicating whether you want update e-mails sent to you from the Web site. If you want them cluttering up your e-mail inbox, go ahead and check the box.

3. **Click the link of the location from which you want to download the software.**

4. **If your computer asks you for a location on your hard drive where you want to store the downloaded file, choose a destination folder. Otherwise, your browser downloads it to a default location.**

5. **Click Save or OK.**

   The file starts to download to the location you specified.

The waiting is the hardest part

This is a good time to flip on the tube and nuke up some macaroni and cheese.

Digital music players can be fat — or phat, for you hip-hop fans — and thus slow to download. MusicMatch, one of the more popular all-in-one-programs, weighs in at 6.4MB. At a 56K modem connection, that means about 30 minutes . . . or nine videos, with commercials.

The art of installing

After the program downloads to your computer, the next step is to install it. Installations vary depending on the particular software, so I can't cover installation in detail. However, here are a few tips that may help you along the way:

- ✔ Shutting down all active programs before you install new software is a good idea. Otherwise, the installer may get confused.

- ✔ Usually, to begin the installation process, you simply double-click the installer icon. In Windows, the installer is usually an .exe (or executable) file; on a Mac, you should see *Install* or *Installer* as part of the file name. Some programs come compressed, meaning that you have to unzip (Windows) or unstuff (Mac) to use them.

- ✔ A typical installer leads you through the process, asking you a variety of questions. You can usually accept the default answers as you go, unless you have specific reasons for not doing this. For example, in Windows, most programs install themselves in your Programs folder on your hard drive, which is fine. However, most players ask you if you want to make them your default player, which you may not want if your favorite player is another program.

- ✔ Odds are, you have to accept a user license agreement before you can install the software. If you decline the agreement, the installation cancels. Most agreements have the same boilerplate legal language that you need a dictionary to understand, but you may still want to at least glance through it for anything particularly strange.

- ✔ Most programs include a Read Me file that includes updated information on the program and installation, such as new features, bug acknowledgements, and installation bugaboos. I suggest you peruse these Read Me files just in case, and then delete them.

- ✔ Many programs require you to restart your computer. If you're prompted to do so, go ahead. Just make sure you save any work in other open programs.

How It Sometimes Works Instead

If you do encounter problems with installing or running the software, don't panic. You have plenty of ways out. And don't worry if the Read Me file seems spare and convoluted — remember that these programs are written by computer geeks.

This section highlights some common problems you may run into.

The player won't play!

Think of a digital music player as if it was your stereo. Just like your tape deck needs tapes, your player needs files. Right now, you have the player, but no music. See Chapter 7 for where to find songs and how to listen to them.

Yeah, but what about the samples?

Some players come with sample song files already built in. Look inside the folder to make sure the songs are in fact there. Each player comes with a song list window and a Play or Listen button. Try clicking the song in the song list and then clicking play. It should be that easy.

You may have to browse to where the songs are located on your hard drive in order for them to appear in the song list.

Even the previews aren't working!

Sounds like a hardware problem. Are you sure you have the proper setup tools that you read about in Chapter 2: a sound card, speakers, and cables?

If so, check the obvious stuff. Make sure that the cables are plugged in securely and the speakers are connected. Are the speakers turned on and the volume turned up? Make sure that your computer's volume is turned up high enough.

Try restarting your computer. Sometimes your computer gets a little confused and forgets how to play sounds. Restarting clears your computer's memory and hopefully clears up the confusion. Make sure that you can hear your computer's startup sound through your speakers.

When all else fails

If all your hardware checks out, you may have to try the download again. Data, like all streams, gets dirty. The digital music player you just sucked down may have become corrupted along the way, or the installer file itself was corrupted to begin with. Try a different download site to get a different copy of the software. If, after all that, the player still doesn't work for you, you're better off trying another player entirely.

Who to call

If you have a problem with the player, odds are you won't be able to call anyone at all. Check the bottom of the home page for an e-mail address for the person who was gracious (or ungracious, as the case may be) enough to put the goods online. If that doesn't work, try yelling "Hey, lemonade!" because you probably need a drink to help you cool down.

Who to curse

No one. Here's the deal: Like my friend Roth used to say, you get what you pay for. In the case of music players, you're probably not paying a dime — beyond the cost of your Internet connection time.

So chill. If the first player doesn't work, the second — or third or fourth — will. Fortunately, most major players like MusicMatch and WinAMP boot up without a glitch.

Human Resources

Here's the good news. No, the great news. Like the Internet itself, music online became a phenomenon because of the passion and enthusiasm of carbon-based human beings. Though you may get frustrated while trying to install and manipulate your new player, you can find plenty of digital music lovers out there who can lend a helping hand.

Usenet

One of the best places to find a lively, ongoing discussion about the trials and tribulations of digital music players is within the Usenet: the collection of *discussion groups* (or *newsgroups*) where surfers post messages for each other online.

Just pose your question as specifically as you can (such as with a succinct subject heading like "Need help with WinAMP") and then post your question in the message area. Don't worry about how simple your question may seem; at some point or another, everyone's a newbie.

Here are some examples of where you can look for help:

✔ `Alt.binaries.sounds.music` is a wide-open area for discussion of all things related to digital music.

✔ `comp.music.misc` is a good place for general questions about music and computers.

✔ `Microsoft.public.music.products` is a place to seek out info related to Windows-based players.

Chat and message boards

Need a quick fix? *Chat rooms* (online places where you can converse in real-time with other surfers by typing messages) are not necessarily the liveliest places for digital music tips, but you can usually find at least a few enthusiasts hanging around. And message boards are where surfers leave messages for each other over a long period of time.

Here are a couple of places to surf when you need to pick the brain of another music buff:

✔ **imusic.com** (`www.imusic.com`) has countless discussion groups available to online music fans. If you don't know the answer to a technical question, maybe someone here does.

✔ **MP3.com** (`www.mp3.com`) has its own thorough message area (see Figure 4-1). Here, you can find a lot of other newbies, plus experts from the MP3.com offices. With over 10,000 posts, this site is like its own mini-Usenet. A great place to start.

Lists and news

Mailing lists — e-mail-based discussion groups — are convenient places to find helpful techies, but don't swamp the participants with every little question. And don't forget that if you post a message to the group, everyone's going to see what you have to say. Use these lists sparingly for best results.

Check out these lists for general help with MP3 or RealAudio:

- ✔ **Real.com** (www.real.com) offers a mailing list that keeps RealPlayer users up to speed on the latest and greatest technical advances.

- ✔ **The MP3 Place** (www.mp3place.com), as shown in Figure 4-2, is an MP3 site that has its own informative newsletter run by the site's Webmasters. Because the latest hardware and software are often the topic of conversation, you have a good chance at finding some helpful tips. To subscribe, visit www.mp3place.com/newsletter for details.

- ✔ **Wired News** (www.wired.com), the online daily news service from *Wired* magazine (see Figure 4-3), has been covering MP3 since the story first broke. Subscribing to the daily news brief is a good way to keep informed of new players and, more importantly, new technical issues.

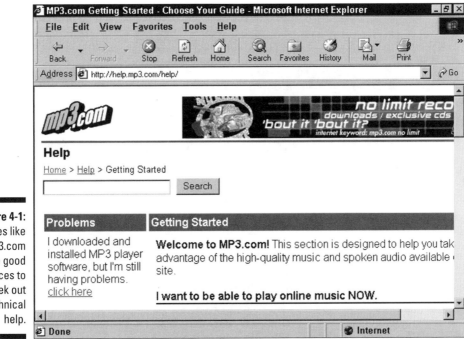

Figure 4-1:
Sites like
MP3.com
are good
places to
seek out
technical
help.

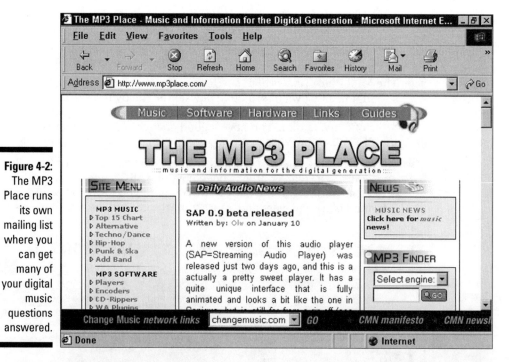

Figure 4-2:
The MP3 Place runs its own mailing list where you can get many of your digital music questions answered.

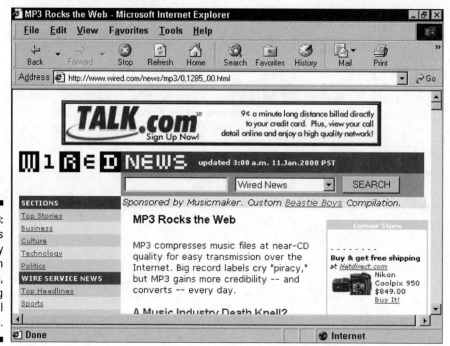

Figure 4-3:
Wired News offers daily coverage on tech news, including digital music.

The Golden Rule

Repeat after me: "Music online is a community. Music online is a community. Music online is a community." If you have problems, you definitely have someone out there to lean on.

Just one catch: Don't expect drive-by advice. To glean the most you can from the group, stick around, participate, and become involved. Like all revolutions, this one starts with you. And, maybe, a guitar.

Part II
Surfing Safari: Finding Music (and Music Stuff)

The 5th Wave   By Rich Tennant

"Guess who found a Kiss merchandise site on the Web while you were gone?"

In this part . . .

*T*his part explores how to start thinking like a music detective — how to find songs and how to network with other digitized musicians and fans. You explore the search sites and enter the burgeoning community of Net listeners and artists.

Chapter 5

Becoming a Digital Music Maven

In This Chapter

▶ Starting your quest

▶ Reaching out for help

▶ Knowing your rights

*Y*ou probably mastered the art of being an offline music fan or musician long ago. Becoming a digital music maven, though, requires a little readjustment in the way you think and, most importantly, the way you search.

The main thing that's different is the rate of change. Offline, you pretty much stick to the tried-and-true pattern of being a fan: You buy a record in a record store, see a concert in an auditorium, and listen to music on your stereo.

Online, not only has all that changed, but all that is continuing to change. Just when you master one form of digital music technology, a new one comes along to shake things up. By learning some basic skills, you can be prepared to ride the waves — no matter how they ebb and flow. In this chapter, you find out how to realign your thinking to make the most out of the digital music frontier.

Becoming Digital

Being a digital music fan is essentially a relationship. There's you. And there's the music. And like any relationship, the more you put into it, the more you get back. The Internet is a big, tricky maze, but if you know how to travel, the journey can offer some irresistible rewards.

After you equip yourself with the necessary hardware and software, the fun can really begin. Whether you crave some new music or some concert tickets, t-shirts or community, you can find it online. In fact, you can find so much online that your online experience can get overwhelming.

Some of my friends get frustrated when they go online because they feel that they can never find what they want. Others feel the opposite way — spending absurd amounts of time online because they can't stop finding stuff they're interested in.

The key to being digital is knowing why you're online in the first place. Here are the four basic types of online music fans:

- ✔ The surfer
- ✔ The hunter
- ✔ The collector
- ✔ The creator

If you're surfing casually

Music fans and musicians have turned hanging out into a fine art. They hang out in record stores. They hang out at each other's homes. They basically live to relax and unwind with their favorite music.

Online, the equivalent of hanging out is what I call *the casual surf*. The casual surf is basically what you do when you have time but nothing much on your mind. Maybe you're in the middle of the workday, and you're feeling burned out. Maybe it's after work and you want to unwind.

Literally millions of people hang out online at any given moment. They're not quite *doing* anything; instead, they're just being. Being digital. One way to avoid the inevitable frustrations of not being able to find online everything you want at the exact moment you want it is to just give yourself some hang-out time.

Here are some tips for letting go and having fun when you're heading out into the surf:

- ✔ **Follow tangents.** Web sites are filled with links to other pages. See where they take you. Maybe you start out at a Beatles page and end up finding out about a whole new artist who appeals to your tastes.

- ✔ **Drop e-mails.** Scroll down to the bottom of home pages you like and look for the address of the person who created it. Don't be shy; the person created the Web page and provided an e-mail link for a reason — to meet people just like you.

- ✔ **Try out new styles.** Web sites are filled with recommendations. If you're just hanging out online, try downloading a few totally random songs. Some of the best discoveries are made just this way.

If you're hunting for stuff

Sometimes, you may be hanging out online and gradually notice that your posture is changing. Instead of leaning back, you're hunched forward. You're typing more quickly. Beads of sweat form on your forehead. You're engaged. You're hunting.

Hunting is way different from surfing or hanging out. Hunting is when you can taste what you want on the tip of your tongue. And you absolutely can't get up from your chair until you find it.

No matter what you're hunting for — songs, information, radio shows, and so forth — you're a lot better off if you pinpoint exactly what you want before you set off on your quest. Consider questions such as these:

✔ Are you looking for a specific song?

✔ Are you looking for a specific artist?

✔ Are you looking for a genre of music?

✔ Are you looking for a certain piece of merchandise — a Backstreet Boys T-shirt, a KISS lunch box, a Wu Tang Clan video game?

The more you can narrow your search on sites like AltaVista, as shown in Figure 5-1, the easier time you have finding what you want. This concept is especially important when you're heading off into search engines (see Chapter 7 for a detailed look at conducting these types of searches).

If you're collecting stuff

When the objects of your hunt start filling up your hard drive (or your home), you've probably moved on to *collecting*. Becoming a collector can happen easily enough. I know one guy who collects hundreds of MP3s every week.

If you find yourself moving into this territory — or you're just interested in getting anything and everything related to your favorite band — here are some things to consider before you start your quest:

✔ **Try to find other fans devoted to the same band or type of music.** If they exist, you may consider joining some mailing lists, newsgroups, or even launching your own Web site. (For more information, see Chapter 8.)

✔ **Decide what you want to do with the stuff you collect.** If you're looking to amass a home collection of music and merchandise, you may want to check out some auction sites, such as eBay (www.ebay.com).

✔ **Don't get burned.** If you really, really start sinking deeply into collecting, you want to make sure you're not violating any copyrights by, for example, downloading a bootlegged concert recording. See "Knowing the Legalities" later in this chapter for more details.

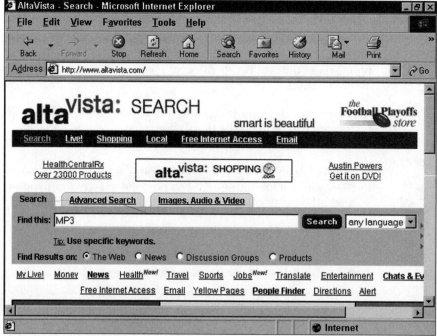

Figure 5-1:
Keep your
search
narrow on
sites like
AltaVista.

If you're creating music

These days, more than ever before, musicians can reach fans directly. If
you're one of the legions of people who are creating music for the Net or just
using the Net to promote yourself or your band, here are some considerations for digital living:

- ✔ **Establish your goals.** Who do you want to listen to your music? Your
  family? Your friends? Heads of record companies? Michael Jackson?

- ✔ **Think about your audience.** If you were a fan, where would you go to
  find something online? Web sites? Search engines? Mailing lists? Surf
  around and do some research before you start on your quest.

- ✔ **Learn to convert your music into digital format.** If you plan to distribute your music online, make sure you nail down the tools that you need
  to convert files to digital music. See Chapter 10 for more information.
  You may even want to find someone to do the job for you.

- ✔ **Be patient.** Results from your efforts may happen overnight or over
  months. The more active you become on the Internet, though, the more
  likely you are to get e-mail feedback from people around the world.

Linking to Win: I Link Therefore I Am

One of the best ways to become a digital music maven is to master the world of links. *Hyperlinks* are like embedded footnotes; each one takes you to a different place that, hopefully, somehow relates to the site you're on.

Sometimes, you may see a link but not have any real idea where it may take you. Before you waste your time downloading the site, run your cursor over the link and look in the status bar at the bottom of your browser. As your cursor passes over the link, you see the URL of the site. The URL may at least give you a sense of whether you're going to an individual's home page or to the Web site of a major commercial service.

In Figure 5-2, you see a link to the Webmaster's e-mail address — a great way to let the Webmaster know what you think of the site.

Of course, after you hit a few dozen links, you can start to feel a bit lost. Where did I start anyway? How do I get back? Here are a couple of quick steps worth jotting down in case you lose your way:

✔ Click the Back button of your Web browser until you get back to where you started or to some other familiar landmark.

✔ In Internet Explorer, click History on the main button bar to see all the places you've been along your way (see Figure 5-3). To return to any of those particular spots, just click the site.

✔ In Netscape Navigator, choose Go from the menu bar to display a menu detailing all the sites you've visited (see Figure 5-4). Choosing a specific site takes you back to that place.

Navigator's Go feature is only good for your current browsing session; if you quit the program, the Go menu is cleared. On the other hand, Explorer's History feature logs your travels for days, weeks, or even months, depending on how you configure the option.

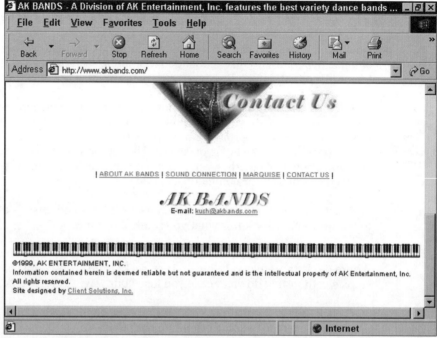

Figure 5-2:
The Webmaster's e-mail address often lurks near the bottom of the home page.

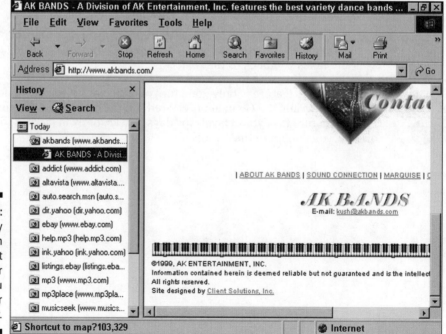

Figure 5-3:
The History button on Internet Explorer helps you find your way.

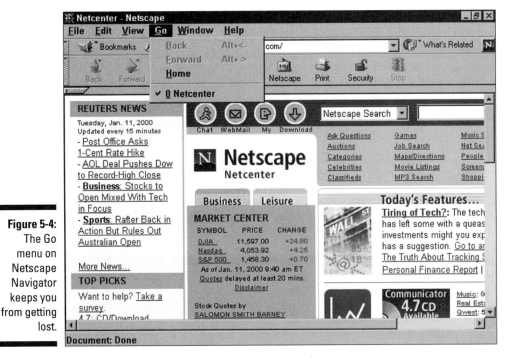

Figure 5-4:
The Go
menu on
Netscape
Navigator
keeps you
from getting
lost.

Networking the Human Way

Don't be fooled: All this technology isn't just a matter of machines. For every
bit, every byte, every file, every program, someone behind the scenes
worked long and hard to bring it to you. Digital music mavens look at the
online world as a thinly veiled global community. To help you get what you
want when shopping, searching, or collecting stuff online, keep the following
two adages in mind.

Software is human

Music software is constantly changing. It grows, it evolves, and, yes, it dies. In
this sense, the software is truly human — sort of a reflection of the people
who make it. Here are a few tips for dealing with software that sometimes
seems all too human:

- ✔ Revisit sites monthly to see if the software you previously downloaded has been upgraded or changed.

- ✔ Sign up for e-mail updates that alert you to important innovations and, possibly, bugs.

- ✔ Don't expect the software to be perfect. Behind every piece of software, after all, is an imperfect human.

Humans are software

I know, that sounds like a line from a bad sci-fi movie, kind of like "Soylent Green is people." But what I mean is that one of your best resources for music online is other people. And people are essentially software — growing, changing, and working out bugs.

When buying, downloading, posting, auctioning, or doing basically anything online, don't forget to reach out to the people who make the wares. Most of the time, they want to hear from you. Also, talk to other users of the software. They may actually know more about the software from using it than the creator does! Other users can provide plenty of useful tips.

Knowing the Legalities

Anyone embarking on the quest for music online needs to know about legalities. Here's the deal.

Is digital music legal?

Any digital music format, including streaming media or MP3, is perfectly, totally, and completely legal. How you *use* a digital music format, however, can be against the law.

The issue here is copyright. In a nutshell, copyright law protects any song or piece of art or lyric created by your favorite band. Because they own their work, the artists have the right to decide how their work is used — and how much they get paid by the person who wants to use the work.

What this means — and this is very important — is that no one can legally exchange digitally-converted versions of existing music without the permission of the artist.

For example, the multitudes of artists on MP3.com have given their permission for people to sample their songs. Madonna, however, doesn't want you to get "Like a Virgin" for nothing. So if you see a site offering her songs, you can rest assured that they're probably illegal copies.

You may wonder about making audiotapes at home. We've all been doing that for years. How is MP3 any different? Basically, it's not. You are allowed to make copies of music or other forms of art for your own personal use (because, presumably, you paid for the CD in the first place); you just can't distribute them to others or receive them from others.

See Chapter 16 for more information on copyright issues.

Yeah, but does anyone really get arrested for this stuff?

Jeffery Levy did. In 1999, the 22-year-old University of Oregon student went down in history as the first person convicted of piracy under the No Electronic Theft act. He was caught by university officials for posting almost 1,000 illegal MP3 songs on his Web site. Though he faced three years in prison and up to $250,000 in fines, Levy instead received two years probation and limited Internet access.

Still, Levy has been the exception. Most people never get arrested or even caught. But that doesn't mean they're free from prosecution. Record labels are becoming a bit more diligent about tracking down illegally distributed music. Often, they issue cease-and-desist letters to Webmasters who are violating copyright laws. That usually does the trick, but if the Webmasters refuse to abide by the letter, the label gets more serious, often going to the courts.

The Recording Industry Association of America (www.riaa.org), whose Web site is shown in Figure 5-5, has filed numerous lawsuits against people who post pirated songs on their sites. As a result, these pirates usually end up shutting down their sites voluntarily rather than face prosecution.

How else is piracy being fought?

Another piracy fighter is the Secure Digital Music Initiative or SDMI (www.sdmi.org). Over 100 companies, including members of the RIAA, support this idea.

The SDMI, whose Web site is shown in Figure 5-6, calls for placing a special digital watermark on music released on CDs. If someone makes a pirated digital version of this music, digital music players equipped with SDMI protection features prevent the illegal songs from being played.

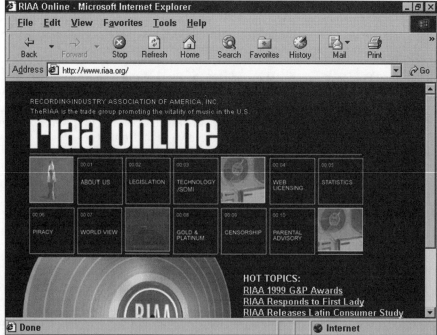

Figure 5-5:
The Recording Industry Association of America monitors copyright infringement of digital music.

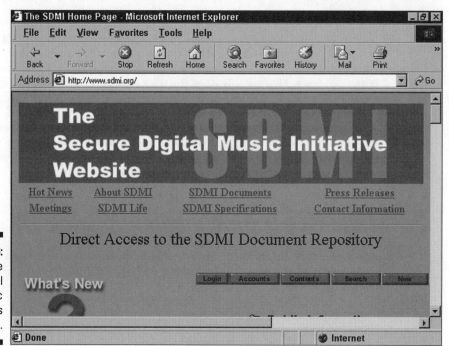

Figure 5-6:
The Secure Digital Music Initiative's Web site.

SDMI's concept is still being developed; there's no telling if and when such a measure may be adopted. But clearly, a lot is at stake for electronic music distribution. Not everything online is meant to be free.

What does all this mean to me?

What all this means is that you take a risk every time you download an illegal song. And, for whatever it's worth, you also deprive the artist of earning money for the music that you like enough to download.

The good news is that as more independent artists, such as Public Enemy (see Figure 5-7), embrace the MP3 format, the freedom of music becomes more widespread.

With major performers like Alanis Morissette and Chuck D giving their permission to have their music distributed in digital format, you can expect more digital music to choose from.

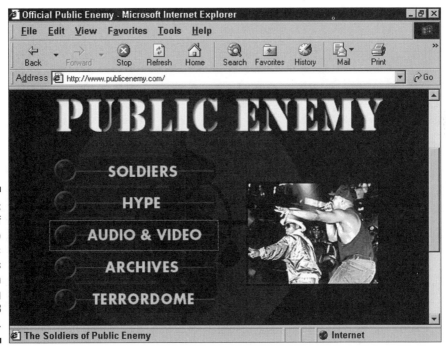

Figure 5-7:
Chuck D of the hip-hop group Public Enemy has been pioneering MP3 activities.

Chapter 6

Shopping for Music Online

- -

In This Chapter

▶ Practicing smart, safe online shopping

▶ Buying all kinds of music online, including digital music

▶ Buying merchandise, concert tickets, and more

- -

A lot of people think that being a music fan online means spending all your time downloading songs. Well, they're half right. Yes, you probably spend a lot of time listening to music, but with the growth of electronic commerce, or *e-commerce,* you have a wide range of merchandise to choose from.

Record stores, concert ticket sellers, T-shirt vendors — they're all heading to the Internet.

Never has updating and maintaining your collection been easier, whether you're, say, a hardcore Elvis Presley aficionado or a casual John Coltrane enthusiast. With some smarts and skills, you can successfully navigate the wires to find everything and anything you do and don't need (but really want to have).

When you think of shopping for music online, the first thing you probably imagine is shopping for CDs. And you can find plenty of CDs out there. No more jumping into the car, driving to the mall, rifling down the crowded aisles just to find out that the local music store doesn't have that title you're looking for.

Don't forget, though, about the other formats: DVD, vinyl, cassettes, and, yes, even 8-track tapes. They're all out there. Plus, many people are selling digital music in the form of MP3s and other types of digital audio, such as Liquid Audio.

In this chapter, you find out how to get the most out of the e-commerce music marketplace. You see how to buy tickets on the Web, how to navigate online CD stores, and even get yourself some downloadable digital tunes to-go.

Shopping Smart

Before you venture onto the Net to score your tenth-row-center Tom Waits tickets, you may want to brush up on the basics of online shopping.

Just as you would think twice before buying a bootleg concert recording from a stranger in the streets, you want to exercise similar caution online. The Federal Trade Commission (www.ftc.gov) — see their Web site in Figure 6-1 — regularly updates its site with the latest in consumer e-commerce protection information.

Here are some essential online shopping tips to keep in mind:

- ✔ Search the FTC site for info about fraudulent dealers.
- ✔ Never disclose personal passwords or credit card numbers to an unknown party.
- ✔ Use a secure browser.
- ✔ Always pay with credit cards.
- ✔ When buying or selling on an auction site, take advantage of escrow services.
- ✔ Avoid promotions that seem too good to be true; they usually are.
- ✔ When buying merchandise, such as musical instruments, be sure to check out the stuff offline in an actual music store. Then move online to score the best deals.

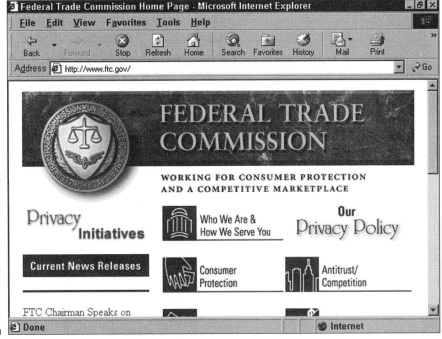

Figure 6-1:
The Federal
Trade
Commission
is a good
source for
information
pertaining to
online fraud.

Understanding Shipping Costs

A lot of people think that shopping online doesn't necessarily make sense, because of the inevitable shipping and handling charges. The good news is that these fees tend to hover around $3 to $5 for most music purchases.

And, even better, you often find a cap on shipping costs; at CDNOW, for example, the top fee is around $5, no matter how many CDs you order.

The bottom line: If you're going to shop for music or music-related goods online, you may as well buy more than one product at a time. Because you're paying for shipping anyway, you save money in the long run if you have the crews toss a few more items into your box.

Buying Music from the Megasites

So you wanna buy some CDs? Odds are, you eventually end up going to one of the megasites. The megasites are the online superstores of CD shopping, where you can find everything from the latest Madonna record to a reggae classic by Peter Tosh.

Table 6-1 lists those stores that are available only on the Net.

Table 6-1	Internet-Only Megasites
Site name	*URL*
Amazon.com	www.amazon.com
Artist Direct Superstore	www.ubl.com
Buy.com	www.buy.com
CDNOW	www.cdnow.com
Tunes	www.tunes.com

Table 6-2 shows the megasites that are simply online versions of offline retailers.

Table 6-2	Web Sites for Offline Retailers
Site name	*URL*
Barnes and Noble	www.bn.com
Borders	www.borders.com
HMV	www.hmv.com
Tower Records	www.towerrecords.com
Virgin Megastore	www.virginmega.com

For a more detailed review of these sites, see the *Music Online Directory*.

The following subsections take you through one of the bigger sites out there, CDNOW. Rest assured, the steps you use here will come in handy at most of the other sites as well.

Searching on a megasite

Here's the good and bad news about CD megasites:

- They have a ton of CDs.
- They have a ton of CDs.

No, that's not a typo. Going into a store where they have everything is great, but you may become frustrated when you're trying to find one thing in particular.

CDNOW, like most megasites, is smart enough to have its search engine on every page. In CDNOW's case, the search engine is conveniently located at the top and bottom of every page (so you never have to click too much and get a nasty sore wrist). Figure 6-2 shows the CDNOW home page, with the search engine ready and waiting.

To search CDNOW, follow these steps:

1. **Choose one of the following criteria from the drop-down menu: Artist, Album Title, Song Title, Record Label, Video Title, or Actor/Director.**

   As an example, try a search for the CD *This Year's Model* by Elvis Costello. You could choose Artist and search for Elvis Costello, but that would return every album he ever made. So, in this case, you're probably better off choosing Album Title.

2. **In the text box, type the name of the artist, album, song, label, movie, or actor/director.**

   In this example, type **This Year's Model**.

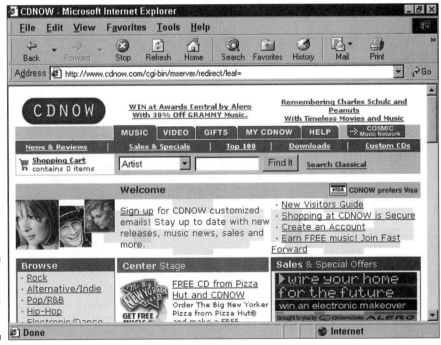

Figure 6-2: The CDNOW home page.

3. Click the Find It button.

The search for *This Year's Model* actually unearths two different results: *This Year's Model* by Elvis Costello and *This Year's Model* by Pizzicato Five, as shown in Figure 6-3.

4. Click the title of the CD you're looking for.

Because you know you're looking for Costello's album, go ahead and click that title. The information page for the CD appears, as shown in Figure 6-4. If you're ready to buy this CD, then jump ahead to "Making a purchase," later in this section.

The previous example was easy, but what happens if you know only the album name and not the artist? How would you know which one to buy?

Consult the experts. CDNOW, like most megasites, has all kinds of music trivia buffs who manage the site behind the scenes. Take advantage of them. If you know only a few lyrics to a song or a title or even something vague like, "It's a happy song that came out last summer and it was in that end-of-the-world movie," e-mail customer service and they'll put their troops to work.

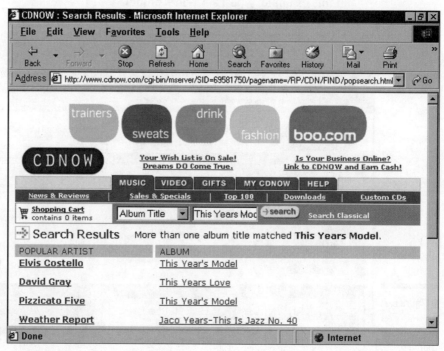

Figure 6-3:
The results of the search.

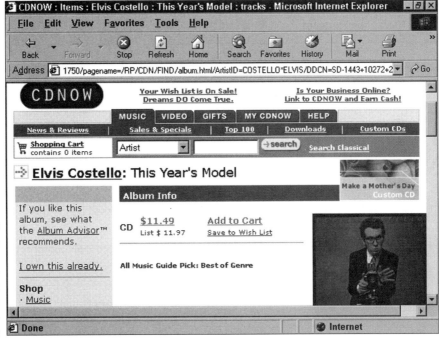

Figure 6-4:
The page
showing the
album you
searched
for.

If all else fails, try some of these methods for refining your search:

✔ Change the spelling of your search phrase. Maybe you're typing in **Melvin Cosell** instead of **Elvis Costello**.

✔ Replace numbers and symbols with letters: Use *and* instead of *&* or use *one* instead of *1*.

✔ Double-check that you chose the proper search criteria in the drop-down menu — odds are, you won't find many artists named *This Year's Model*!

✔ If you're searching for a soundtrack or compilation, expand the search by typing in **Various Artists** and then narrow the search from there.

✔ If you're sure of the artist's name, try typing that in. CDNOW returns every album ever made by the artist.

Browsing for tunes

Maybe you don't know what you want. You just feel like window-shopping.

If you know what genre of music you feel like buying, have a surf around the site's main categories. In CDNOW's case, you can find those genres listed on the left side of the home page. Here are some of the genres you can browse on any music site:

> ✔ Rock
>
> ✔ Hip-hop
>
> ✔ Country
>
> ✔ Folk/blues
>
> ✔ Jazz
>
> ✔ Kids/family

Each section may have its own specials and sales!

You can also seek the experts' advice. On CDNOW and most megasites, look for reviews from major music sources, such as *Rolling Stone* or *Billboard*.

Getting recommendations

Most sites offer some kind of recommendation tool that can suggest music to you based on your interests.

At CDNOW, this tool is called the Album Advisor. Basically, you punch in some artists you like and the computer spews out other similar sounding bands. The results are a hit or miss proposition, but this tool can be a fun way to get turned on to new tunes.

For some reason, CDNOW buries this tool in the Gift section — don't worry, you don't have to be buying a gift to use it. Follow these steps to use the Album Advisor:

1. **On the CDNOW home page, click the Gifts tab at the top of the page.**

   A page comes up listing all kinds of gift-buying options.

2. **Click the <u>Album Advisor</u> link.**

   The Album Advisor search page appears, as shown in Figure 6-5.

3. **Type in up to three names of artists you like.**

   No rules here — just type in anyone who strikes your fancy.

4. **Click Recommend.**

   The site reveals a list of links to artists who strike a similar note.

Other sites, such as Amazon.com, have message boards on which surfers can trade opinions with each other. Other fans are often a great source for recommendations — don't be shy about sending them e-mail.

Figure 6-5:
CDNOW's
album
advisor.

Listening to audio clips

In the old days, you could wander into record stores and go into listening booths: tiny vestibules equipped with turntables and vinyl to sample.

The online equivalent these days is audio clips. At a site such as CDNOW, you often see a little speaker symbol next to a song, which means that a clip is available for you to check out.

Here are some worthwhile tidbits to keep in mind about audio clips:

- ✔ They're free.
- ✔ They rarely include the entire song.
- ✔ To listen to them, you probably need RealPlayer, Windows Media Player, or some other compatible music player. For more information about downloading and installing these music players, see Chapter 3.

Making a purchase

After you find what you want, you can put the item in your shopping cart by clicking an Add to Cart button — or something similar. A *shopping cart* is the virtual equivalent of the cart you push around your local department store. Usually, you can access your shopping cart from any page on the site, to see the names of the items you selected, the prices, and the subtotal of all the items.

Shipping and taxes are not calculated until you check out.

Just as you can adjust the contents of a real-world shopping cart, you can adjust your online selections in a couple of ways:

- ✔ Click Change Quantity to change the amount of items you want.
- ✔ Click Remove Item to delete selections.

Before you make your purchase, you need to create an account on the site. When setting up an account, you need the following information:

- ✔ Login name
- ✔ Password
- ✔ Shipping address and contact information
- ✔ Billing address (if different from your shipping address)
- ✔ Credit card number and expiration date (if you want the site to store this information for more convenient checkout)

Setting up an account is a free process and an added convenience later — with an existing account, you won't have to re-input your information for each subsequent purchase. Not only does setting up an account save you time, it also means that you won't have to send your information over the wires again, which decreases the likelihood that someone will intercept the information.

Most megasites use *secured servers* for the actual transaction part of your order. This means that your credit card number and other vital info should be safe from hackers.

Buying Customized CDs

Mix tapes have always been a passion for finicky music fans; now, you can find a load of CD customization sites that can burn your selected songs on to a disc. The catch? Don't expect to find all your favorite Top-40 hits.

The sites that offer such services must get permission from the artists or record labels to include the songs in these do-it-yourself compilations. Plus, most new releases aren't yet available.

For the most part, either the bands that offer their music in this format are on smaller, indie labels or the songs are classics from decades gone by.

Still, for some old-school fun, this is a groovy way to have your hand in your own CD production. Table 6-3 list sites that offer customized CDs.

Table 6-3	Customized CD Makers
Site name	*URL*
Custom Disc	www.customdisc.com
EMusic	www.emusic.com
Musicmaker	www.musicmaker.com

For a more detailed review of these sites, see the *Music Online Directory*.

Creating a custom CD with MusicMaker

The process of creating your own custom CD is pretty much the same on all sites. MusicMaker (see Figure 6-6), for example, burns a customized CD based on choices you make from over 150,000 songs. In the United States, the minimum order is $9.95 per disc, which gets you about five songs; each additional song after that costs $1.

To create your disc with MusicMaker, you first need to select your songs. MusicMaker has a few ways you can do this — all available from the main home page. You can

- ✔ Search by a specific artist or song title.
- ✔ Browse according to genres, including boogie woogie, children, techno, television, and zydeco.
- ✔ Browse the Top-100 list of songs.
- ✔ Browse the Top-100 artists.
- ✔ Click Suggested Compilations to see what the experts suggest, if you're really feeling lazy.

Figure 6-6:
MusicMaker
lets you
order your
own
customized
CD compila-
tions.

After you decide which songs you want, follow these steps:

1. **Click the name of the desired song or artist.**

   A page listing the individual tracks appears. If you want more information about the song, click Info. If you want to hear a sample clip, click Play.

2. **Click Add to add the song to your list.**

   When you select a song, the Your Custom CD box at the top of the page displays each new track, the length of the track, and the time remaining on the CD, as shown in Figure 6-7.

3. **Continue searching and selecting songs until you're done (or your disc is full).**

Don't worry about choosing the order of the tracks as you're accumulating songs. Wait until you select all your tracks and then click the View/Edit button on the right side of the page. You see a page that lets you not only reorder the tracks, but also delete unwanted tracks.

Personalizing your custom CD

The songs are only the first part of your CD. After you select your tracks, you may want to get stylish by adding art, liner notes, and other accoutrements.

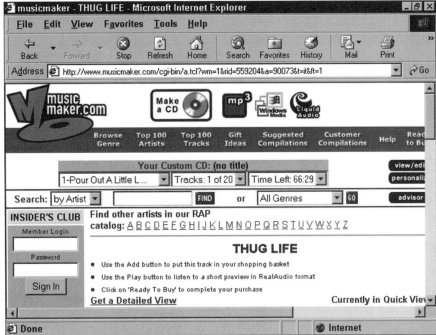

Figure 6-7:
Find songs
for your
customized
CD.

To personalize your CD on MusicMaker, follow these steps:

1. **Click the Personalize button on the right side of the page.**

   The Personalize Your Custom CD page appears, as shown in Figure 6-8.

2. **Scroll down to #1 and type a title for your CD in the text box.**

   Dave's Mix. Dave's Blend. CD à la Dave. Whatever.

3. **In #2, select an image for the face of the CD.**

   MusicMaker includes over a dozen images, from a teddy bear to balloons. Whichever one you choose will appear on your disc.

4. **In #3, select cover art.**

   A lipstick kiss? A teddy bear? You choose.

5. **In #4, type your own liner notes.**

   This could be a Happy Birthday wish, if the CD is a gift, or maybe just your own thoughts about the global significance of your personal mix. Have fun with it.

6. **Click Proceed to finish and check out.**

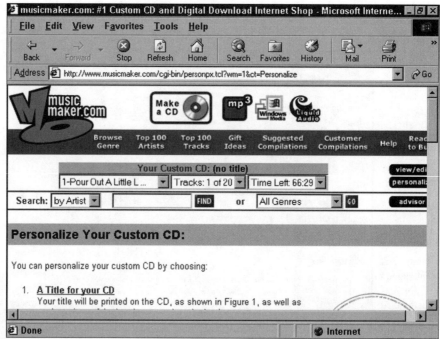

Figure 6-8:
Personalize
your CD.

When you're done, your masterwork is shipped to you within three business days and may take up to two weeks to arrive, depending on the delivery method you choose.

If you think you may return here often, you can set up your own personal account. Doing so gives you special discounts, plus updates through a special MusicMaker e-mail newsletter.

Finding Independent, Imported, and Rare CDs

The expression "hard-to-find" was obviously invented long before the Internet. Nothing is hard-to-find anymore, now that so many people have taken to selling online.

MusicFile (www.musicfile.com), as shown in Figure 6-9, is one of the best sites for searching for rare items. Recently acquired by Amazon.com, MusicFile has all kinds of obscure vinyl and plastic (that's LPs and tapes). You can even post your needs on the message boards in the hope that another fan, with the magic music, surfs on by. Then it's up to you to make a deal.

Other sites for rarities include Dr. Wax (`www.drwax.com`) and the Independent Distribution Network (`http://www.idnmusic.com/index.html`).

Check out these sites if you're looking for any of the following:

- ✔ Out-of-print records
- ✔ Discontinued formats like 8-track tapes or 78 rpm records
- ✔ Imported records from other countries
- ✔ Special collectibles, such as red vinyl records or interview discs

Joining Music Clubs

At some time, almost everyone has filled out one of the ubiquitous magazine postcards to join a record and tape club. For just a penny (or something like that), you get several CDs, as long as you promise to buy a certain number of CDs somewhere down the line.

Columbia House (www.columbiahouse.com), as shown in Figure 6-10, is probably the biggest music club out there. Popular for years offline, Columbia House brings all its services to its gargantuan Web site. You can browse through all the latest hits and specials or read up on special artists in editorial features.

While you're there, you can also sign up for DVD and computer game clubs if you have the extra pennies.

Here are some special online features you get when joining a club:

✔ You can search the club's entire catalog instead of relying on the smattering of selections listed in the paper catalog.

✔ You can receive updates on new releases and reissues of classic albums and tapes on CD.

✔ You can find expanded news and biographical information on different artists.

✔ You can find links to artist Web sites.

✔ Best of all, you can decline the automatic selection so that you don't have to send back that annoying little card every time you want to turn away a CD.

Figure 6-10:
The music membership club from Columbia House lets you buy music at special prices.

Buying Digital Downloads

Many people on the Internet take an entrepreneurial approach to digital music — they let you download, but for a price. The idea works in much the same way as those pay-to-download deals for software: You, the customer, charge the cost to your credit card, and then you can suck down the goods.

This approach does have its advantages for the consumer: Not only can it save you trips to the record store, but also the shipping charges on ordinary online purchases.

The pay-to-download process is still a work in progress, though, so keep in mind that the rules and wares are constantly changing. For example, before you download a new song, you may need to upgrade your specific digital audio player.

EMusic (`www.emusic.com`) is firmly entrenched in the future of music distribution. As shown in Figure 6-11, the Web site deals exclusively in selling downloadable MP3 songs. As is usually the case, selections run along the lines of electronica, hip-hop, and indie rock.

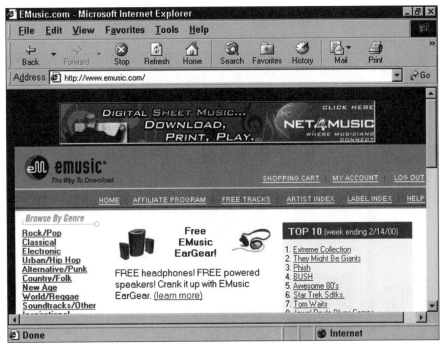

Figure 6-11: Buy downloadable MP3 songs at EMusic.

To get the music, you must have your own MP3 player and a credit card. Pick the song you want, and EMusic charges about 99 cents. An entire album is around $8.99; a short-version album, like an EP, is around $4.99.

Before you begin downloading, you have to create an account. You do this by clicking the <u>My Account</u> link on the home page and then filling out the necessary information:

- ✔ Name
- ✔ Password
- ✔ E-mail address

After you set up an account, follow these steps:

1. **Browse by clicking the genre you're interested in on the left side of the page.**

   You can also browse by artist or record label by clicking the appropriate index link at the top of the page.

2. **When you find the album you want, click the name to see a list of every song on the album (see Figure 6-12).**

   This list includes the price per song. You can also listen to a short clip of the track before you purchase.

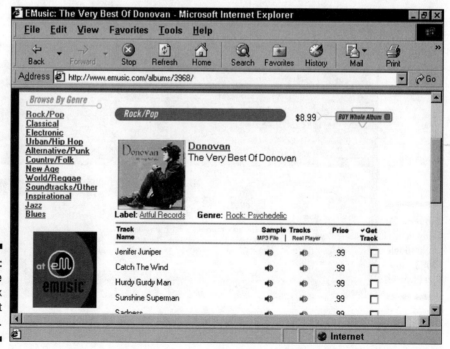

Figure 6-12: Choose which track you want to buy.

3. **Check the box(es) of the song(s) you want to purchase.**

4. **When finished, click Add to Cart.**

   A page showing the contents of your shopping cart appears.

5. **Click Proceed to Checkout to finish the purchase.**

6. **After paying for your order, follow the link to the download page.**

7. **Click the song to download the track.**

   The song is stored on your hard drive and you can log off.

Downloading a four-minute song on a 56K modem takes about eight minutes.

You have only three attempts to download each song. If your modem keeps disconnecting or the dog keeps pulling the plug, you have to e-mail customer service to get another chance at your download.

When you purchase MP3 songs, the music is still subject to the same copyright protection as any MP3 song. You can't legally give the music to someone else. For a primer on the legalities for digital music, see Chapter 5.

Buying Concert Tickets Online

Wouldn't it be nice to buy concert tickets without having to listen to busy signals or wait in long lines? These days, you can cut to the chase and shop for seats online.

The Ticketmaster Web site (www.Ticketmaster.com), as shown in Figure 6-13, has more tickets than any other site. And it has all the services you need — from a personalized My Ticketmaster tool that updates you on when your fave band comes to town, to electronic tickets that are printable from your own PC.

Table 6-4 lists other online ticket sellers. See the *Music Online Directory* for reviews of these sites.

Figure 6-13:
Ticketmaster is one of many sites that lets you select and purchase concert tickets online.

Table 6-4	Online Ticket Sellers
Site name	**URL**
Culture Finder	www.culturefinder.com
Sold Out	www.soldout.com
Ticket Web	www.ticketweb.com
Tickets.com	www.tickets.com

The techniques that you use to find and purchase tickets on Ticketmaster.com can be applied to other sites as well.

Locating your concert

You can use the following methods to find your particular event on Ticketmaster.com:

✔ **Search by event name:** Type in the name of the performer or concert in the Search For text box. To narrow your search by state, select your chosen location from the Choose State drop-down menu.

✔ **Browse by genre:** Click any of the genres on the left side of the main home page. Genres include rock, country, urban, jazz/blues, world music, and oldies.

✔ **Select from some of Ticketmaster's most popular events:** These events are listed in the center of the main home page.

✔ **Do a Power Search:** Go to www.ticketmaster.com/powersearch/. This page enables you to narrow your search by date, city, artist name, and even location of ticket outlets.

Buying tickets

To buy tickets, follow these steps:

1. **Find the concert you want to attend by using one of the search methods in the previous list.**

   The artist's tour schedule appears.

2. **Click to highlight the concert you wish to attend.**

3. **Click Buy Tickets.**

   A purchase page appears, as shown in Figure 6-14, describing all the important details of the show: venue information, date, time, ticket prices, and seating chart (if available).

4. **Scroll down the page and type the number of seats you want to purchase.**

5. **Scroll down and select the ticket price and seat locations from the drop-down menus.**

   Choose Best Available to purchase tickets that are as close to the stage and as near to the center aisle as possible.

6. **Select method of delivery.**

   Generally, you can choose one, two, or three-day delivery or Will Call (which means tickets are left at the door of the event — a good way to avoid shipping costs).

   Prices for delivery vary, but are listed on the page.

7. **Click Continue.**

   After a brief pause, your selected seat and billing information appear. This billing information includes handling charges and convenience charges (fees that the company makes you pay for using this super service).

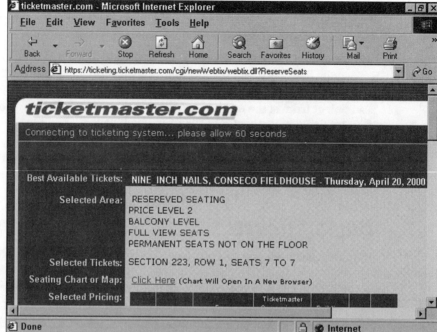

Figure 6-14:
Information
about your
tickets.

8. **Fill out your billing information and click Continue to complete your purchase.**

   Your order is then processed, and your tickets are sent happily on their way.

Finding Videos and DVD

Of course, sometimes you don't want to just listen to music; you want to watch it. Virtually any site that sells videos or DVDs also offers music and concert titles.

DVD Express (www.dvdexpress.com), as shown in Figure 6-15, carries everything and anything that's in DVD, including a great selection of concert films, music video compilations, and music-related documentaries. A bonus of DVD music videos is that they often come packed with groovy little extras.

For $22, the DVD of Pink Floyd's quintessential midnight movie, *The Wall*, comes with previously unreleased footage and interviews with the band.

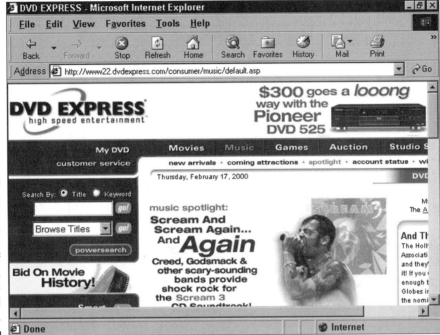

Figure 6-15:
DVD
Express has
a large
selection of
high-quality,
music-
related
DVDs.

Buying Other Cool Stuff

There's no end to the cool, music-related paraphernalia that you can purchase online.

Hankering for a *Yellow Submarine* lunchbox or a Dolly Parton oven mitt (okay, maybe that doesn't really exist)? Or maybe you want to crank up that guitar or bang your drum.

The Net offers all kinds of pit stops to pick up the mundane and sublime of music stuff: from posters to percussion instruments. Check out the *Music Online Directory* for a complete list.

Table 6-5 lists just some of the collectibles you may want and where you can find them.

Table 6-5	Sites for Other Really Cool Music-Related Stuff	
Stuff You Want	**Where to Get It**	**URL**
Posters	123Posters	www.123posters.com
Collectibles	Rockabilia	www.rockabilia.com
Jukeboxes	Jukeboxes, Etc.	www.jukeboxesetc.com
Instruments	Sam Ash	www.samash.com
Sheet music	Sheet Music Direct	www.sheetmusicdirect.com
T-shirts	Kung Fu Nation	www.kungfunation.com
Stereos	Circuit City	www.circuitcity.com

My advice: Shop with your ears offline, and then move online to find the best deals.

Chapter 7

Finding Free Music: Info, Songs, Videos, and More

....

In This Chapter

▶ Finding music info

▶ Finding MP3s

▶ Finding streaming audio

▶ Finding concerts and Net radio

▶ Searching through newsgroups

....

*O*dds are, if you're venturing onto the Net as a music fan, the main thing that you want to find is the music. Who can blame you? Musicians and music fans have never had easier access to music, whether in MP3, streaming audio, or another digital format. You may want to start out by simply getting general info on your favorite artist, or perhaps you want to dive right in.

Don't be disappointed if you can't find free songs from your favorite contemporary artists. Because of sticky copyright and contract issues, many popular bands don't release their music online. For now, at least. But take heart — you may be pleasantly surprised at how much high-quality music by unsigned or unknown artists you can find on the Internet. In this chapter, you discover how to sniff out the good stuff.

Getting Ready to Find Music Online

Before you get down and dirty trying to find free music online, you may want to ask yourself a few questions:

✔ Do you have all the necessary hardware? (See Chapter 2 about turning your PC into a stereo.)

✔ Do you have the required software? (See Chapter 3 for information about streaming audio and MP3 players.)

To be a true digital music detective, you need to keep in mind all the different kinds of music you can find online, such as the following:

- Previously released songs
- New songs
- Samples from upcoming albums
- Songs by unsigned artists
- Live songs from concerts released exclusively online
- Entire albums
- Illegal songs (see Chapter 5 for more information on legalities)
- Real-time broadcasts of music festivals
- Music videos

Searching for Music-Related Stuff Online

If you're just starting out on your quest — or just don't know what you're looking for to begin with — you may want to begin with the biggest target possible. This means hitting up some of the larger search engines rather than narrowing your search right off the bat.

Search engines

A lot of people like to head straight for their big, trusty search engine, such as AltaVista (see Figure 7-1), when they're searching for any kind of information. When searching for music, a large search engine isn't a bad place to start — even if it isn't necessarily the most efficient.

The key to using search engines is to have the most specific idea possible of what you're looking for. The best way to begin is to enter the name of your favorite artist, which calls up a list of related sites that can start you on your quest for music stuff. Table 7-1 lists the most popular search engines that you may want to hit up for general music information.

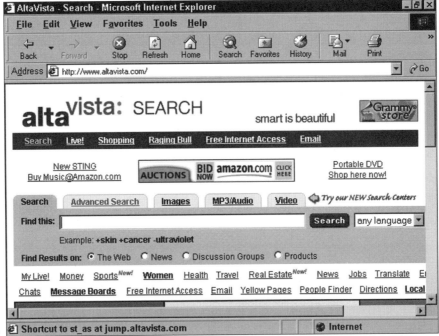

Figure 7-1:
AltaVista,
like other
large search
engines, is a
quick way to
begin a
search.

Table 7-1:	Popular Search Engines
Search engine	*URL*
AltaVista	www.altavista.com
Excite	www.excite.com
GoTo	www.goto.com
Lycos	www.lycos.com
Yahoo!	www.yahoo.com

Don't forget to think about all the bands that your selected artist has appeared in when you're entering information. For example, if you're searching for information about Neil Young, try all of these options:

✔ Search under **Neil Young**

✔ Search under **CSNY**

✔ Search under **Buffalo Springfield**

✔ Search under **Stills and Young**

When you find what you're looking for, you may get a reasonably huge list of sites (especially for Neil!). To continue your journey, start off by visiting the artist's official site. What is an official site? It's a site created and maintained by either the artist or the artist's record label.

Though official sites aren't always better than fan sites, they tend to offer the most updated and reliable information. As a common rule, most bands have registered their own name as the domain name — for example, Radiohead's URL is www.radiohead.com. This is always a good clue that the site is official.

Some official sites include the following:

✔ David Bowie, www.davidbowie.com

✔ Creed, www.creednet.com

✔ Metallica, www.metallica.com

Music hubs

For a step down into the trenches of online music information, you can also start at the *music hubs*. These sites are, in effect, the portals of music online — directory services dedicated to bands, songs, musicians, music news, merchandise, and just about anything else that's related.

The ARTISTdirect Network (www.artistdirect.com), as shown in Figure 7-2, is one such hub — a sprawling (and expanding) suite of Web sites dedicated to helping music fans find the songs and information they most need and desire. The network currently contains four main sections:

✔ **UBL:** The Ultimate Band List — a massive resource for band information

✔ **iMusic:** A sprawling community for music fans (see Chapter 8 for more information)

✔ **Downloads Direct:** A small site featuring new music downloads

✔ **Superstore:** Links to e-commerce music sites

The Ultimate Band List (UBL)

The Ultimate Band List (www.ubl.com), as shown in Figure 7-3, is one of the biggest and oldest resources for finding information on your favorite artists. You could literally spend weeks surfing through all the links.

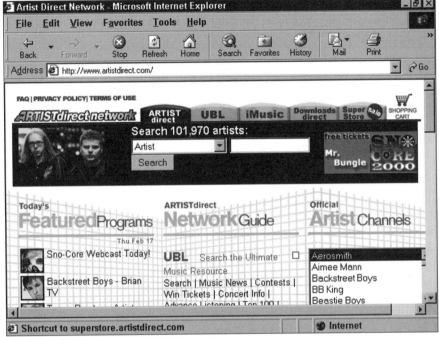

Figure 7-2:
ARTISTdirect includes a search site, a superstore, music downloads, and a music community.

Figure 7-3:
The Ultimate Band List's search engine gives you plenty of info on your favorite artist.

If you go to the UBL just to browse, you can start out with any of the links on the main menu near the top of the home page. Here's a list of each link and what it gives you:

- **Artists:** This link takes you to artist profiles, charts, message boards, and interviews prepared by and for UBL.

- **Contests:** This link takes you to any contests that UBL is currently running. In the past, surfers could win anything from autographed CDs from top-selling artists to concert tickets.

- **Music News:** This link takes you to the latest music news headlines about artists and labels.

- **Concert Info:** This link takes you to live event directories. You can search by venue, artist, or dates. You can also get a list of reviews from other fans about current shows.

- **Hear New Music:** This link takes you to a list of MP3 and other digital music downloads — searchable by your favorite artist.

- **Featured Programs:** This link takes you to live audio programs run by UBL. These include 24-hour streaming radio and TV broadcasts.

- **Community:** This link takes you to UBL's message boards and chats.

- **Add/Edit New Content:** This link takes you to a Web page where you can add your own information about the music scene.

UBL is perfect for those who want more information on a specific artist. To conduct a search for your favorite artist, follow these steps:

1. **Select what you want to search for (for example, artists) from the first text box's drop-down list.**

2. **Enter the keyword for your search.**

   As an example, search for the band Rush. The resulting page lists all the artists whose names contain the word *Rush*. If you're doing a search for Nirvana, you go directly to that band's page, because no other band names contain the word *Nirvana*.

3. **Click the name of the band you're searching for to go to its page.**

   If you see a red-highlighted link that reads <u>Store,</u> clicking it takes you directly to products available for purchase online.

When you get to your artist's page, you have additional links to click to receive more information. These links are available only if pertinent information exists for your selected band. On the Rush page, for example, you can click the following links:

- **Biography:** Shows a UBL bio of the band.

- **Artist Websites:** Lists official sites (prepared by Rush or Rush's record label) and unofficial sites (made by fans).

✔ **Tour Dates:** Provides current tour information for Rush, courtesy of the recording industry tour guide, Pollstar. If a band is not currently touring, you don't find any information on tour dates.

✔ **Downloads:** Takes you to any downloadable files for the band.

✔ **Reviews:** Provides reviews of Rush's albums and concerts. Some of the reviews are from quasi-professional sources, such as Wall of Sound; others are courtesy of fans like you.

✔ **Audio/Video:** Provides links to audio and video files available for download on the Net.

✔ **Lyrics:** Provides song lyrics from the band's various albums.

✔ **Tablature:** Lists links to pages of sheet music.

✔ **Mailing Lists:** Provides links to mailing lists that give you news and information about the band.

✔ **Newsgroups:** Provides links to Usenet message boards devoted to your favorite band.

✔ **Message Board:** Takes you to a discussion board on your favorite band, which is run by UBL.

✔ **Artist Showcase:** Shows you any special information, news, or contests relating to the band.

✔ **Buy Music and Merchandise:** Entices you to shell out cash for albums and other goodies. You can find links to various e-commerce deals for your band on the main page.

✔ **Listening Room:** Takes you to any special audio happenings — such as a preview of a new Rush album.

Downloads Direct

The Downloads Direct section of the ARTISTdirect Network features new and different songs for you to download. Songs are categorized according to genre: pop, rock, electronic, hip-hop/r&b, and alternative.

The selection isn't great, but this section is a good place to check for new, exclusive tracks by popular artists ranging from Bjork to Counting Crows. Songs come in a variety of formats, such as the following:

✔ MP3

✔ Liquid Audio

✔ RealAudio

✔ Windows Media

Unfortunately, the site doesn't tell you which format the music is in until right before you download it.

Finding MP3s

Okay, okay, okay: I'll cut to the chase. Where can you find all those free and amazing MP3 files you keep reading about? This section shows you where and how to locate those tunes.

Understanding bootlegs

Like any greatly hyped revolution, MP3 has suffered a bit from overexposure. Lots of people I speak with assume that they can find Top-40 songs by all their favorite artists.

As mentioned in Chapter 4, copyright and contract issues prevent most major hits from being made available on the Web as free MP3 files. After all, the record companies are in this business to make money, and giving away copies of their hit tunes isn't exactly the best way to bring in the cash — they prefer that you buy the CD.

That said, you may find links to many free MP3 files by famous pop artists. Odds are, these are illegal, or *bootleg*, copies of the songs, and the Webmaster is violating copyright law by posting them. Nothing can stop you from downloading them, but just be aware that you are participating in an illegal act if you do.

Sometimes, when you click one of these hyperlinks, you may find that the file has mysteriously vanished. That's probably because the Webmaster buckled under the pressure from the artist's record label to remove the file.

To play it safe, stick to songs downloaded from well-known sources, such as those discussed throughout this book.

Unearthing songs from MP3.com

You can find tons of MP3 sites on the Net, but the mother ship of all MP3 sites, MP3.com (`www.mp3.com`), as shown in Figure 7-4, is the place to start your journey for new MP3 music. And I emphasize the word *new*. What you won't find here are songs by bands whose work is already lining your record shelves. Instead, MP3.com mainly features music by independent and unsigned artists.

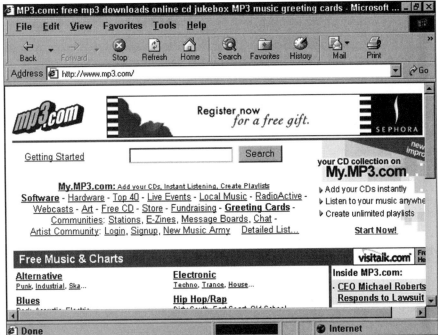

Figure 7-4:
MP3.com
has thou-
sands of
free songs
for the
download.

Yes, there is definitely a reason why some of these bands don't have record deals — they're just not very good. But you may be able to find a star in the making — or just a band that's worth listening to but perhaps is outside the radar of the popular music machine.

A recently revamped interface makes it easy to browse through the typical categories, as well as some of the more obscure categories, such as East Coast Hip-Hop and Rock en Español.

You can also search by artist, region, and musical genre. And you can also check out a list of the most frequently downloaded songs.

To listen to a file on MP3.com, you have a few options:

- ✔ Click **Hi-Fi Play** to listen to the song instantly if you have broadband Internet access, such as DSL, cable modem, or T1.

- ✔ Click **Lo-Fi Play** to listen to the audio if you have lower than a 56K modem.

- ✔ Click **Download** to download the MP3 file to your hard drive or a disk.

- ✔ Click Artist Radio **Lo-Fi** or **High-Fi Play** to hear each and every available song by the chosen artist played instantly (though, fortunately, not at the same time).

Downloading MP3 files from MP3.com

Music Web sites generally have different procedures for downloading songs. Always check the site for special instructions.

Downloading music files from most sites is usually a point 'n' click affair. For example, here's how to download songs from MP3.com:

1. **Find the song you want to download.**

2. **Click the <u>Download</u> link to begin downloading the song.**

   You see the size of the file next to the <u>Download</u> link.

   Your computer prompts you for the location where you want to save the file.

3. **Browse to the location where you want to save the file and click OK.**

   The song downloads to your hard drive.

Unlike other sites, MP3.com offers some added features, such as giving you the option to e-mail a song to a friend or store it for future access. To do this, click the link for My.MP3.com. After you set up your account, the site enables you to do cool stuff like the following:

- ✔ Make massive playlists for songs you want to hear when you visit MP3.com.
- ✔ Have your MP3 songs stored at the site instead of downloaded to your hard drive.

For general download and installation information, see Chapter 4.

MP3.com isn't the only place to suck down the latest MP3 tracks. For a more detailed list, see the *Music Online Directory*.

Scouring MP3 search sites

Outside the main MP3 music hubs, you can have a go at search engines tailored specifically for finding digital audio. Like any search engine, getting good search results means being a good searcher — using appropriate keywords and combinations to unearth the songs you're craving.

Table 7-2 lists a few of the more popular MP3 search sites. Check out the *Music Online Directory* later in this book for more information.

Table 7-2:	MP3 Search Sites
Site name	*URL*
2Look4	www.2look4.com
MP3Now	www.mp3now.com
Listen.com	www.listen.com

Searching for MP3s on other sites

In addition to MP3.com, try searching for MP3s at the following sites:

- **AltaVista** (www.altavista.com): Click the MP3/Audio tab at the top of the home page.

- **Yahoo! Digital** (digital.broadcast.com): Click the Audio link on the left side of the page to browse through many music categories.

- **Lycos** (music.lycos.com/mp3/): Search through the massive Lycos MP3 library (see Figure 7-5).

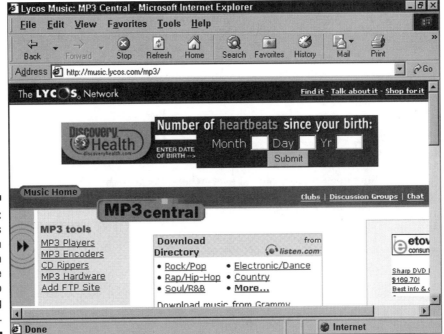

Figure 7-5:
Lycos has its own search engine dedicated to finding MP3s.

At these sites, you just type in the desired song or artist name and then weed through the results. Unfortunately, no hard and fast way exists to figure out which files are bogus and which are not. Many of these songs are, yes, illegal, so you may find that the links are faulty.

See "Downloading MP3 files from MP3.com" earlier in this chapter for further details.

Problems?

Okay, you go through all the necessary hoops to download an MP3 file and it won't work. Don't fret — it's probably not your fault. Here are a number of good reasons why MP3 downloads can give you a headache, an error message, or both:

- **Time limits:** To prevent swamps of traffic, some Webmasters set their computer servers on timers to go on and off throughout the day. Unfortunately, they don't often post when they're open for business.

- **Overcrowding:** Think of a computer server as a water tap — it can fill only so many glasses of water at a time. If too many people are trying to download MP3s, the server can overload. When in doubt, try again to connect later.

- **No free meals:** Other Webmasters are stubborn about MP3s; they don't want to give you a free deal unless you give them something in return. This is a popular practice of people dealing in illegal MP3s.

- **Password problem:** Another way MP3 Webmasters try to limit traffic is to require passwords. Make sure you have the correct password to access a site.

Finding Streaming Audio

Streaming audio is almost everywhere. Because this format has been around longer than MP3, it is, without a doubt, the most ubiquitous of digital music formats. Streaming audio doesn't just mean songs. You can also find the following:

- Music news
- Concerts
- Interviews with artists
- Festivals
- Radio broadcasts

Here's some great news about streaming audio — you may find more stuff available by big name artists. The reason is simple: You can't really steal (otherwise known as download) the music. Because streaming audio is essentially broadcast onto your desktop as a one-time affair, artists don't have to worry about anyone illegally copying or distributing the music.

But here's some really bad news about streaming audio: 56K or less modems don't offer the kind of bandwidth necessary to really enjoy hi-fi broadcasts. However, with the increasing popularity of digital subscriber lines, cable modems, and the like, more and more people are able to enjoy these bandwidth-hogging broadcasts.

As with MP3 or any other digital music format, you can search for streaming audio by using the popular search engines, such as Yahoo! or Excite. However, you may do better by going to a more specialized site. In the subsections below, I examine the features of a couple of the most popular streaming audio sites.

Real.com Guide

Run by RealNetworks, the company behind RealPlayer, the Real.com Guide (www.realguide.com), as shown in Figure 7-6, clues you into all things Real (in the RealAudio and RealVideo formats, that is). The main page compiles category listings of events from sites across the Web, including live performances, radio stations, and news.

For a more detailed look at Real music offerings, click the <u>Music</u> link on the left side of the page.

The Music page breaks down streaming audio into options that include the following:

- **Artists:** Over 500 from the Backstreet Boys to Verve

- **Genres:** Sites according to style — from jazz to world music

- **Live Concerts:** Mainly rock shows, including those archived from previous nights

- **News/Reviews:** Up-to-date daily music news and reviews

- **Record Labels:** Links to streaming audio on record label sites

- **Shopping:** Links to e-commerce sites with Real audio previews

- **Shows:** Audio entertainment shows made specifically for the Net, such as Bo Lewis's Big Band Dance Party, which is devoted to swing music

- **Videos:** Links to music video sites, including MTV

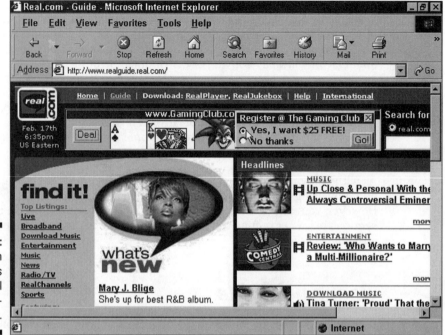

Figure 7-6:
Real.com
Guide lets
you get Real
with stream-
ing audio.

If you don't find what you're looking for in these sections, Real.com Guide also offers its own search engine. Again, the more specific you can make your search, the better your results.

WindowsMedia.Com

You can find streaming tunes in the Windows Media format at Microsoft's WindowsMedia.com (http://windowsmedia.microsoft.com), as shown in Figure 7-7. The main page shows you the major types of streaming goods out there, from weather reports to daily jokes. Here are a couple of the options:

✔ Click Music to get to the site's collection of music-related links. You can find music previews for major artists, such as Puff Daddy and the Foo Fighters. Some bands, such as the Violent Femmes, have made entire albums available for your streaming pleasure.

✔ Click Radio to get to Webcasts from radio stations across the world. Many times, you may be listening to the same broadcast that someone in the station's actual locale is hearing. You can search for stations according to location or format (FM or AM).

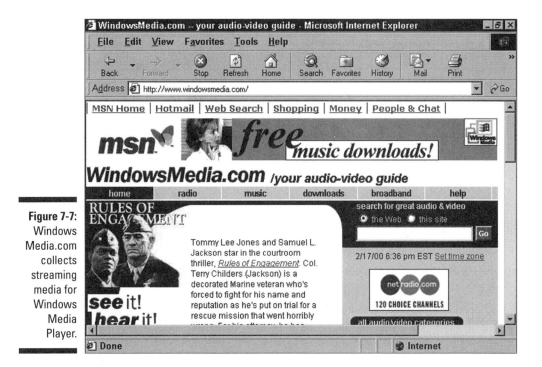

Figure 7-7:
Windows
Media.com
collects
streaming
media for
Windows
Media
Player.

Finding Music Videos

With streaming media players like RealPlayer, Windows Media Player, and QuickTime Player (see Chapter 3 for more information about installing these players), surfers can now tune in to music videos online. Now, you don't have to wait for MTV or VH-1 to show your favorite video; you can just boot it up from the Net.

That's the good news.

The bad news is bandwidth. Just like hi-fi audio, music videos are fat with data, and they have a little trouble squeezing through an average modem. The result is choppy viewing.

Just as a video gets started, you may see the singer suddenly freeze. No, he's not breakdancing; he's just stuck in transfer.

If you have a broadband connection, such as a digital subscriber line, T1, or cable modem, you receive a fairly nice, consistent image.

Table 7-3 lists sites that feature streaming music video.

Table 7-3:	Sites with Streaming Music Video
Site name	*URL*
MTV	`www.mtv.com`
VH1	`www.vh1.com`
Much Music	`www.muchmusic.com`
Launch	`www.launch.com`
Streamland	`www.streamland.com`

MTV has — no surprise — a massive collection of videos available on its Web site (`www.mtv.com`). On the main page, as shown in Figure 7-8, you can search for a specific band or use the drop-down menus to scroll to an artist by name.

Surfing the MTV site is like being in a video music library. In addition to all the popular videos you see on TV, you can find all kinds of arcane clips from MTV's archives as well — including in-studio gigs.

Figure 7-8:
The MTV
home page.

Some of these clips are in the old-fashioned MOV format, which means they aren't streaming media. MOV is clunky and less pristine than RealVideo or Windows Media, but it gets the job done. Don't worry about the format — your media player can play all those old formats. You do have to wait for the whole download, however: An average-length song can be as long as a half hour.

Not all songs are available in full-length format; some are only available as short clips.

As with streaming audio, you cannot save streaming video — such as a music video at MTV — to your hard drive. Sorry.

To browse MTV's massive list of archives, follow these steps:

1. **Choose the appropriate Find a Band drop-down menu and scroll until you find the band you're looking for.**

2. **Click the band's name.**

   You see a page listing all the band's available videos from MTV's vault, as well as exclusive online videos and interviews.

3. **To view a video, click the song name.**

Chapter 8

Hanging with the Music Online Community

In This Chapter

▶ Finding other fans and musicians online

▶ Surfing general and niche music interest sites

▶ Tapping mailing lists and newsgroups

▶ Chatting it up

Music fans and musicians were among the earliest pioneers on the Net. Today, thousands of communities, from sprawling Web sites to insider mailing lists, thrive online. This chapter looks at how you can find and join these groups.

Why do it? Why blow so much time trying to connect with other people online when you've got plenty to choose from offline? Well, I can think of several reasons.

In music online communities, you can do the following:

✔ Trade digital music files

✔ Meet other fans

✔ Meet musicians

✔ Network with people in the music industry

✔ Chat with stars

✔ Stay informed about music news and information

Most of all, you can find other people who share your interests. If you're, say, the only Pixies fan in Poughkeepsie, you can find countless other fans of the group with just a few clicks. If you're the only Grateful Dead fan in Toulouse, you can seek out Deadheads online.

This chapter shows you how to find a community online, no matter what your musical tastes. Now get going.

Big Cliques

Online, there are little clicks, there are big clicks, and then there are community cliques. As opposed to individual Web sites dedicated to different bands, these sites act as networks or community groups or whatever other social analogy you can think of.

Big cliques are places you can go to surf between, say, a gathering of diehard 'NSYNC fans and rabid followers of Korn. These include the following:

- ✔ iMusic
- ✔ Web rings
- ✔ Clubs
- ✔ Newsgroups
- ✔ Mailing lists
- ✔ Chat

iMusic

Run by ARTISTdirect, the company behind the Ultimate Band List (see Chapter 7 for more information about the UBL), iMusic (www.imusic.com) is home to over 1.5 million music fans of all shapes and sizes. Figure 8-1 shows iMusic's home page.

You can search for message boards by typing in the band name in the artist search section. Or you can join in on any discussion topics — from Beck's latest release to Lil' Kim's latest garb. You can also find long-running discussions on such erstwhile topics as rock versus rap or misheard lyrics.

Searching for artists on iMusic

At the top of the page, a pull-down index menu lets you search by the following criteria:

- ✔ Artist name: the name of the musician
- ✔ Message boards: for info on discussion groups
- ✔ Soundtracks: for movie soundtrack information

Figure 8-1:
iMusic is a
hub of over
1.5 million
music fans.

Searching by artist name gives you the most links to places to explore on iMusic. Follow these steps:

1. **Select Artists from the iMusic Index pull-down menu.**

2. **Type the name of the artist in the search text box.**

   For example, say you're searching for Madonna.

3. **Click Find.**

   A page appears listing all related links on iMusic. In this case, you see a link to the Madonna Artist Showcase and the Madonna Message Board.

Navigating links on iMusic

The *Artist Showcase* is, essentially, the mission control of all the links on iMusic for a specific artist. You can find links to the following:

- ✔ Tour dates
- ✔ Biographical information
- ✔ Music downloads
- ✔ Artist's Web sites
- ✔ Reviews

✔ Mailing lists

✔ Newsgroups

Though all these links are listed together, note that only the tour dates, biographical information, downloads, and links to artist's Web sites are maintained by iMusic; all the others are created by various denizens of the Net (and thus may not be as reliable).

Setting up an iMusic user profile

If you really want to get into the action at iMusic, you need to create a user profile and jump into the lively message board discussions.

A *user profile* is basically your vita: a page of personal information about your musical likes and dislikes. iMusic members make extensive use of these profiles, because the profiles provide the only means members have of getting to know each other.

To create a user profile, follow these steps:

1. **Click the <u>User Profiles</u> link (listed in the upper-left corner under Featured Communities) on the iMusic home page.**

   This link takes you to the page listing all the user profiles on iMusic.

2. **Click <u>Here To Create Or Modify Your Own User Profile</u>.**

   You see a rather ugly yellow form that lets you create or modify your user profile, as shown in Figure 8-2.

3. **Click the Add A New Password button.**

   A page appears with three text boxes for your name, e-mail address, and password. You also have the option to receive the iMusic newsletter.

4. **Type your name in the first text box.**

   This doesn't have to be your real name — just choose a nickname you want other members to call you.

5. **Type your e-mail address and password in the remaining text boxes.**

6. **Select Yes or No as to whether you want to receive iMusic's e-mail newsletter.**

   If you're looking to be an active part of the community, the newsletter is a good way to stay informed.

7. **Click the Submit Password button.**

   A page appears telling you that your information has been added. Your name and password appear in the text boxes.

   If the name you type is already taken by another member, you see a page telling you to choose a new name. Your nickname must be unique.

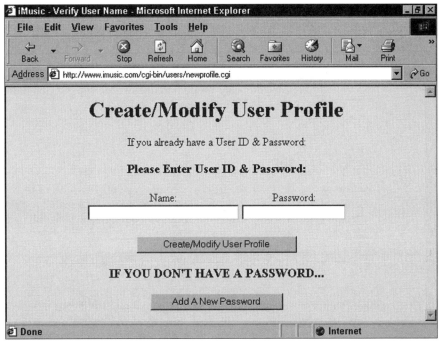

Figure 8-2:
Create or
modify your
user profile.

8. **Click the Create/Modify User Profile button.**

   The New/Update User Profile page appears, on which you input all the details of your personal profile, such as your real name, likes, dislikes, links, your Web page (if you have one), and even your motto. (Though I wouldn't suggest "Rock on, dude!" unless you want to sound like a dweeb.)

   This page asks for more info than you probably ever want to give to someone you meet online, but all this information is optional. If you prefer, you don't have to fill out anything at all. Be sure to heed iMusic's warnings about entering your last name and other info that's too personal, such as your telephone number.

9. **Type in your information and then click Submit Profile.**

   Your user profile appears on another page. Congratulations. Now go make some friends.

Communicating with other fans at iMusic

After you have your user profile, you can either chat it up live with other members or jump in to the heated discussion on the iMusic message boards.

First, scroll down to the bottom of the iMusic home page. From here, do one of the following:

✔ Click **Message Boards** to see a list of categories for discussion — from country to blues, from Madonna to Frank Zappa. After you find a topic you want to chime in about, type in your comments at the bottom of the page and then click Post Comment.

✔ Click **Chat** to call up a list of topical chat rooms. After clicking a room, you need to enter your user name and password. Type in this information, and then click Post as User Name to enter the lair.

Web rings

Web rings are kind of like support groups for fans. Instead of merely having dozens of separate sites devoted to a single artist, the sites are linked together — you start at one site; then go to the next; then the next, until you find yourself back where you started.

Generally, one individual starts a Web ring. Then that person contacts other people who have similar Web sites and asks them to join the ring. After enough sites have joined, the ring's founder may create a Web ring home page that serves as the ring's official starting point. From there, you can usually click a <u>Next</u> link (or <u>Previous</u> link when you're in the ring) to take you to the next site in the ring. Most Web ring home pages have a page that lists the links to all the pages in the ring, so you can choose a specific site to go to instead of clicking through the entire ring.

When you get to each site, you likely find a little banner saying that the Webmaster is a proud member of that particular Web ring. Web rings are continually expanding with new sites.

WebRing (www.webring.com) is a huge directory of Web rings. Its RingWorld Directory provides links to a number of topics. You can find the launch pad for music-related Web rings (see Figure 8-3) under the Arts and Humanities section, or simply go directly to www.webring.com/ringworld/arts/music.html.

Table 8-1 lists some of the music-oriented Web rings you can find in the RingWorld Directory:

Table 8-1:	Music-related Web Rings	
Web ring	*URL*	*Description*
Lyrics Ring	http://tinpan.fortunecity.com/tripper/811	For song lyrics for rock, pop, and hip-hop music
The U2 Web Ring	www.interference.com/u2webring	For the rock band U2

Web ring	URL	Description
The Organ Web Ring	www.organweb ring.com	For organ fans and musicians
The Bluegrass Acoustic Music Web Ring	www.blueaudio.com/ ring.htm	For fans of bluegrass and related acoustic music
The REM Web Ring	www.remrock.com/ remweb	For fans of the quintessential college rock band, REM
The Female Singer/ Songwriter Web Ring	www.geocities.com/ sunsetstrip/back stage/9036	For female musicians such as Jewel and Tori Amos
The Arabic Song Web Ring	http://members.tri pod.com/asring	For people who enjoy Arabic music

To add your site to a Web ring, look for a link that takes you to that particular group's ring homepage. Once there, you should be able to find a link to submit your Web site to the ring. The submission process is usually pretty simple: Just fill out your vital details — Web address, e-mail, and so on — and send it along. Within a couple days, you find your site added to the ring.

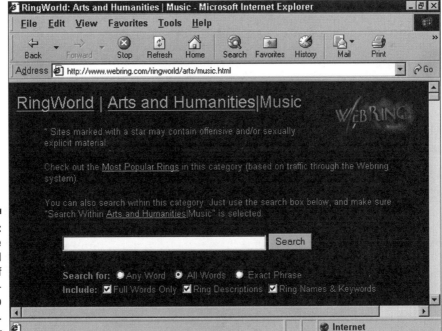

Figure 8-3:
The RingWorld Directory of music-related Web rings.

Yahoo! Clubs

Lately, the major search engines have been getting into the community game with their own special interest clubs. Yahoo! has capitalized on its popularity with its own active communities; you can find music-related communities at `http://clubs.yahoo.com/music`, as shown in Figure 8-4.

Basically, anyone can start a club, complete with chat, message boards, Web pages, and multimedia files. Club topics range from car audio to songwriter. Starting a club is a good way to meet other fans and musicians. You only have to do as much as you feel like to maintain a club, but the more you get involved, the more active your club will probably become.

Here's how to create your own club:

1. **Go to the Yahoo! music clubs page at** `http://clubs.yahoo.com/music`.

2. **Click the category of music sites that best represents the club you wish to create.**

   A page appears, showing the list of existing clubs in that category.

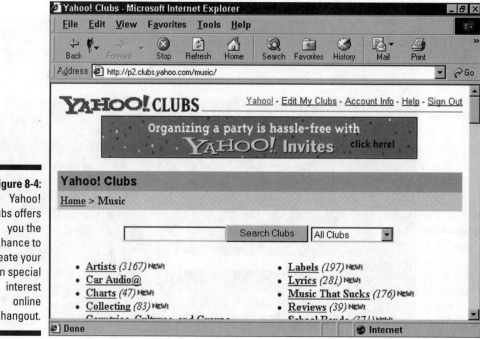

Figure 8-4:
Yahoo! Clubs offers you the chance to create your own special interest online hangout.

3. **Click the Create a Club button near the top of the page.**

   A page comes up asking you to sign in using your Yahoo! user ID and password. If you don't have a Yahoo! user ID, click the <u>Sign Me Up!</u> link to register for free. When you register, you receive a free Yahoo! e-mail account.

4. **Enter your user ID and password, and click Sign In.**

   The Create a Club page appears, asking you to confirm you club selection and to confirm your Yahoo! e-mail address.

5. **Click the Email Instructions button.**

   Yahoo! sends instructions to your Yahoo! e-mail address for setting up your club. Don't ask me why they don't just give you a generic instructions page — I just work here.

6. **Go to the Yahoo! main page at** `www.yahoo.com`.

7. **Click the <u>Check Mail</u> link at the top of the page.**

8. **If you are prompted for your user ID and password, enter them and click Sign In.**

   Your Yahoo! e-mail page appears, showing whether you have any new messages.

9. **Click <u>Inbox</u>.**

   You should see an e-mail message titled "Get Your Club Started."

10. **Click the <u>Get Your Club Started</u> link to open the e-mail message.**

    You see a link to your special area of Yahoo! in which you set up your club.

11. **Click the link.**

    Whew! Could they make this more complicated? Don't fret — you're almost done.

    When you click the link, the Create a Club page (finally!) reappears in a new browser window, as shown in Figure 8-5.

12. **Choose a name for your club.**

    When naming your club, keep in mind that thousands and thousands and thousands of people will run their eyeballs over just as many club names. Keep your club name simple.

13. **Choose your location. (This is optional.)**

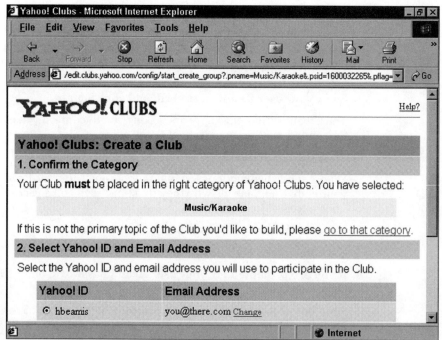

Figure 8-5:
Create your
music club
on Yahoo!

14. **Choose whether you want your club listed in the Yahoo! Club Directory.**

    Odds are, you do.

15. **Review the Terms of Service, take some aspirin for the headache they give you, and click Accept or Decline.**

After you create your club, you can invite friends to join. You may be shocked at how many people actually come to visit your club. Your days of loneliness are over.

Tapping newsgroups

Newsgroups are a lot more than just news. More specifically, this area of the Internet — sometimes called *Usenet* — is full of ongoing conversations. At least 50,000 different newsgroups are out there, and people leave, or *post,* messages for each other on almost every topic you can — and can't — imagine.

To read messages on a newsgroup, you need a *newsreader.* Most new e-mail programs, such as Outlook Express, have a built-in newsgroup feature. But Web browsers, such as Netscape Navigator and Internet Explorer, also have built-in newsreaders. For more on using newsreaders, check out *Internet For Dummies,* 7th Edition, by John R. Levine, Carol Baroudi, and Margaret Levine Young, and published by IDG Books Worldwide, Inc.

For music fans, hundreds of discussions take place in newsgroups on everything from Abba to xylophones.

A detailed list of some popular music-oriented newsgroups is available in the *Music Online Directory.* If you want to search yourself, I suggest you start out at Deja.com (www.deja.com), as shown in Figure 8-6. This site lets you search and peruse newsgroups in a relatively organized way.

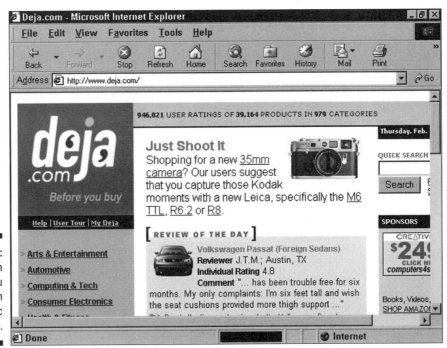

Figure 8-6: Deja.com helps you sift through music newsgroups.

Here are some tips when surfing newsgroups:

- **Get the FAQs (Frequently Asked Questions).** Newsgroups are essentially tiny online communities. And like all communities, the people who hang out there have their own ways of doing things. Before you start asking them stuff that may ruffle their feathers, check out the Usenet Hypertext FAQ Archives at `www.faqs.org`.

- **Lurk a while.** Before you dive into the conversation, listen to what other participants have to say. Think of it as going to a party and killing time at the cocktail bar before you decide whom to talk to. *Lurking,* as it's known in netspeak, is a good way to get a feel for the crowd.

- **Keep it simple.** When you have a question or a point, be brief. Nothing is more annoying than a big long message clogging up the message boards. Unless you're really, really eloquent, most people won't have the patience to read what you have to say.

- **Think about your subject.** When you post a message, you have the chance to include a subject name. Again, the flood of messages in newsgroups is so heavy that you're best off trying to be succinct, sharp, and — it never hurts — clever.

- **Watch the bootleggers.** When you start surfing MP3 newsgroups, you may find many, many, many people who claim — and may be telling the truth — to have, say, the entire Led Zeppelin catalog on bootleg digital audio. Be careful. As I discuss in Chapter 5, the legalities over copyright infringement are worth considering.

Subscribing to mailing lists

Sometimes called *listservs, mailing lists* are e-mail–based discussion groups on niche topics.

To join a mailing list, you usually have to send an e-mail to the person running it; often subscriptions are handled by robot applications, so you simply send in a request and then automatically get added to the list. Sometimes, you have to get special permission from the list master.

Here are the kinds of mailing lists you can find out there:

- **Moderated or unmoderated:** *Moderated lists* are hosted by someone who basically keeps the conversation in line. They steer you to a topic or act like a resident expert, suggesting topics to pick up on. *Unmoderated lists* don't have such a watchdog; anything goes in unmoderated lists.

✔ **Public or private:** *Public lists* are open to anyone. *Private lists* are just that — lists that require some kind of special access, usually an invitation by the creator in the form of a password.

✔ **Edited or unedited:** A host for a site may state ahead of time that all messages must be sent to him or her before going out to the group. And, in this case, the host may request the right to edit your posts for space and brevity.

After you join a list, the messages show up in your e-mail inbox along with your other messages.

Think of mailing lists as more private versions of newsgroups. Instead of just being out there in the Wild West of the Net, they're going discreetly into the mail boxes of people who have chosen to subscribe.

A good way to choose music mailing lists is to start out at Liszt (`www.liszt.com/select/Music/`), as shown in Figure 8-7. Like Deja.com for newsgroups, Liszt collects mailing lists on hundreds of topics. You can either browse through the categories of Liszt's mailing list resources or do your own search by band name or musical genre.

Figure 8-7:
Liszt is a
good place
to search
for music
mailing lists.

Other mailing lists can be found across the Web, such as on individual sites or Web Rings. For some suggested mailing lists, see the *Music Online Directory*.

Nothing in life, including your online life, is forever. If you decide that you don't want to be on a mailing list anymore, you can always unsubscribe. Each mailing list has its own protocol for how to unsubscribe, but generally unsubscribing is as easy as sending a request to the administrator.

Chatting It Up

Music fans and musicians love to talk. Talk about their favorite bands, albums, songs, concerts, song lists, you name it — if it hums, they talk about it. The Net has many resources for talking with other fans or, as it's called in netspeak, *chat*.

In case you're unfamiliar with the concept, chatting is when you exchange typed messages with other people in real-time. Chatting is just like having a conversation, only you use your keyboard rather than your mouth.

Here are different types of chat environments:

- ✔ **Instant messaging:** Programs, such as ICQ and AOL Instant Messenger, that enable you to chat with other individuals in real-time over the Net.

- ✔ **Internet Relay Chat (IRC):** Open discussions over the Internet. These are live, text-based chats on literally thousands of topics. To participate in IRC, you need an IRC client. For more information, see *Internet For Dummies*, 7th Edition, by John R. Levine, Carol Baroudi, and Margaret Levine Young, published by IDG Books Worldwide, Inc.

- ✔ **Web-based chat rooms:** Chat spaces provided within a particular Web site.

- ✔ **Virtual chat:** Chat rooms that use graphical icons to create a more animated environment.

Here's a look at the main chat options that would interest a music fan.

ICQ

ICQ (www.icq.com), which, when pronounced, sounds like "I Seek You" (get it?), is unquestionably the hottest chat program on the Net. The program, which you can download for free from www.icq.com/download/, enables you to chat with other surfers around the world in real-time.

After you install the program on your computer and add your friends' names to the database, you can leave the program running. The program automatically alerts you when your friends come online, and you can chat with them.

ICQers also fill out profiles that earmark their special interests, including music. If you go to `www.icq.com/networks/Music`, as shown in Figure 8-8, you find a list of categories for music interests. Recent topics include the following:

- ✔ Heavy metal
- ✔ Girl bands
- ✔ Easy listening
- ✔ Woodstock

Sometimes, the topic areas list accompanying home pages created by some of the like-minded users.

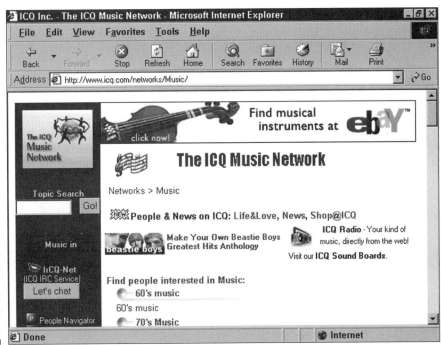

Figure 8-8:
ICQ is a popular way for Net surfers to chat online.

Web-based chat

Many Web sites feature built-in chat areas, where fans can send real-time messages to each other online.

To participate, you generally don't have to download any special program. The chat program is usually written in the Java programming language, which your browser can process. You can then interact in real-time with others using just your browser.

Internet Relay Chat (IRC)

Internet Relay Chat is another chat option in which so-called *IRC channels* replace chat rooms. These channels are freewheeling places to shoot the breeze on any topic you can (and can't imagine).

People also use IRC to trade software files. Here are some of the things that they trade:

- **Digital images:** Bands, concerts, groupies
- **Audio:** Legal and illegal MP3s, Liquid Audio, or other digital formats
- **Other files:** Lyrics, sheet music, text

To participate, you need to download an IRC client. For Windows, try mIRC at www.mirc.com; for Macintosh users, Ircle (www.ircle.com) is good.

After you install the client, check out Liszt's collection of IRC channels (www.liszt.com/chat) for music sites.

The Palace

Since its launch in 1995, The Palace (www.thepalace.com), shown in Figure 8-9, one of the first and largest *virtual chat* sites, has shrewdly tried to give chatters something to look at without sacrificing the necessary fantasy.

The formula remains the same as when it began — visitors choose an icon (sometimes known as an *avatar*) to represent themselves as they chat through word balloons. Some users scan in photographs of themselves; others use images of anything from Bart Simpson to a pizza slice. Whatever strikes your fancy is fine, but if you want to meet other music fans, the more niche you can get, the better (for example, use a tie-dye shirt if you're going into a Grateful Dead chat). And individual bands have joined the party — groups from Korn to the Cure have launched their own Palace sites for their fans' perpetual costume party.

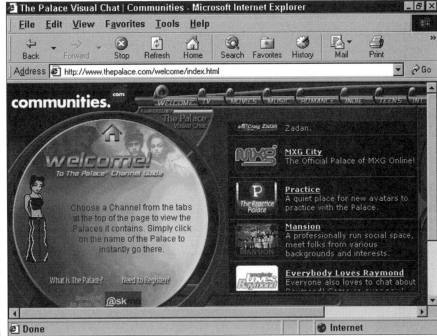

Figure 8-9:
The
Palace's vir-
tual chat
has been
used by
bands such
as Korn and
the Cure.

Part III
MmmmmmP3 Bop

In this part . . .

This part looks specifically at how you can take advantage of the versatile and compelling new music format known as MP3. You find out how to use an MP3 player and how special software helps you organize playlists. Then, you dive into the world of portable MP3 players, CD burners, and other hardware.

Musicians discover how to encode and format their own MP3 music, and they find out how to market and promote their music online.

Chapter 9

Playing with Your MP3 Music

MP3 players are software programs that enable you to listen to digital music recorded in the MP3 format. With MP3 players, you can do the following:

✔ Listen to MP3 songs on your computer.

✔ Make playlists that organize your favorite songs.

✔ Use special equalizer programs to adjust the audio playback.

In Chapter 3, I introduce some of the major players, including Winamp, MusicMatch, and Sonique, as well as discuss basic functionality. This chapter looks at the basics of using and customizing MP3 players, as well as options for storing music files. I also show you specific software that enables you to organize your playlists according to your tastes and moods. I then explore the options for storing MP3s, whether on disk, online, or even on your own home-burned CD-ROMs, and show you the expanding menu of portable MP3 player hardware.

Music fans, start your engines.

Pulling Not-So-Stupid MP3 Tricks

Sure, you can listen to MP3 music. You can make playlists. You can tweak your on-screen equalizer. But that's just the beginning. MP3 fans and techies stay up long into the night to find new, weird, and flat-out wacky things they can do with MP3 songs.

Here's a look at some of the things you can do:

- Mix your MP3 tracks like a real DJ.
- Download psychedelic light shows that move to the music.
- Add audio effects, such as reverb or bass, that affect how you hear the music on playback.
- Change the *skin* that your player uses, so that instead of looking at a plain gray panel, you can look at a panel colored with zebra stripes or banana peels.
- Use DJ software that lets you mix the songs while you listen.

You can pull off these feats by downloading specialized MP3 players or by using *plug-ins* — special add-on programs, such as skins or DJ wares, that you can use with popular MP3 players, such as Winamp or MusicMatch.

Plug-ins

Plug-ins are nifty little modifiers that attach to programs and allow the programs to do more than they originally could. Plug-ins exist for Winamp and other types of programs as well, such as Web browsers.

To install a plug-in, all you have to do is download it; through the installation process, the plug-in lands in the appropriate folder so that you can play with it, if you want, when you boot up the main wares.

Here are the four types of plug-ins that you can add to your MP3 player:

- *I/O (Input/Output) plug-ins* handle various aspects of sound input and output. Input plug-ins help you do stuff like take songs in a different format — such as Windows Media — and play them through your MP3 player. Output plug-ins enable you to modify the way you listen to songs, similar to an equalizer program.
- *Graphical plug-ins* do things like create little light shows while you listen to a song. You can even watch Bart Simpson skateboard in rhythm across your screen.
- *DSP (digital sound processor) plug-ins* give you the power to take a basic audio track and modify it with echo, reverb, and other studio tricks.
- *Miscellaneous plug-ins* can do everything from translating your Winamp controls into French (or Romanian!) to making your player full-screen on your desktop.

Plug-ins tend to be homemade by MP3 fans. The good news is that you can find some highly creative and entertaining wares; the bad news is that sometimes they can be buggy or unreliable.

To play it safe, I recommend getting your plug-ins through Web sites that have already sifted through the good, the bad, and the ugly. Winamp's site (`www.winamp.com`), for example, has its own section devoted to the latest plug-ins.

Examples of current plug-ins for Winamp include the following:

- **Sexy Analyzer** (`www.geocities.com/SiliconValley/Peaks/9546/`): This graphical Winamp plug-in takes a song's frequency and displays it in a stunning visual display — something like running music through a color spectrum.

- **Geiss** (`www.geisswerks.com`): This popular plug-in, as shown in Figure 9-1, is like having your own MP3 light show. This plug-in creates a pulsating, kaleidoscopic visual display that morphs according to the changing music.

- **DFX** (`www.fxsound.com`): This audio-enhancing plug-in operates on the assumption that even the best MP3 players don't sound nearly as good as they could. DFX restores high-fidelity features and, more or less, gives your MP3s a nice, hearty sonic boost.

- **Nice MC** (`http://nicemc.webhostme.com`): This plug-in turns your Winamp player into a video player. With this plug-in, you can boot up digital videos off the Web using your MP3 controls, without the hassle of running another program at the same time.

Figure 9-1:
Geiss — a
psychedelic
Winamp
plug-in.

Gimme some skins

Skins are colorful, kooky, and just plain fun programs that change the appearance of your MP3 player. Programs like MusicMatch and Winamp come with their own built-in skin options. (For example, in Winamp, click the <u>Skins & Plug-Ins</u> link at the top of the Winamp home page.)

For more fun, you can sample some of the sheaths being created by amateur MP3 fans across the Net.

Here's how to install a skin for Winamp:

1. **Launch Winamp.**

2. **Right-click the lightning bolt in Winamp's bottom-right corner.**

3. **Choose Skins⇨<<Get more skins!>>.**

   Your default Web browser launches and takes you to Winamp's skins page.

4. **Browse the skin library to find the skin you want.**

5. **Click <u>Download</u>.**

   Your chosen skin automatically downloads to the Skins folder on your hard drive, and Winamp's appearance changes to that skin. Figure 9-2 shows a sample zebra skin.

Figure 9-2:
A zebra
skin.

You can find skins in the Winamp skin library based on the following:

- ✔ Movies
- ✔ Games
- ✔ Sports
- ✔ Recording artists
- ✔ Celebrities
- ✔ Universities
- ✔ TV shows

DJ wares

Looking to give your MP3 files a spin? A bunch of new and cool software on the Net lets you play DJ with your digital tunes. Just download the software and go to town.

For the most part, these wares are pretty much a novelty — something to pass the hours late at night while you're waiting for your MP3s to download. The point is to have fun creating mixes that you can enjoy or play for your friends. If you're really motivated, you can even save your mixes and upload them for others to check out online.

Here are some of the DJ programs that you can check out.

Tactile 12000

```
www.tactile12000.com
```

Boy, does this program look cool. The Tactile 12000 interface, as shown in Figure 9-3, feels almost like playing a computer game with its two turntables. You can do all the DJ tricks, such as cross-fading between tracks. This program is worth playing around with — if only to see the vinyl fly under the needles.

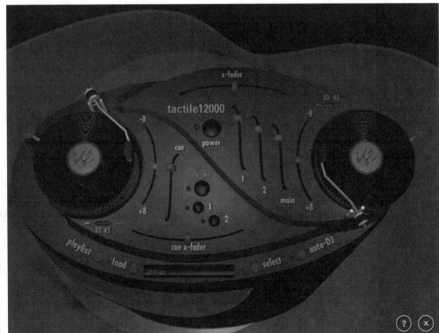

Figure 9-3:
The stylish
Tactile
12000 player
turns you
into an
MP3 DJ.

Copyright (c) 2000 Tactile Pictures

PCDJ

www.visiosonic.com

PCDJ provides a good crash course for first time DJs. Download the software and twiddle the knobs on what looks like a radio panel. You can adjust the pitch, fade between songs, and, for $29.95, soup up the wares with PCDJ Mix Master, which enables you to rip MP3s as well as play them.

Virtual Turntables

www.carrotinnovations.com

Though the program costs $42 to register, Virtual Turntables, as shown in Figure 9-4, is beefy enough to serve greenhorns and experts alike. Not only do you get all the basic goodies of pitch bending and file search, but you can also futz around with special controls to make songs play at the same number of beats per minute.

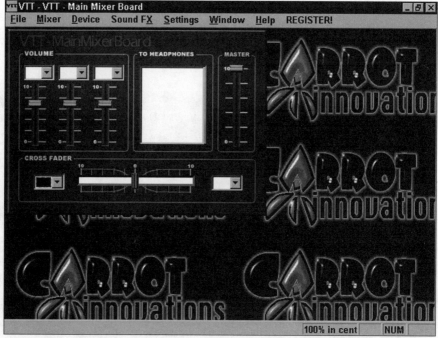

Figure 9-4:
The Virtual Turntables program is another MP3 DJ program.

Taking MP3s on the Run

To experience a killer format like MP3, you need something equally killer to play it on. MP3 portable players let you take the show on the road.

All MP3 portable players function basically the same way. After you download your MP3 songs, you transfer them directly to the player by hooking up the hardware to your PC. Usually, you can store at least an hour's worth of songs.

Some devices even come with their own storage disks. Yep, kind of like CDs.

MP3 itself is legal, but making MP3 files of copyright-protected songs is not. You may have heard about some lawsuits against the Diamond Rio, one of the first portable players. To make a long story short, the court ruled that the Rio and other MP3 players are legal. Don't worry.

Here are the overall pros and cons of MP3 portable wares:

✔ **Pros:**

- *No skipping:* Because the songs are in digital files and not on CD, you don't have to deal with annoying skips if, say, you listen to your player while jogging over a pothole.

- *Lightweight:* Because you don't have to lug around CDs or tapes, MP3 players tend to be extremely light.

- *Highly portable:* The absence of CDs and tapes makes the players very portable; they're often smaller than a deck of cards.

- *Expandability:* Some devices accept cards, such as SmartMedia cards, that let you store additional songs.

✔ **Cons:**

- *Limited storage:* At this point, many players can store only the songs that you download directly into the player. Generally, you get about an hour of music.

- *Inflexibility:* The downside of not having CDs or tapes is that listening to a large variety of music at any given time is difficult.

- *Difficulty of use:* After you get the songs into the players, they're not so difficult to operate. Basically, they have the same Play, Pause, Stop, Rewind, and Fast Forward functions of a normal music player. The problem is that you need to physically plug the player into your computer in order to download the music. This process is becoming easier, but you still must be prepared to untangle some cables in the back of your PC.

Okay, that's all you really need to know about portable MP3 players. Now, take a look at the latest, greatest players. Keep in mind that you can often find upgrades to these machines. So be sure to check with the manufacturer's Web site for the most recent versions.

Diamond Rio 500

www.diamondmm.com

One of the most ubiquitous players out there, the Diamond Rio caused quite an uproar when it was originally released. Now that people — especially wary record industry executives — have gotten used to the idea of portable digital players, the Rio is just one of many.

The new Rio 500 ($269), from Diamond Multimedia, stores almost twice as many songs as its predecessor, thanks to 64MB of built-in memory. The Rio 500 is also the best buy for Mac fans, because the Rio 500 is now fully compatible with Apple products.

The Rio 500 comes with its own special port that lets you connect it to your PC without unplugging your printer. The Rio 500 also supports special SmartMedia cards that let you add up to 32MB to the 64MB of memory that it comes with.

jazPiper

www.jazpiper.nl

Made in the Netherlands, the jazPiper is available with 32MB of memory ($169) or 64MB ($249). It boasts higher than average sound quality, with added features like its own built-in equalizer functions. The jazPiper can also hold up to a couple hours of music in WAV format.

If you want to know what you're listening to, the jazPiper has a sleek display that tells you the song title and artist name. The player is also compatible with SmartMedia cards if you want extra memory.

Nomad II

www.nomadworld.com

Created by Creative Labs, the Nomad II is quickly gaining ground on the Diamond Rio. Like the Rio, you can get it in both 32MB ($170) and 64MB ($250) formats.

The Nomad II, as shown in Figure 9-5, gives you special goodies, such as an FM tuner and a remote control (in case you stuff your player in your backpack and don't feel like unzipping to change tunes).

Figure 9-5:
The
Nomad II.

Best of all, the Nomad II comes with its own docking station. Instead of having to snake cables around the back of your PC, you simply slip the Nomad into the docking station, which stays hooked to your PC — just like the cradles that PalmPilots come with. You must also recharge the Nomad in the docking station, because it uses rechargeable AAA batteries.

Lyra

www.lyrazone.com

RCA became the first major electronics manufacturer to leap into the MP3 portable player market with its Lyra device, as shown in Figure 9-6. The Lyra is a great looking player, with a nice, big display showing you artist names and song titles. For $200, the Lyra is unique because it supports both MP3 files and RealAudio files.

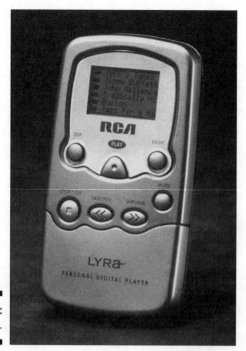

Courtesy of Thomson/RCA

For better and worse, the Lyra encrypts every song that's loaded into the device so that each track can be identified with a serial number. That means you have to wait for a lag every time you download a new song.

Turbo MP3

www.turbomp3.com

Boasting the biggest LCD screen on the market, the Turbo MP3 player is nice to look at and conveniently slim in size. The basic unit comes with 32MB of memory but can support SmartMedia cards.

While each song plays, the screen displays total track time, time elapsed, bit rate, sampling frequency, volume level, and battery charge remaining. The Turbo MP3 also has different types of play modes, including modes that let you repeat specific songs or your entire collection.

Personal Jukebox PJB-100

www.pjbox.com

You want big? You got big. The PJB-100 dwarfs other MP3 players by storing a whopping 4.86GB of songs, which translates into about 80 hours or 1,200 individual tracks. It even comes with its own playlist organizing software to help you keep track of your tracks.

Despite the storage size, the PJB-100 is surprisingly portable, easily fitting in the palm of your hand or a backpack.

All this memory costs you though — in the neighborhood of $800. They don't call it a jukebox for nothing.

I-Jam

www.ijamworld.com

You want small? You got small. The $179 I-Jam, as shown in Figure 9-7, is one of the tiniest MP3 players on the market, measuring in at about 3" x 2".

The small size comes at a price. The I-Jam has no onboard memory; instead, you have to play all your songs on multimedia cards (if you're used to playing CDs, this won't be much of a stretch).

Still, I-Jam has neat features, such as its own FM tuner and a candy-colored assortment of stylish shades.

Figure 9-7:
The I-Jam
player.

raveMP

`www.ravemp.com`

The $199 raveMP tries to be more than just an MP3 player. This sleekly designed device also stores telephone numbers, voice messages, and text.

The basic player comes with 64MB of storage that you can expand to 96MB using special flash memory cards. Like the Nomad II, it also sports its own easy-to-use parallel port docking station.

Mplayer3

`www.mplayer3.com`

The $195 Mplayer3, from Pontis, also tries to save space by not offering onboard storage; instead, you play songs by inserting multimedia cards into slots within the machine.

The Mplayer3 is also one of the few players that, in addition to Windows, is Linux and Macintosh compatible.

NEX

`www.frontierlabs.com`

The $180 NEX player is just about the size of an average pager, which means the NEX player is small. But it still packs a formidable punch, offering 64MB of storage that you can expand using memory cards.

The headphones that come with the machine aren't the best, but the volume controls deliver some of the loudest tunes on the market.

Hitting the Road

Okay, taking your MP3 player into your car and slapping on the headphones is probably not a good idea. Now, you don't have to worry — a new breed of MP3 players made specifically for the automobile are crashing on to the market.

Digital audio players for cars are still evolving. Prices and options should be better very soon.

In the meantime, here's a look at a couple of players.

Auto PC

`www.autopc.com`

Clarion's Auto PC is paving the way for MP3 road warriors. Right now, the Auto PC is still a bit in development, but this $1300 Windows CE OS system offers AM/FM stereo, CD, and CD-ROM support. MP3 compatibility is supposed to be around the corner.

Because Auto PC is a computer, you can also get nifty add-ons, such as a Global Positioning Satellite (GPS) navigation system.

empeg car

`www.empeg.com`

For $950, the empeg car player is removable and portable. To get the tunes, you connect the device to your PC and download the songs using Windows-compatible software. The empeg also sports its own FM tuner.

To control the music, you use a small remote control that's about the size of a credit card.

Storing Your Songs for the Road

The nice thing about collecting MP3 music is that you don't have to clear off a shelf, buy a bookcase, or litter your coffee table. Digital music means digital storage — clean, neat, and compact on your PC hard drive or removable disk.

In general, you have the following options for storing your MP3s:

✔ Your hard drive

✔ Your own self-made CDs (see Chapter 10 for more information about burning your own discs)

✔ Online, through special services like those offered at MP3.com

Of course, you're not going to lug your PC or removable drive around when you're listening to MP3 portable players. For these hit 'n' run devices, you're better off using some of the brand new disks made specifically for digital audio.

More and more MP3 players come equipped to handle these micro disks, so now's as good a time as ever to become familiar with them. Like ordinary disks, you slip them right into the MP3 portable player's slot.

Here's a look at some popular formats.

CompactFlash cards

`www.compactflash.org`

CompactFlash storage cards, as shown in Figure 9-8, have actually been around since 1994. Measuring in at less than half the size of an ordinary floppy disk, these cards can store all kinds of digital information: audio, images, and text.

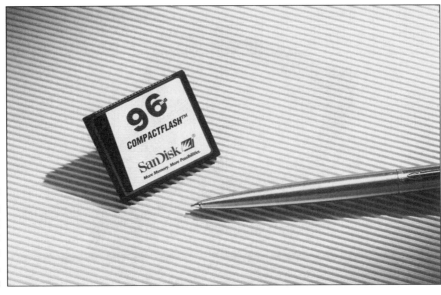

Figure 9-8:
A Compact
Flash
storage
card.

To get your songs from your PC onto a CompactFlash card, you need to get a PC card adapter. The adapter, which holds the CompactFlash card, fits right into an empty PC slot inside your computer. Once in, you dump the songs and go on your way.

Most MP3 players use a Type 1 CompactFlash card, which can hold up to 128MB of music.

SmartMedia cards

www.simpletech.com/flash/smartmed.htm

These cards are even smaller than CompactFlash cards. Many MP3 players are compatible with SmartMedia, as shown in Figure 9-9. Like CompactFlash, the cards require that you purchase a special PC card adapter so that you can dump your MP3 songs from your computer to the disk.

Players such as the Rio, however, have their own specifications with regard to compatibility. Because of certain copyright-protection features, SmartMedia cards have to be specially formatted to work only for the Rio.

Figure 9-9:
SmartMedia
card.

Chapter 10

Making Your Own MP3s

*O*ne of the best things about MP3 is that it's a two-way revolution. You can download digital audio from the Internet and, just as good, you can create your own MP3s and upload them.

To a certain degree, you need to be ready to roll up your sleeves and get technical. Making MP3s is not quite as point 'n' click easy as listening to them. But with a little know-how, you can create digital audio from any of the following sources:

- ✔ CDs
- ✔ Cassette tapes
- ✔ WAV files
- ✔ TV broadcasts
- ✔ Video tapes
- ✔ Microphone live recordings
- ✔ Albums
- ✔ And, yes, 8-tracks

This chapter gets your computer ready to rock for MP3 production and then takes you through the steps you need to follow in order to create your own MP3 tunes.

Understanding the Jargon

Okay, you have to learn some jargon. Basically, here are the four key terms you need to know:

- ✔ **Ripping:** Ripping sounds kind of crude, but it's actually a lot more refined. This term refers to when you transfer music from a compact disc to your computer's hard drive. This is probably the most common method of converting CDs into MP3s.

- ✔ **Encoding:** Encoding is less common. This is what you do when you need to convert WAV audio files into MP3 format.

- ✔ **Burning:** Burning is the reverse of ripping. Burning a CD means that you transfer information to a compact disc. To do this, you need — you guessed it — a *CD burner:* a special device that enables you to record audio on specially formatted *writable* compact discs.

- ✔ **All-in-ones:** All-in-ones refer to software programs, such as MusicMatch, that do the works of MP3 functions: playing, ripping, and encoding.

That's it! So now if someone says, "Hey, dude, can I rip your tunes, encode your files, and burn your disc?" you know what he means.

Dealing with Legalities

When you start creating your own MP3s, you enter the sticky, tricky world of copyright infringement. The good news is that you can copy whatever audio you want — from CDs, movies, tapes, and so on — for your personal use. But if you sell or give away CD copies of an artist's copyright-protected music, you're breaking the law.

Wares to Begin

In Chapter 2, I explain how to get your computer ready for listening to online music. You can use many of those same principles and techniques to ready your computer for creating MP3s.

Here, we go through the necessary steps to get you started, from getting set up with the right hardware and software, to hooking up your stereo and testing that everything's hunky-dory.

Hardware

To create MP3s, you need these basics:

- ✔ **A computer.** If you bought your computer in the last five years, it should be up to speed. Both Macintoshes and Windows PCs can do the trick, although, as usual, more options exist for PC owners.

- ✔ **A CD-ROM drive.** Here's the tricky thing: Even if you have a high-speed CD-ROM drive, say 24x, that doesn't mean you can create MP3s at a faster rate. The speed of a CD-ROM drive refers to how fast it can play music, not create it. Sometimes, you may want to rip the music at a slower rate to avoid gaps in the music sequence. (FYI: about 35 percent of CD-ROM drives cannot support functions like ripping. For a good list of compatible drives, visit www.tardis.ed.ac.uk/~psyche/cdda/.)

- ✔ **Sound cables.** You need sound cables to hook up your computer to any external source, such as record players, VCRs, microphones, tape decks, television sets, DVD players, and so on. For about $10, you can pick up a Y-cable from Radio Shack. Tell the clerk what kind of device you're connecting, and she'll give you the proper cable.

Software

Here's some good news: You don't have to switch from one program to another when making your own MP3s. Unless you're a really persnickety music geek, you can find a host of all-in-one programs that let you do all the tricks with just one click.

To stay on top of the latest rippers, encoders, and all-in-ones, log on to http://software.mp3.com.

Here's a look at some of the latest all-in-one software.

MusicMatch Jukebox

www.musicmatch.com

In addition to being a popular MP3 player, MusicMatch Jukebox (for PCs) lets you rip and encode your CDs, WAVs, or Windows Media files. For an extra $29.99, you can upgrade the Jukebox to create a slightly higher-quality audio experience.

When recording otherwise, you have an option of switching from FM-radio quality to near-CD quality (the better the quality, the longer the transfers).

Media Jukebox

www.musicex.com

The Media Jukebox (for PCs) is aimed at the slightly more discerning MP3 creator. First off, Media Jukebox plays its own specially formatted MusicEx files, which ensure copyright protection for artists who want to be safe and secure. Be warned: this means you probably won't find the widest selection of your desired songs.

On the ripping side, Media Jukebox lets you encode up to 320bps without having to shell out any extra bucks for an upgrade. The interface may not be as pretty as MusicMatch's, but it gets the job done at a nice velocity.

RealJukebox

www.real.com

The popular PC player for RealAudio and RealVideo formats is surprisingly one of the user-friendliest MP3 all-in-ones. RealJukebox is easy to use and easy to upgrade, though not quite as powerful as some of the other programs.

The basic free player enables you to rip MP3s, but not at as high quality as, say, Media Jukebox. But you can upgrade for $30 to the RealJukebox Plus Gold for better quality.

SoundJam MP

www.soundjam.com

Macintosh MP3ers are in luck with SoundJam MP, an all-in-one player/encoder that enables users to make and play their own digital tunes. You can manage your playlists and hear streaming audio as well.

On the encoding side, the free player lets you encode up to 30 songs during your first 14 days of using the player. After you register and pay for the upgrade, you can encode more songs.

Cool Edit 2000

www.syntrillium.com

Not necessary, but not bad to have, Cool Edit (for PC) is a sound-editing program that, for $70, makes a nice addition to your MP3-making artillery. You need this program only if you're recording music from external sources.

You don't need Cool Edit if you're just recording from CDs. Basically, the program takes your PC's sound-recording features and turns them into a mini pro-sound studio. You can add effects such as reverb, chorus, and echo. You can splice, cut, paste, and essentially micromanage your incoming audio.

Hooking up sound cables

To get audio from an external device to your computer, you have to plug the sound cable from the device into the line-in jack of your computer.

Whenever you connect sound devices, be sure to turn down the volume on both ends (or, better yet, turn off the power on both machines). You don't want to blow out your eardrums or even a speaker.

Follow these steps to connect an external device to your computer:

1. **Plug the cable into your chosen output source.**

   The cable plugs into the RCA jacks on the back of the device. The red end goes into the red jack, the white end into the white jack.

2. **Plug the cable's other end into the computer.**

   This end goes right into the line-in jack in the back of the machine.

   Macintoshes come with sound built in, so you plug the cable into the external microphone jack.

Testing your connection

After you hook up your external source to your computer, you may want to do a test run to make sure everything's kosher. To test your connection, follow these steps:

1. **Set the volume on your Windows PC by choosing Start⇨Programs⇨Accessories⇨Multimedia⇨Volume Control.**

   The Volume Control dialog box for Windows appears (see Figure 10-1).

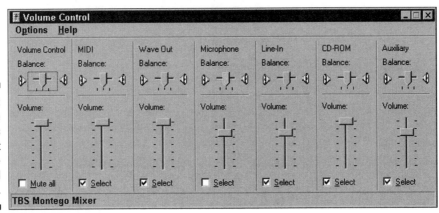

Figure 10-1: Volume Control lets you adjust the incoming sound levels.

2. **Choose Options⇨Properties.**

    The Properties dialog box appears (see Figure 10-2).

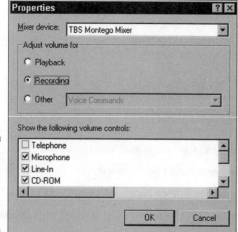

Figure 10-2:
The Volume
Control
Properties
dialog box.

3. **Select the Recording radio button.**

4. **Make sure that the Line-In box is checked.**

5. **Click OK.**

    The Recording Control dialog box appears.

6. **Check the box next to Select under Line-In (see Figure 10-3).**

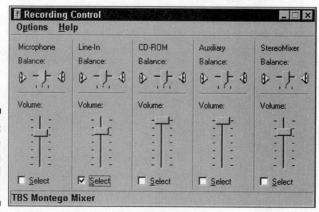

Figure 10-3:
The
Recording
Control
dialog box.

7. **Lower the volume of the Line-In channel.**

   Remember what I said earlier about not blowing out your eardrums?

8. **Play music from the source.**

9. **Adjust the volume slider while the incoming music plays.**

If you don't hear anything, make sure all your cables are properly connected.

Ripping the Tunes

Ripping music isn't as crude as it sounds. Basically, ripping is the MP3ers' slang for taking some offline music and converting it into digital format. Think of it as ripping the analog out of the song, or ripping out the 20th century for the 21st, or the old for the new, or . . . you get the idea.

Why rip? Here are some reasons:

- ✔ **Easy storage:** You can preserve all your old albums, tapes, and other analog music.

- ✔ **Easy access:** You can take all your records on the road.

- ✔ **Easy organization:** You can keep a nice, clean file listing of all your goods.

Here's how ripping works:

1. You rip songs from a CD, tape, or some other outside source and store the digital files on your hard drive. At first, these songs appear in WAV format; Macintosh files appear as AIFF files. Theoretically, there's nothing wrong with WAVs or AIFFs; digital music mavens, in fact, used this format for years. But WAV and AIFF files are really, really big. The MP3 format enables you to compress these files down into bite-sized — byte-size, actually — chunks.

2. You then encode or convert the WAV files to MP3 format.

Programs such as MusicMatch Jukebox and Media Jukebox handle all this stuff for you with just the click of a button — or a few buttons, at least.

This section shows you how to record files using MusicMatch Jukebox; other programs have similar steps. For a complete list of the latest, greatest ripper software, head over to http://software.mp3.com/software/featured/windows/ripper/, as shown in Figure 10-4.

Can you listen to MP3s on your home CD player?

The short answer is yes, but with some effort. If you simply copy MP3 files onto a disc and then slide the CD into your stereo, you won't hear anything. The files, you see, have to be uncompressed so that your CD player can make sense of the sounds.

Instead, you have to decompress the MP3 files, using something like MusicMatch Jukebox, into WAV or AIFF files. Then, you have to convert these files into audio files that work for your stereo. CD burners usually come with software that enables you to do this. Check out Chapter 3 for more information on CD-burning software.

To improve the sound quality of your ripped files, try the following:

✔ Close any unnecessary open windows.

✔ Close all unnecessary applications to make more CPU power available.

✔ Close other programs that may be writing information to your hard drive.

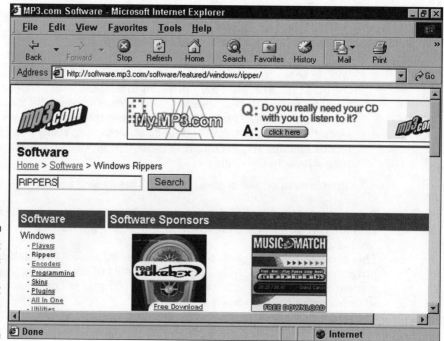

Figure 10-4:
MP3.com's list of the latest ripping software.

Recording from a CD with MusicMatch Jukebox

Ripping a song from a CD couldn't be easier with wares. Most programs function the same way: Put in a CD, press record, and wait.

Here's a more specific look at recording from a CD with MusicMatch:

1. **Launch MusicMatch by double-clicking the MusicMatch icon on your desktop.**

   The recording window appears, as shown in Figure 10-5.

2. **Insert an audio CD into your CD-ROM drive.**

   Wanna see something really cool? Connect to the Internet before you insert the CD. After your CD-ROM drive begins to read the audio disc, MusicMatch sends the disc's serial number to CDDB, an online CD information database, and gets the CD title and track info from the database.

   If MusicMatch doesn't come up with a match for your CD, just double-click the track names and enter the names yourself.

3. **To begin recording, click the name of the track you want to convert, or click All to record the entire disc.**

   A Recording Status window displays information relating to how the conversion is proceeding. A green square appears next to a song after the song is converted.

After you finish, you can find your songs by clicking the Library button on your MusicMatch Jukebox player; just click a track to play it.

Figure 10-5: The recording window of MusicMatch.

Often, you may read about CD quality versus near-CD quality. What does this mean? In the case of MusicMatch, the difference is basically a matter of speed and money. Near-CD quality recordings are made by compressing the songs into tinier packets than CD quality ones; this compression saves space on your hard drive — for the price of a small decline in song quality.

For a fee ($29.99), you can upgrade to MusicMatch Jukebox Plus, which includes features like faster burning and encoding.

Recording from external sources with MusicMatch

Converting vinyl, cassette tapes, TV show theme songs, or anything else you're hungry for works basically the same as converting CDs.

To record from an external source using MusicMatch, follow these steps:

1. **Connect the output cable from the source (turntable, tape deck, and so on) to the input jack in your sound card.**

   For more information about connecting cables, see "Hooking up sound cables" earlier in this chapter.

2. **Adjust the recording sound levels.**

   Again, see "Hooking up sound cables" earlier in this chapter for information about volume controls.

3. **Launch MusicMatch Jukebox.**

   The MusicMatch Jukebox appears on your desktop.

4. **Click the Record button.**

   The first time you record, the program goes through a one-minute initialization process.

5. **Choose Options⇨Recorder⇨Source, as shown in Figure 10-6, and select the option for line-in to record from an album or cassette.**

6. **Begin playing the music from your output source.**

   You receive a green box at the end of the recording progress bar if the song has recorded successfully.

7. **Click Stop on the recording software when the output source is finished playing.**

Figure 10-6:
The Options
menu on
MusicMatch
lets you
control input
sources.

For the best sound quality, encode the files at 128 bits, 44kHz stereo, which means the file stores more information about how the song specifically sounds; the higher the bits and kilohertz, the better the sound. Some shareware programs, such as RealJukebox, limit encoding to 96 bits, though you probably can't tell the difference.

Burning Your Own CDs

Funny how sometimes digital music can be a bit too digital. MP3s may be terrific for storing music on your computer, but odds are, you still have to use CDs in your car, your stereo, and your boom box.

Yes, all kinds of cool, portable MP3 players are coming out (for the skinny, check out Chapter 9). But these players probably won't become commonplace for another few years.

In the meantime, you can have the best of both worlds, thanks to the new and burgeoning line of CD burners — CD-ROM hardware devices that let you create, or *burn*, your own CDs.

Here are some things to consider before you begin burning:

✔ Burners, like regular CD-ROM drives, come in different speeds. The faster the burner's drive, the faster you can record. Save yourself some time and frustration by getting the fastest machine you can afford.

✔ You can get either internal or external burners. An external burner is nice if you're traveling or switching back and forth between desktop and laptop computers. An internal burner sits nicely in your computer's case and draws power from the computer.

✔ Some CD-burning programs come with a simulation mode, which enables you to test-burn the information. In doing so, the CD burner goes through the motions of burning, only it doesn't turn on the laser that actually burns the information on the disc. Running through a simulation before actually burning a CD is a good way to avoid ending up with a shiny — and expensive — coaster.

✔ CDs for your stereo cannot store as many songs as MP3 CDs; you can squeeze literally hundreds of MP3s on a CD-ROM, but only a couple dozen songs on an audio CD.

Types of CDs to burn

Remember when you first ran out and got a CD player? Man, was that cool. Music was suddenly neat, clean, and, literally, compact. Unfortunately, it was also stubborn. For years, average music fans didn't have the means to record music on their own CDs.

Fortunately, times have changed.

Now, you can record your own CDs, and the prices of CD burners are coming down, down, down. Thing is, you need to buy special discs that allow your CD burner to do its work. In addition to recording music, you can record computer games and other data.

CD-recordable discs

Also known as *CD-R* discs, *CD-recordable* discs are one-hit wonders. These discs enable you to burn information on them once and only once. After that, you can listen to them until you're blue in the ears. You just can't record over them again.

CD-R discs can store both MP3 files or regular audio files. MP3 files can be played only on MP3 players; audio files can only be played on your home or portable stereo equipment.

CD-rewritable discs

CD-RW, or *CD-rewritable,* discs are like your good old reliable cassette tapes. Unlike CD-Rs, these babies can be recorded, played, recorded, played, and so on, up to roughly a thousand times, according to most manufacturers. As a result, they're a little more costly than CD-Rs.

However, CD-RW discs, unlike CD-Rs, cannot be played on a home stereo.

Because CD-R drives have been around longer than CD-RW drives, you may find that older CD-R machines can't read CD-RW discs.

Can you listen to MP3s on your home CD player?

The short answer is yes, but with some effort. If you simply copy MP3 files onto a disc and then slide the CD into your stereo, you won't hear anything. The files, you see, have to be uncompressed so that your CD player can make sense of the sounds.

Instead, you have to decompress the MP3 files, using something like MusicMatch Jukebox, into WAV or AIFF files. Then, you have to convert these files into audio files that work for your stereo. CD burners usually come with software that enables you to do this. Check out Chapter 3 for more information on CD-burning software.

Chapter 11

So You Wanna Be an MP3 Star?

In This Chapter

▶ Taking yourself (or your band) digital

▶ Getting your MP3 music online

▶ Promoting your MP3 music

*N*ot so long ago, a typical band found it pretty hard to get an audience. They had to get together. Practice. Find a club. Get booked. Attract an audience. Make a demo. Lick envelopes. Make cold calls to record executives. And, throughout it all, hope that they would get noticed.

Sounds like a lot of work.

These days, anyone with a computer, a modem, Internet access, and — of course — some musical ability can record music and release it to the world online in MP3 format. Artists can easily make their music available to listeners all around the world. And at a greatly reduced cost.

This chapter looks at how musicians can get their MP3 music online and, hopefully, have people hear it.

Taking Your Music Online

Wouldn't it be nice if you had some kind of teleporter, like the one on *Star Trek,* that could transport your band onto the Net? Just imagine: You step on a platform, strum your guitar, and — zap — you're digitized.

Although the process of making MP3s (see Chapter 10) is getting easier, that's only one step in the game. If you want to be an MP3 star, you need to follow a whole sequence of steps:

1. Record your music on regular audio tape, digital audio tape, or CD.

2. Transfer the recorded music to your computer using the methods in Chapter 10.

3. Convert (encode) the resulting WAV or AIFF files into MP3 format.

4. Find a Web site to host your music.

5. Promote your music.

6. Monitor how many times your music is downloaded.

7. Update the site with new music.

8. Start all over again.

Before you set off into the great digital frontier, you need to keep a few things in mind:

- **Don't be intimidated by the technology.** You don't have to be a techie to put your music online. MP3 digitization is becoming more and more a point 'n' click process.

- **Get ready to work for success.** Getting your music online is only the beginning. You are circumventing the red tape of the corporate music business machine, but you're still entering a marketplace that's highly diffused and competitive.

- **Be prepared to invest a lot of time in promoting your music.** If you really want to go for it, get ready to put as much — if not more — energy into letting people know about your MP3 music as you spent on creating it.

Communing: Is There Anybody Out There?

Before you get started, you may want to look at what other people are doing with MP3. Independent artists, or *indies*, and pop stars are using MP3 to promote themselves.

An *indie,* for the sake of this chapter, means any independent-minded artist who wants to have more control over his or her destiny. Indies are probably frustrated with the traditional music channels. MP3 offers an opportunity to truly be in control.

Not surprisingly, pop stars are chomping at the bit for this kind of action as well. Some of them release their music exclusively online. Some do it to supplement the tunes that are being handled by their record companies.

Here are just some of the well-known artists who have been experimenting with MP3 distribution:

✔ Tori Amos, `www.toriamos.com`

✔ Alanis Morissette, `www.alanismorissette.com`

✔ Chuck D, `www.publicenemy.com`

✔ They Might Be Giants, `www.tmbg.com`

✔ Beastie Boys, `www.beastieboys.com`

✔ Prince, `www.npgonlineltd.com`

✔ Sarah McLachlan, `www.sarahmclachlan.com/index2.html`

✔ David Bowie, at `www.davidbowie.com` (see Figure 11-1)

Figure 11-1:
David Bowie's Web site has featured MP3 versions of his songs.

Getting Your Songs Online

So you have your MP3s recorded; now, you need to find somewhere to post them. The possibilities are endless . . . and confusing. Should you create your own Web site? Rent space from someone else? Put your songs in an MP3 database?

This section looks at some of the different options you have for getting your music on the Net through MP3 hosting services, search engines, digital music sites, and even your very own Web site.

Using MP3 hosting services

Don't have the energy to make your own site? You can find plenty of services out there that can host your tunes — and even help you get paid.

 The good news is that you generally don't have to agree to any exclusivity when posting your MP3 songs. In other words, post your songs on as many of these sites as you want.

MP3.com

MP3.com is not only the mothership for finding MP3 music, but it's also the place to start for uploading your music.

For no cost, MP3.com puts your songs inside its massive database. And I do mean massive — at least 100,000 songs at last count. All these songs are legal, too, which means you can't upload your Rolling Stones CDs to MP3.com; the music needs to be your own.

And don't worry, no record executive is behind the scenes passing judgment as to whether you're worthy of getting on MP3.com. All artists are welcome.

Here are the general steps for adding your tunes to MP3.com:

1. **Head over to** `www.mp3.com/newartist/` **and go through the login process.**

2. **After you sign up, upload your MP3 song(s) and fill out some basic information about yourself or your band: genre, background, and so on.**

   If you have your own Web site, you can add it as a link. You can also strike a deal with MP3.com that allows them to sell your CDs — if you've got 'em.

   MP3.com then adds your music to the database. Simple as that. When surfers click your name, they go to a page that lists all your songs, biographical information, and anything else that you make available. For a sample, see Figure 11-2.

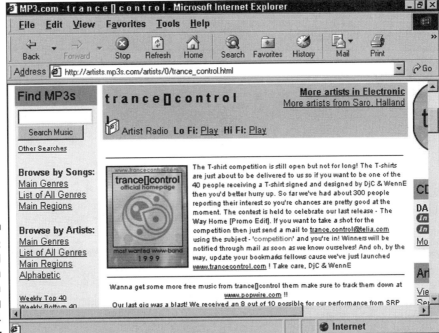

Figure 11-2:
A typical
MP3.com
page for a
participating
artist.

3. **Monitor your stats to see how many people are checking out your goods and — more importantly — downloading your tunes.**

If enough people download your music, you may be eligible for MP3.com's Payback for Playback program, which is currently dispersing $200,000 to bands with frequent downloads. Some artists have earned up to $5,000 in one month. How does it work? MP3.com keeps track of the downloads and then cuts you a check according to the amount of action you get.

Change Music Network

Based in New York City, the Change Music Network (www.changemusic.com), as shown in Figure 11-3, makes no bones about its self-described "revolutionary" mission.

"The Change Music Network is dedicated to radically transforming the face of music creation, distribution and promotion," it posts. "Using the internet and the latest in digital music technologies, the network is ground zero for the revolutionary changes in the way people listen, make, share and sell all genres of music." Power to the people!

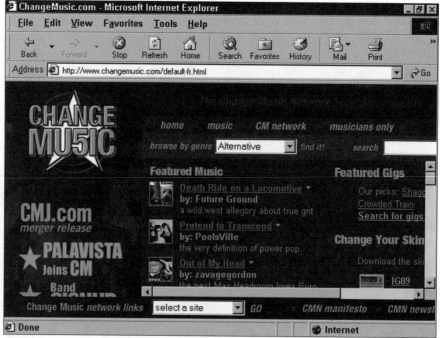

Figure 11-3:
Change
Music offers
free Web
pages and
song space
to MP3
artists.

Any artist who joins the free service gets the following goods:

- ✔ **Song space:** You can upload as many MP3s as you want onto the site.

- ✔ **Web page:** You can post band photos, lyrics, tour schedules, astrological signs, or whatever else you can think of.

- ✔ **Links:** Change Music includes your songs in its cross-references. So when someone is trolling for, say, alternative rock songs, they find your page (if that's the kind of music you play).

In addition, Change Music has a network of related sites that can enhance your MP3 experience. The sites include the following:

- ✔ MP3 Park (www.mp3park.com) — for the latest MP3 wares

- ✔ MP3 Place (www.mp3place.com) — MP3 tutorials and help

- ✔ Customize.org (www.customize.org) — MP3 software accessories, such as skins and plug-ins

- ✔ Findsongs (www.findsongs.com) — an MP3 search engine

Lycos Listening Room

Lycos is first and foremost a search engine. But these days, Lycos is also aiming to be an MP3 player — in the mover-and-shaker sense of the word.

The Lycos Listening Room (`http://listeningroom.lycos.com`) offers artists free exposure for their songs — plus a built-in audience of over 1 million surfers who search for MP3s on a regular basis.

In addition to receiving a free Web page for your MP3 songs and information, you can keep up with statistics on how many people download your songs. You can also view message boards on which your music may be the daily topic of conversation.

A simple registration page takes you through the steps. The information that Lycos asks you to include would be helpful on any MP3 site:

✔ Band genre

✔ Band history

✔ Press reviews

✔ Photos

✔ Band description

Riffage

Riffage (`www.riffage.com`), as shown in Figure 11-4, spotlights MP3 artists with a decidedly college feel. Musicians can log on to the site to post their own songs, which are placed in Riffage's burgeoning database.

Modeled in part after Amazon.com, Riffage is big on community. It encourages fans and artists to review and recommend MP3s to each other. So if you create your own MP3 space here, you're likely to become part of the ongoing party.

The big selling point for bands is the selling point. Unlike MP3.com, which gives 50 percent of sales to artists, Riffage offers bands 85 percent of sales. This is the place to go if you're really into merchandising, because you can literally sell just about anything related to your band through the site.

Downloads Direct

Part of the sprawling ARTISTdirect Network, which includes the Ultimate Band List and the iMusic community (see Chapter 8), Downloads Direct (`http://content.ubl.com/downloadsdirect/`) places you in the company of big stars and wannabes alike. Figure 11-5 shows the Downloads Direct home page.

Figure 11-4:
The home-
page for
Riffage.

Figure 11-5:
The home-
page for
Downloads
Direct.

You can upload your songs, band info, and pictures for free. Downloads Direct then lists you according to genre. The cool thing is that someone who comes to the site to get the latest Smashing Pumpkins MP3 song may stumble across your song, too.

Downloads Direct also runs creative MP3 upload themes, such as "Upload Your Broken Heart" — a Valentine's Day special that encouraged artists to contribute their saddest and truest love songs. Selected participants are then featured in special promotional displays on the site.

Building your own site

Of course, the ultimate MP3 do-it-yourself expression is your very own Web site. Here, you can totally and uninhibitedly promote yourself, your band, and your music.

Even if you decide to put your songs on a site like MP3.com, having your own Web site is a good idea. Your site becomes your headquarters, and you can link your site to all the other places from which you make your music available.

To make your own site, you need to do the following:

- ✔ Plan it
- ✔ Build it
- ✔ Launch it
- ✔ Hype it
- ✔ Live it

Plan it

Like any good project, a Web site benefits from a master plan. Before you start hacking code, whip out an old-fashioned pen and paper and start brainstorming. Also, be sure to have a look at what other people are doing with their sites.

The skinny on HTML

If you're thinking of building your own Web site, don't get freaked by clunky Web page jargon such as *HTML* and *JavaScript.* If you can punch buttons on your computer keyboard, you can make a surprisingly cool site. But if you need some friendly advice, check out *Creating Web Pages For Dummies*, 4th Edition, written by Bud Smith and Arthur Bebak and published by IDG Books Worldwide, Inc.

Before you worry about what you can and can't accomplish technologically, let your imagination run wild by answering the following questions:

- ✔ Is this site going to be primarily for fun or for business? Do you plan to sell your CDs and use your site as a marketing tool, or is it going to be just for fans? Or both?

- ✔ Do you want your site to have a specific look? Should it be conservative in design or wild and crazy?

- ✔ Do you want the site to include sound? Do you want visitors to hear a snippet of your band when they first load your home page?

- ✔ What kind of stuff do you want on the site? Fan photos? Early demos? Lyrics and transcriptions?

- ✔ How much time do you want to spend maintaining the site? Because this is your site, you can spend as much or as little time as you want (one hour a month, just to make slight changes; or five hours a day, if that's your thing).

After you have a good plan, you're ready to plug in.

Build it

HTML (which stands for Hypertext Markup Language) is the computer language that describes how Web pages appear in browsers. If you are a closet computer geek and like getting your hands dirty with code, all you really need to start creating your Web page is a text editor, such as WordPad for Windows or SimpleText for the Macintosh, and a book on HTML. *HTML 4 For Dummies*, 2nd Edition, written by Ed Tittel and Natanya Pitts and published by IDG Books Worldwide, Inc., is an excellent primer on HTML.

However, most musicians aren't geeks and don't have the time to learn HTML. Fortunately, you don't need to hack through that mind-numbing code; HTML-editing software can do all the dirty work for you, making it as easy as using, say, a word processing program.

You can create your own pages with such free tools as FrontPage Express, which offers basic HTML-editing features. If you decide you want to go hog wild with your site, you can graduate to one of the HTML-editing super-programs, such as FrontPage 2000, Dreamweaver, or HoTMetaL. These programs can cost a couple hundred bucks, so invest in them only if you're serious.

You can also check out the free Web-hosting services, such as Tripod (www.tripod.com) and Yahoo! Geocities (www.geocities.com), which offer fill-in-the-blank templates that let you design a page with pictures, wild colors, and even your own theme song within minutes. These sites also let you upload pages that you've created on your own.

Launch it

After you build your Web nest, you need to find somewhere to roost. In order for other people to see your site, you need to put it on a computer that surfers can access through the Internet.

Don't worry about serving up your pages from home — you don't have to. Countless companies give away their own computer space for nothing, which means that you make your pages and then upload them to the computer that *hosts* the site. Visitors access your site via a Web address that the company provides to you.

Be sure to check with your Internet service provider to see if free Web server space comes with your Internet connection. Most ISPs, such as EarthLink, provide several megabytes of disk space for your Web pages and give you your own Web address to boot. You may already have a place for your Web site and not know it!

If you use a Web-hosting service, such as Yahoo! Geocities or Tripod (see Figure 11-6), you can upload your pages. These services also give you the benefit of belonging to a community of like-minded users. And the cost to you? Nada. These sites make their cash through advertising that — you guessed it — often ends up on your page whether you like it or not. Much of this advertising is unobtrusive, however.

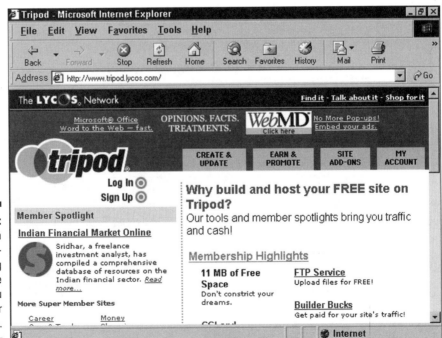

Figure 11-6:
Tripod is a free Web-hosting service where you can put your home page.

If you want your own succinct, personalized Web address, such as www.yourbandname.com, you can get one . . . for a price (assuming the name isn't already taken). Just go to Network Solutions (www.networksolutions.com), as shown in Figure 11-7, where you can register your personalized Web address. The cost of personalization is about $100 every two years.

Hype it

After you launch your site, you want people to visit it. Start off by registering your site with popular search engines such as Excite (www.excite.com) and Yahoo! (www.yahoo.com). At Yahoo!, for example, choose the category from their enormous list that best describes your site — such as tango music — and then suggest your page for inclusion.

Within a few weeks, you should see your site listed, though there seems to be no rhyme or reason as to what Yahoo! decides to include. If you put your site on a free Web-hosting service, your site is grouped into a community of similarly themed sites, along with weekly event schedules, message boards, and chat happenings.

As in any other 'hood, the best way to get known is to become involved: E-mail other Webmasters who run similar sites and offer to exchange links — in other words, include a link to their sites on your page if they include links to your site on their pages.

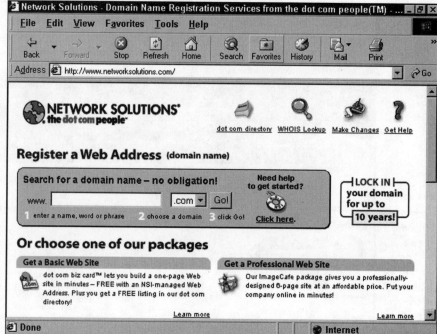

Figure 11-7: Register your personalized Web address at Network Solutions.

Live it

The amazing thing about creating a Web site is how many people stop by; don't be surprised if you get even a hundred visitors your first week. Of course, after people start cruising by, you may feel obliged to keep sprucing up your place: fixing errors or bugs, removing old content, and adding new stuff.

Don't worry if you get sick of the whole thing and need a fresh start; you can always delete it and start all over again. Just be sure to let regular visitors know what you're up to.

Promoting Your MP3 Music

Well, you've come far. You became a musician. You recorded some music. You converted your music into MP3. You found somewhere to put your music online. Now you have just one thing left to do.

Get people to listen to it.

In effect, promotion is the most challenging aspect of being an MP3 musician. Technology, after all, can be learned. Web sites can be mastered. Music can be traded. But the act of marketing, managing, and creating that elusive "buzz" around your music is no easy proposition.

That's the one catch of MP3. Though you can instantly reach listeners around the world, you're doing so — for better or worse — pretty much on your own. One benefit of the corporate music machine is that it is, alas, a corporate music machine. It has money to spend on marketing and promotion, and professionals to handle that stuff. They can get you on MTV or on the local radio show.

The do-it-yourself approach means that you have to work a little harder to get noticed online. This section details some D-I-Y promo tricks you can try.

Contests

Across the Web, sites like MP3.com and eMusic regularly offer special promotional contests. Yeah, contests can be a little cheesy, but they can get you and/or your band some exposure.

One band, Red Delicious, won a promotional contest on MP3.com and got a big prize and a great break: an opening bill for Tom Petty on his concert tour.

Usually, popularity contests are the standard. A site announces a theme, such as Valentine's Day, and you have to upload your track. Listeners tune in and vote on which songs they like best. Then the song with the most votes gets, for example, a prominent link of the site's home page.

To stay up on the latest contests, surf the major MP3 hubs:

- ✔ MP3.com (www.mp3.com)
- ✔ EMusic (www.emusic.com)
- ✔ Winamp (www.winamp.com)
- ✔ MusicMatch (www.musicmatch.com)
- ✔ Change Music Network (www.changemusic.com)

Newsgroups

Okay, so you're trying to reach other music fans — specifically, fans who like listening to MP3 music. Want a sure-fire captive audience? Try newsgroups.

As I describe in Chapter 8, newsgroups are where MP3 fans congregate, talk music, and trade files. And newsgroups are popping up for every new interest or new niche.

Think you can't find some likeminded MP3ers? You have hundreds of newsgroups to choose from; here are just a few:

- ✔ alt.binaries.sounds.mp3.indie: dedicated to indie rock
- ✔ alt.binaries.sounds.mp3.jazz: for jazz fans
- ✔ alt.binaries.sounds.mp3.latin: for Latin music enthusiasts

In these newsgroups, you can download and upload your choice of MP3 songs. And you can post little pithy messages that hype you or your band.

To access newsgroups, you need a *newsreader*. The e-mail programs for the two major Web browsers, Microsoft Internet Explorer and Netscape Communicator, also read newsgroups. You can also get a dedicated news-reading program, such as Agent for Windows (www.forteinc.com) or Newswatcher for the Mac OS (www.macorchard.com). Follow the program's instructions for connecting to newsgroups.

Your newsreader gives you the option to post a new message to a group. Simply type out your message, attach your MP3 song to the message, and upload your song to the group. Simple as that.

If you're promoting your band, you're sure to be downloading other bands' MP3s — at least to check out the competition, right? Doing this can be a bit more complicated, though. Sometimes, Internet service providers don't like so many big fat files hogging up their server space. Instead, they break up files into several parts, requiring listeners to get each piece and then reassemble them. That can be tricky. Here's what to do when using, say, a newsreader such as the one built into Outlook Express:

1. **Log on to your news server and find the newsgroup you want to download from.**

   A list of unread messages appears.

2. **Highlight all the files that share the description of the song you want to download, as shown in Figure 11-8.**

3. **Right-click on one of the highlighted files and choose Combine and Decode from the pop-up menu.**

   A dialog box appears asking you to organize the files in numerical order (see Figure 11-9). A pain, yes. But it shouldn't take you too long.

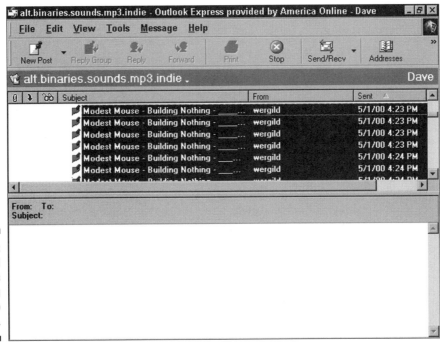

Figure 11-8:
Highlight all the pieces of the song you want to download.

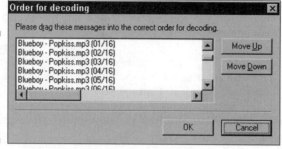

Figure 11-9:
Organize
your song
files numeri-
cally when
asked.

4. **Click OK.**

   The files are combined into a single file.

   When finished, a message window appears that shows the entire MP3 file as an attachment.

5. **Right-click the file's name and choose Save As from the pop-up menu.**

   The Save As dialog box appears.

6. **Navigate to the place on your hard drive where you want to store the song.**

7. **Click OK to save the file.**

After the song downloads, navigate to the song's location on your hard drive and double-click the file. Your MP3 player launches and plays the song for you.

Mailing lists

As I describe in Chapter 8, *mailing lists* are subscriber-based discussion groups that occur via e-mail. You can use mailing lists to network — in both senses of the word — with other bands: exchanging information and swapping songs.

For a complete list of MP3-related mailing lists, visit Liszt (`www.liszt.com/select/Music/Lists_for_Musicians/`), the mailing list directory.

When you're online — and especially when you're participating in mailing lists — you have to pay attention to *netiquette,* or etiquette for the Net, which is simply a standard, acceptable way of behaving. Here are some important things to keep in mind:

- ✔ **Respect list privacy.** Though you may see a list for polka dancers, the list may be meant only for three polka fans in Lawrenceville, New Jersey. Do your research before blindly trying to subscribe to a private list.

- ✔ **Lurk.** If you find that a list is open to the public, hang out for a bit and get a feeling for the discussion before you begin posting. Is the discussion wild? Conservative? Combative? Supportive?

- ✔ **Don't send ads.** Doing so almost guarantees a backlash or, as they're called in netspeak, *flame responses.* Don't crassly promote your band if you don't see others on the board doing the same.

- ✔ **Be human.** People join lists to talk, make friends, and get information. If you take a kamikaze approach to lists — hitting them up, siphoning information, leaving a trail of MP3 songs in your wake — you probably won't be that popular after all.

Surf, surf, surf

To really spread the word, the best thing to do is hit the waves. Get out there. Visit sites. Join discussions. Network. Hang out.

Think of the online world as the offline world without flesh and bone. You may not see the people out there, but they're all over the place. Join discussions on message boards. Find other musicians and offer to link to their pages if they link to yours.

The more effort you put in, the more you get in return.

Cashing In

Can you sell your MP3 songs? Absolutely. However, e-commerce for e-music is still in the early stages. Even major artists currently use digital music as more promotion than anything else.

Some sites, such as MP3.com, have tried to work out deals in which artists can get paid for digital downloads. For the most part, though, users download songs and play them on their computers.

Selling copyright-protected music is one of the biggest challenges that the music industry faces today. Before copyright protection becomes standard — and worth the time and effort — two things need to occur:

✔ Bandwidth needs to increase, allowing for faster, friendlier downloads.

✔ Electronic music needs to be made secure so that artists can actually get paid.

It's only a matter of time. Stay tuned.

Taking Your MP3 Music Offline

Maybe you've recorded some killer tunes in this killer new electronic format, but you still want to ship out CDs the old-fashioned way.

No problem.

After you produce a master tape or disc of your music, you can investigate the many services that can reproduce your disc and even produce artwork. Try Oasis Duplication (www.oasiscd.com), as shown in Figure 11-10, or Global Express Media (www.globalexpressmedia.com). Both of these services can help you to find a designer, poster maker, and even churn out your CDs and tapes.

Figure 11-10: Oasis Duplication can package your tunes.

You can also distribute your music online, even if it's in CD form. Head over to CD Baby! (www.cdbaby.com), as shown in Figure 11-11. Essentially, CD Baby! is like an indie record store online. Send them your discs and CD Baby! sells them for you through their site or 800 number. You get a check for anything they sell.

And maybe you can say you owed it all to MP3, after all.

Figure 11-11:
CD Baby!
sells your
discs or
tapes and
pays you the
revenues.

Part IV
Becoming a Net Radiohead

The 5th Wave   By Rich Tennant

"Would it ruin the online concert experience
if I vacuumed the mosh pit between songs?"

In this part . . .

With the Net, you can enjoy live simulcasts (or Netcasts) of everything from radio stations in Berlin to hip-hop concerts in Detroit. Also, more and more Net-only music shows are being created by and for fans. This part tells you what you need to do to enjoy the wide world of streaming audio (and video) music — how to find these Netshows, how to listen to concerts on your PC, and how you can Netcast your very own show.

Chapter 12

Radio without an Antenna

● ●

In This Chapter

▶ Tuning in to Net radio

▶ Listening to Net-only shows

▶ Finding offline radio shows online

▶ Listening to Net radio shows created by pop stars

▶ Enjoying SHOUTcast MP3 radio

● ●

*R*emember your antenna? That pesky little metal rod that would let you listen only to radio shows within a certain range? Good thing you don't need that sucker anymore. These days, the Internet lets you tune in to radio shows around the world with just your computer and modem.

You can find all kinds of shows out there. Online simulcasts of offline radio programs. Net-only shows made specifically by and for surfers. Even shows created by big name pop stars who want to share their favorite songs — including those by other artists — with you.

Less than five years ago, Net radio was a novelty: choppy, audio-only simulcasts of offline radio that sounded, at best, like a lousy AM receiver in an old Chevy. Today, with fatter bandwidth and phatter audio-visual wares, so-called *netcasting* has evolved into a full-fledged culture and industry.

Okay, maybe you can't quite rock out to Net radio on the beach (yet), but with shrinking hardware and portable peripherals, you will soon. This chapter looks at the sprawling soundscape of Net radio.

Getting Started with Net Radio

Here's the good news: You don't need a lot to make your computer ready to listen to Net radio. And after you're up and running, you have a lot of listening possibilities to choose from.

As far as hardware goes, all you need to enjoy Net radio is the following:

- ✔ A computer
- ✔ A modem
- ✔ An Internet connection
- ✔ External speakers

For a more detailed look at how to turn your computer into a jukebox (or stereo), see Chapter 2.

For software, essentially two standards exist:

- ✔ RealPlayer (www.real.com)
- ✔ Windows Media Player (www.microsoft.com/windows/mediaplayer/ en/default.asp)

For more info on both programs, see Chapter 3.

You can also check out another Net radio movement on the rise: *SHOUTcast* radio. SHOUTcast is a special kind of Net radio program that enables you to netcast your MP3 files over the Internet.

To listen to this kind of Net radio action, you need to download Winamp (www.winamp.com). Chapter 3 also gives you the skinny on Winamp.

To listen to SHOUTcast broadcasts, you must have the Winamp player. Winamp does not let you listen to RealAudio or Windows Media programs.

After you download the software, listening to Net radio is simply a matter of point 'n' click. Find the site you want to tune in to and then look for a hyperlink that you want to listen to. Figure 12-1 shows KHUM 104.7 FM, a Net radio station out of Humboldt, California. Click the appropriate link and your RealPlayer or Windows Media Player automatically begins to play.

Using Net Radio Guides

With so many things to listen to on the Net, you just may go nuts trying to keep everything in order.

You're not the only one who has figured this out. You can find a host of sites that are, in many ways, the *TV Guides* of Net radio sites. These massive resources enable you to sift, search, and organize based on genres, times, tastes, and musical styles.

Broadcast.com

One of the oldest and biggest Netcasting sites, Broadcast.com (`www.broadcast.com/music/`), as shown in Figure 12-2, has been responsible for Netcasting over 20,000 events since it launched in 1995. Broadcast.com is now affiliated with Yahoo!, the massive search engine.

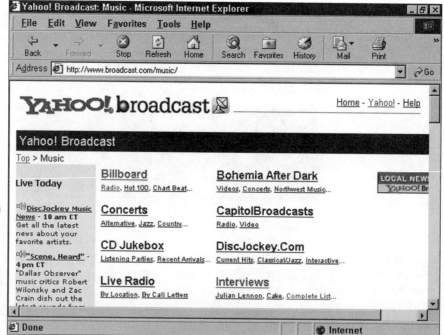

Figure 12-2:
Broadcast.
com's music
page has
links to sites
all over the
world.

For music fans, Broadcast.com is a deep guide that seems to cover every-thing and anything that's flowing down the streams — you can surf between a radio station in San Francisco and one in Saigon with just one click.

You can find links to the following:

- ✔ International radio
- ✔ Interviews with major artists
- ✔ Special shows
- ✔ Music news

Getting around the site is a lot like getting around the Yahoo! home page. For example, say you want to find a radio station from your hometown in . . . Seattle. Follow these steps:

1. **Click the <u>Radio</u> link on Broadcast.com's main page.**

   Doing so takes you to a page listing categories from Adult Album Alternative to Urban.

2. **Click <u>Browse By Location</u>.**

   A page appears listing dozens of cities around the United States.

3. **Click the <u>Seattle, WA</u> link (or any other city you want to check out).**

   You see a page that contains links to all the following stations from Seattle:

   - KJR 95.7 FM — an oldies station

   - KJR-AM, 950 AM — sports radio

   - KUBE, 93.3 FM — Top-40

4. **Click the call letters of the station you want to listen to.**

   In this example, I click KUBE. The station's home page on Broadcast.com appears, as shown in Figure 12-3.

   Sometimes, stations list their program schedules online. Broadcast.com even lets you select your own specific time zone, which conveniently adjusts the times so that you don't end up listening to a morning radio show in the afternoon.

5. **To listen to the show, click the ugly purple button that says "Click Here for the Yahoo! Broadcast" for whichever media player you use.**

   You may see an annoying ad banner come up. Just click it shut.

   Next, you see a file download window appear for a moment. Then your RealPlayer or Windows Media Player launches and begins playing the station's clip.

   You hear whatever is being broadcast live at that moment in Seattle. You can't switch to a program that previously aired or is scheduled for later in the day.

Real.com Guide

Run by RealNetworks, the company behind the ubiquitous RealPlayer, this guide (`http://realguide.real.com/music/`), as shown in Figure 12-4, connects you with thousands of hubs around the world that feature streaming audio and video tunes.

Figure 12-3:
KUBE's
home page.

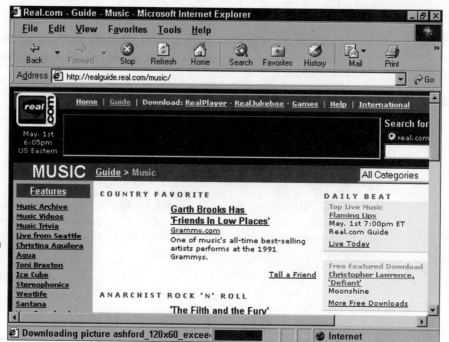

Figure 12-4:
The music
page for
Real.com
Guide.

At Real.com Guide, you can find the following:

- ✔ Nearly 150 record labels
- ✔ Over 60 sites featuring live audio/video music news
- ✔ About 600 streaming media sites devoted to specific recording artists

You also get Take 5, Real.com Guide's very own show devoted to the latest music and entertainment news and releases. Real.com Guide also creates its own niche guides to specific musical topics, such as the Latin pop explosion.

BRS Web-Radio

BRS Web-Radio (www.web-radio.com), as shown in Figure 12-5, specializes in helping you find offline radio stations that are simulcasting their shows on the Net. Here, you can search through 3,000 different stations by call letters, state, or format. You can also find links to international shows from Argentina to Cyprus.

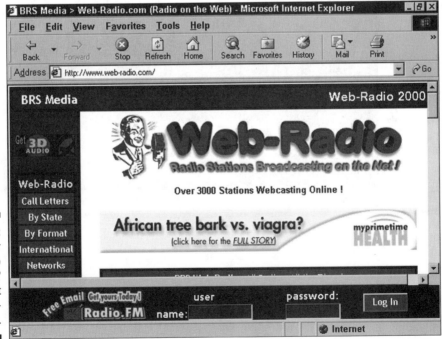

Figure 12-5: Looking for offline radio stations? Check out BRS Web-Radio.

Radio 4 All

Indie-minded microbroadcasters have been running their own low-power radio transmissions around the world for years. Though the FCC recently granted a license that enables so-called pirates to legally occupy certain airwaves, many of these renegades have been doing their own outlaw thing.

Part of that mission is to reach the people by any means necessary. Radio 4 All (`www.radio4all.org`), as shown in Figure 12-6, offers links to these microbroadcasters from Free Radio Quebec to Radio Free Cascadia in Eugene, Oregon.

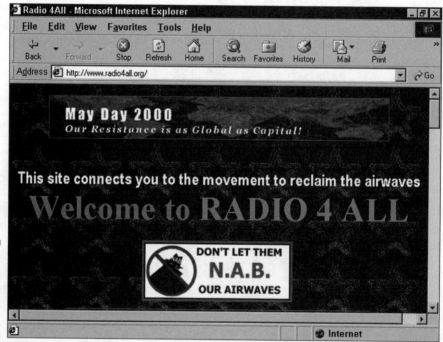

Figure 12-6: Pirate radio hits the Web at Radio 4 All.

Listening to Net-only Radio Shows

With so much power to do your own thing with Internet radio, many intrepid DJs have been creating shows that only appear online.

Sometimes, these shows are like traditional radio broadcasts, playing songs interspersed with chatty banter. Other times, these shows are full-blown multimedia Webcasts — such as KoolOut.com, as shown in Figure 12-7 — mixing everything from chat to message boards, gaming, and video.

Some of these shows, such as 88 Hip-Hop, have become hotspots for celebrity musicians who drop by to perform live or just shoot the breeze.

Other programs include the following:

- ✔ **The Womb** (www.thewomb.com): Electronica music from Miami, Florida.

- ✔ **Hard Radio** (www.hardradio.com): Classic heavy metal from Texas.

- ✔ **Green Witch** (www.greenwitch.com): Do-it-yourself radio programming from San Francisco.

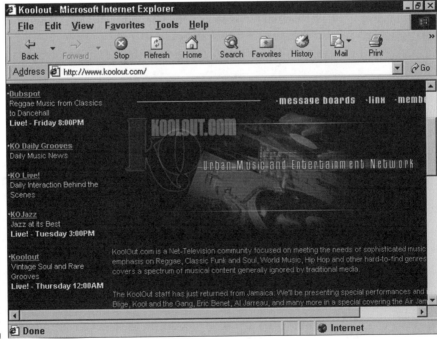

Figure 12-7: KoolOut. com, an urban dance show from Pseudo. com.

Pseudo.com (www.pseudo.com) has created a new school of radio broadcasting that combines audio, video, chat, message boards . . . you name it.

When booting up any of Pseudo.com's shows, surfers get to choose from real-time audio and/or video streams. Rather than dialing a studio line and praying to get through, surfers can directly e-mail in questions or participate in chat.

Here's a look at the lineup:

- ✓ **88 Hip-Hop:** Devoted to hip-hop music and culture
- ✓ **Streetsound:** Electronica tunes, news, and reviews
- ✓ **KoolOut:** For urban dance and R&B

All the flashy animation may make you see stars before you can find the program you want to listen to. Here's a look at how to get around if, for example, you want to check out all the action that awaits you on 88 Hip-Hop. To begin, log on to Pseudo.com (www.pseudo.com) and then follow these steps:

1. **Move your cursor over the blue box that says "Music."**

   A menu appears listing all of Pseudo.com's music shows.

2. **Click 88 Hip-Hop.**

   The 88 Hip-Hop home page appears, listing all the different shows and programs within the section:

   - Click 88 Hip-Hop to get current streams or archives of the main radio show.

   - Click 88 Hip-Hop.com News for news and information.

   - Click 88 Soul for shows dedicated to urban culture.

   - Click Queendom for 88 Hip-Hop's women's programming.

   - Click Fat Beats Radio for the latest in hip-hop music.

3. **When you find the show you want to watch/listen to, click the Play button.**

   Doing so calls up the Pseudo Player Preferences window, as shown in Figure 12-8.

4. **Select your preferred media player, either RealPlayer or Windows Media Player.**

5. **Choose whether to use the Pseudo Player Interface.**

   The Pseudo Player Interface is simply a customized window that essentially makes your streaming media player more in line with Pseudo.com's design.

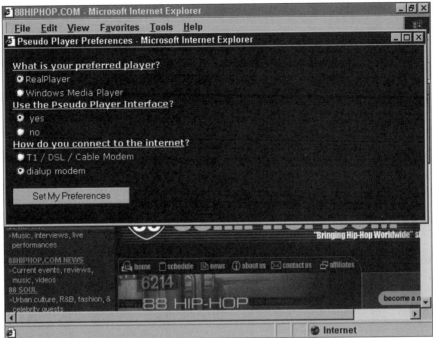

6. **Select the method by which you access the Internet: DSL, cable modem, T1, or dial-up modem.**

7. **Click Set My Preferences.**

   Your media player launches and plays the show.

Don't forget to change your preferences if you upgrade your connection. Doing so gives you a richer display every time you tune into a show.

Rocking to Pop Star Radio

Music fans aren't the only ones taking to the Net radio waves. Popular recording artists, seeing an opportunity to reach their fans in a whole new way, have been creating their own streaming stations online.

And surprisingly (or maybe not), these artists want you to hear more than just their own music. Many of them have hired DJs or have put together their own playlists that let you listen to stuff that may be lurking in their own record collections.

Brainwash

King Coffey, drummer and techie for the band Butthole Surfers, was one of the first rockers to produce his own Net radio show, Brainwash (`www.monster bit.com/brainwash`), as shown in Figure 12-9. For the show, he basically thumbed through his own record collection and put his favorite stuff on the wires for surfers of the world to check out.

Surprisingly, he doesn't feature any tracks by his own band. Guess he's heard enough of them already.

Grand Royal Radio

The Beastie Boys have long been one of the most do-it-yourself bands around. And they were among the first online, and they run their own Web site. They also launched their own record label, Grand Royal (`www.grandroyal.com/ grRadio/index.html`), as shown in Figure 12-10. And more recently, they started their very own Net radio station: Grand Royal Radio.

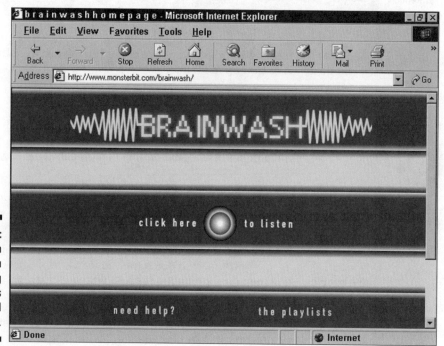

Figure 12-9: Brainwash gets you into King Coffey's record collection.

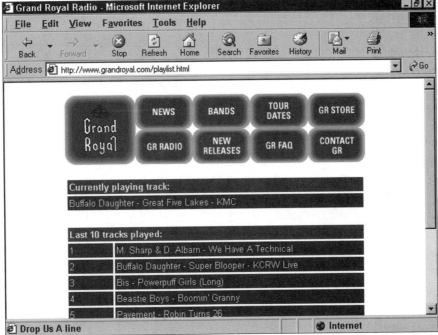

Figure 12-10:
The Beastie
Boys'
favorite
tunes play
on Grand
Royal Radio.

If you like the artists on the Beasties' label — such as Buffalo Daughter, Luscious Jackson, and, of course, the Beasties themselves — you may like the playlist, which features the Boys' new and obscure tracks.

Radio Margaritaville

Supposedly, singer/songwriter Jimmy Buffet got the idea for Radio Margaritaville (www.margaritaville.com), as shown in Figure 12-11, while driving through Australia. Down under, he heard a local radio station that played, as Buffet said, "just good music."

With that mission in mind, Buffet launched his own Net radio station, featuring music by his favorite artists: New Orleans jazz players, reggae artists, and surf musicians, to name a few. You also get a fair share of the man himself, though don't expect Buffet to take up the hosting duties; he leaves that to someone else while he's on the road.

Figure 12-11:
Jimmy
Buffet's
home-style
Radio
Margarita-
ville.

Listening to Offline Radio Stations Online

Every day you listen to radio stations offline: in the car, in the shower, on the beach — wherever you can take your radio.

One question I often hear is "Why would a station that's already on the regular radio go online?" The answer is simple: to reach more listeners. Being on the Web enables stations to reach a worldwide audience, rather than just the audience that's within the station's traditional broadcast range.

Personally, you get the chance to play around with radio stations in a way that you simply can't offline. Depending on the site, you may be able to do the following:

- Listen to archived radio shows
- E-mail in requests
- Chat with DJs and special guests live online

✔ Tune into live streaming video broadcasted from inside the studio

✔ Communicate with other listeners in message boards and chat rooms

Or, at the very least, you can just kick back and listen.

Literally thousands of radio stations are on the Net. Here's a look at two examples of notable places to tune in online. For a more complete list, see the _Music Online Directory_.

KCRW — Morning Becomes Eclectic

KCRW (`www.kcrw.org`), an eclectic station in Santa Monica, California, has attracted an online cult following of its show, "Morning Becomes Eclectic," as shown in Figure 12-12. "Morning Becomes Eclectic" is an interview program that has featured rare appearances and performances by the following artists:

✔ Radiohead

✔ Ben Harper

✔ Tom Waits

✔ PJ Harvey

✔ Ben Folds Five

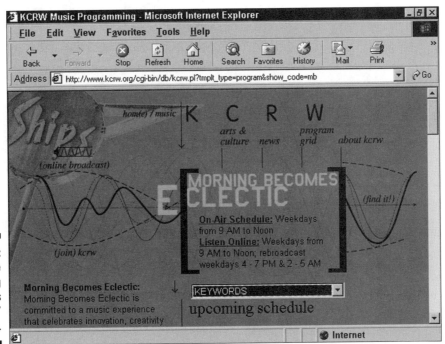

Figure 12-12: The "Morning Becomes Eclectic" home page.

Inspired by the success, KCRW created another show specifically for its online audience called "Hollywood Rap." When this entertainment gossip show became popular on the Net, producers eventually moved it to offline broadcasts.

WWOZ — New Orleans jazz

Live from "Nawlins," WWOZ 90.7 (`www.wwoz.org`), as shown in Figure 12-13, is the place to tune in for your dose of jazz, blues, zydeco, and Cajun rhythms.

Tune into the latest live broadcast, or even browse through the MP3 store to purchase some southern fried music of your own. And during Mardi Gras, WWOZ is the best place to shake your booty without getting crushed by the crowds.

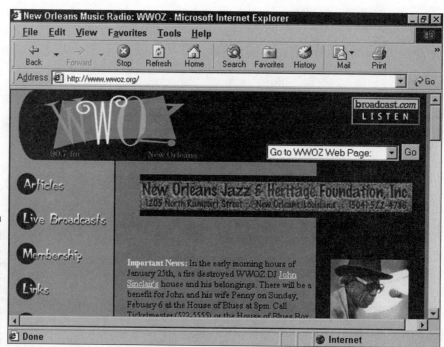

Figure 12-13: Spice up your day with New Orleans music on WWOZ.

Action Radio

Straight out of Toulouse, France, Action Radio (`www.chez.com/action radio/`) is international radio straight to your desktop. You're out of luck if you don't speak the language, but at least you can hear the global language of music. This site features the latest urban beats from the beautiful south of France.

It's the next best thing to being there.

SHOUTcast Radio

The MP3 movement has unsurprisingly spawned its own Net radio movement: SHOUTcast. The idea is simple: If you have a bunch of MP3s, you can let other people around the world tune into them as well.

Created by Nullsoft, makers of the popular Winamp MP3 player, SHOUTcast is a nifty little program that lets anyone — you, me, our moms — broadcast our MP3 collections to any other Winamp users on the scene.

In Chapter 14, I show you how to roll up your sleeves and do your own SHOUTcasting. This section is about rocking out to other people's stuff.

To listen to SHOUTcast programs, you need to install a copy of the Winamp player. You can find the program on the CD-ROM that accompanies this book. You can also get the latest version at `www.winamp.com`.

Finding SHOUTcast radio

After you have Winamp up and running (see Chapter 3 for more information), you can find thousands of SHOUTcast sites by going to the SHOUTcast home page at `www.shoutcast.com`, as shown in Figure 12-14.

The SHOUTcast home page lists the available MP3 streams according to popularity. And just what makes the top 20 popular? Your guess is as good as mine, but you can see the action by checking out how many listeners are vying to listen to the streams.

Because SHOUTcast songs are coming directly from another person's hard drive, only so much space exists for others to tune in. Think of it as a water tap. Out comes the stream, and only so many people can shove their cups under the faucet.

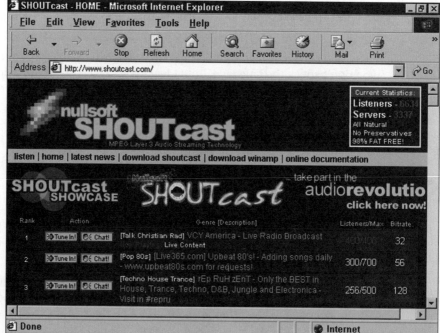

Figure 12-14:
SHOUTcast's
big, bad list
of MP3
radio.

On the main SHOUTcast page, you see a Listeners/Max column, which shows specifically how many people a SHOUTcast "station" can support.

You also see a list of Bitrates, which shows you the speed at which a person is sending out their goods. You need to be copasetic here. Streams pumping out at 128 Kbps are meant for other high-speed surfers. Try tuning into stations that are streaming at your home speed.

At the bottom of the home page, a drop-down menu lets you search by categories, including the following:

- ✔ Alternative
- ✔ Funk
- ✔ Jazz
- ✔ Metal
- ✔ R&B
- ✔ Rap
- ✔ Techno
- ✔ The 1970s
- ✔ The 1980s

Choose All stations to list the mother lode. To get particular information about a specific show, click the highlighted text under the Genre/Description column.

You can download the shareware program RadioSpy (www.radiospy.com) to sort and organize thousands of audio feeds from around the Net. Some cool features include the following:

- RadioSpy notifies you when your favorite SHOUTcasters are online.
- RadioSpy provides daily Net radio music news.
- RadioSpy has built-in chat tools that let you gab with DJs while they Netcast their tunes.

Listening to SHOUTcast radio

SHOUTcast is essentially a point 'n' rock experience. After downloading the Winamp player, follow these instructions to get up and running:

1. **Go to the SHOUTcast homepage and find a stream that you want to listen to.**

2. **Click the Tune In button next to the desired stream.**

3. **Configure your browser.**

   If you use Internet Explorer: A dialog box appears asking if you want to open the file from the current location or save it to a disk. Select Open This File from Its Current Location and click OK.

   If you use Netscape Navigator: You see a dialog box telling you that you are about to play an unknown file type. Don't panic. Click the Pick App button, which calls up an application selection window. Click the Browse button and find the folder that contains the Winamp player. Just double-click the program.

   In either case, the Winamp player launches and the music plays.

Chapter 13

Seeing (and Hearing) Concerts without Tickets

. . . .

In This Chapter

▶ Finding netcasts of concerts

▶ Listening to concerts

▶ Chatting with the stars backstage

. . . .

*N*othing beats seeing your favorite artist in concert. And nothing's worse than not being able to see anything at all. Oftentimes, a concert tour inconveniently bypasses your hometown. Or maybe the show comes when you have other — unbreakable — plans.

That's where concert netcasts come in.

With a few clicks, you can tune into live and archived online broadcasts of musical events and concerts from around the world. All kinds of artists have been cybercast online, including the following hit-makers:

✔ Smashing Pumpkins

✔ Paul McCartney

✔ Alanis Morissette

✔ Wu Tang Clan

This chapter shows you how to get set up, where to find the shows, and what you can do along the way, including chatting with the band backstage.

Getting Ready

Tuning into concerts online is actually a lot less labor-intensive than going to a real show. No driving. No parking. No tickets to buy. No crowds.

The necessary hardware and software

To see and listen to online concerts, all you need to do is have the following (odds are, you already have these):

- ✔ A computer (preferably at Pentium II or higher or a Macintosh G3 or higher).
- ✔ A modem (the faster, the better — ideally, at least 56K).
- ✔ External computer speakers (or a line out to your stereo).
- ✔ An Internet connection.
- ✔ Streaming audio software, such as RealPlayer, Windows Media Player, or QuickTime Player. See Chapter 3 for more information on downloading and installing these players.

See Part I for more info on turning your computer into a lean, mean music machine.

After you're loaded up, all you have to do is find the sites, kick back, and enjoy.

A quick word about speed

Broadband: You hear about it all the time. The term means broad bandwidth or, in simpler terms, really fat streams of data or, in yet other words, fast Internet downloads.

Most of us still live in the B.B. (that is, before broadband) era of the Internet evolution, using pitifully slow modems to access the Internet. A lucky few (and you know who you are) live in the A.B. (after broadband) era; they operate in the world of T1 lines, DSL, and cable modems. These folks can access the Internet at speeds of up to 100 times that of a typical 28.8K modem.

Alas, you may run into some frustration when tuning into a live concert with your regular modem. Here's why: Streaming audio and video is not saved to your hard drive as it downloads. So you can't download it and play it later. You basically just connect and let the music play — much like a typical live radio program.

That means you have to cue up while thousands — if not millions — of other listeners are tuning in. And the more listeners, the more crowded the traffic. The more traffic, the slower the download. The slower the download, the choppier the sound. Hence the frustration.

Concert netcasts can be really cool and really fun. But ultimately, they are still somewhat of a novelty. If you want perfect sound, go to the show.

Finding Concerts Online

With so many events happening in so many places at so many times, you may find that you can't find everything.

But you can come close.

You can find online concerts in a few ways:

- ✓ **Surf specialty sites.** These sites regularly netcast live events.
- ✓ **Visit the home pages of concert halls and nightclubs.** Many clubs and halls netcast their own events.
- ✓ **Search streaming audio guides.** These guides list countless live netcasts.
- ✓ **Join communities that hover around your favorite artist.** Check out Web pages or subscribe to mailing lists. The best way to keep up on a band, of course, is through the fans.

Specialty sites

The easiest way to find live concerts is to visit the sites that have made it their business to bring live events to the Web on a regular basis.

These sites are serious about letting you rock out at home. They send their own crews to every show, wire up the club, and then pump the music — in the form of ones and zeroes — to your PC.

Netcasting concerts is not a perfect science — even broadcasting live shows on TV is not without its potential mishaps. But netcasts, just like TV broadcasts, are the next best thing to being there.

Here are some of the sites that specialize in bringing you online concerts.

LiveConcerts.com

LiveConcerts.com (www.liveconcerts.com), as shown in Figure 13-1, broadcasted its first live event way back in 1996, when it let surfers tune into a California show featuring the Fugees, Ziggy Marley and the Melody Makers, Spearhead, Cypress Hill, and a Tribe Called Quest.

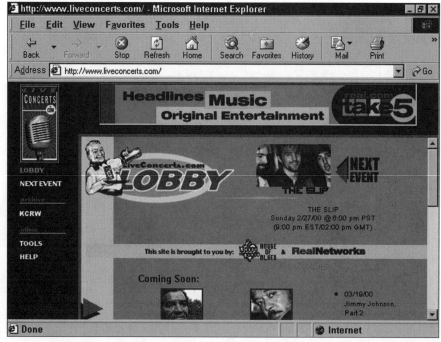

Figure 13-1:
Listen to
upcoming
bands at
Live-
Concerts.
com.

LiveConcerts.com continues to bring bands to the Net. These days, they usually broadcasts an event once a week — though the site has been featuring lesser-known bands recently, including the following:

- ✔ A side project by members of Phish
- ✔ Blues artist Jimmy Johnson
- ✔ Flutist Ken Denson

The site also provides links to an affiliate site for KCRW radio (www.kcrw.com), which features live studio performances on its show "Morning Becomes Eclectic." Past guests include Tom Waits, Radiohead, and PJ Harvey.

L.A. Live

For L.A. Live (www.lalive.com), as shown in Figure 13-2, the challenge has centered on introducing the netcasting technology to the scrappy world of the rock 'n' roll subculture. The company broadcasted its first show — the Screaming Cheetah Wheelies — at the Troubadour.

With several full-length concert netcasts per month at venues across Los Angeles — from the 250-seat Viper Room to the 6000-seat Universal Amphitheater — L.A. Live has featured edgy L.A. artists from Voodoo Glow Skulls to Wank.

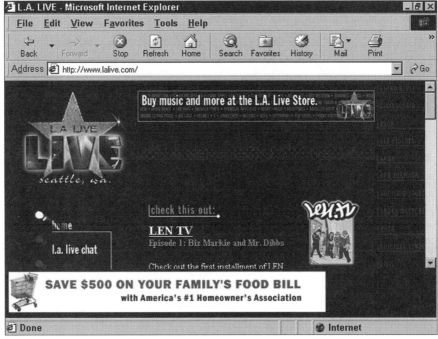

Figure 13-2:
L.A.'s
rock 'n' roll
under-
ground
surfaces at
L.A. Live.

While you're here, you can also peruse the archives of "coffee break" interviews with bands such as Rush and Green Day.

Rolling Stone.com

In addition to providing their fill of news, reviews, and music culture reports, the Web site for *Rolling Stone* magazine streams live concert events (`http://rollingstone.tunes.com/sections/performance/text/default.asp?afl=`), as shown in Figure 13-3.

If most of the shows seem to be from Chicago, there's a good reason: The company that does the Webcasting is Chicago-based. Fortunately, the Windy City gets its share of varied artists, such as Air and Beck.

You can also find interviews and archives, plus a handy Remind Me tool that automatically sends you an e-mail message when your selected band will be simulcast online.

Virtue TV

Based in London, Virtue TV (`www.virtuetv.com`) has offered live Internet video broadcasts since 1998. In addition to interviews with film directors and media personalities, the site offers streaming video concerts — live and archived — from venues around England (and, sometimes, even faraway places like Tokyo).

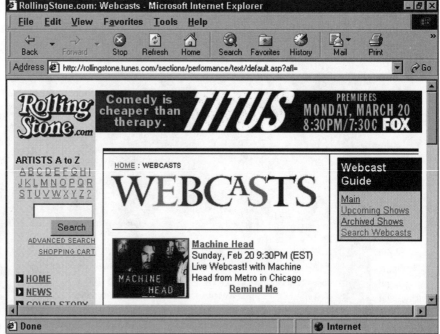

Figure 13-3:
Rolling
Stone
Webcasts
live from
Chicago.

Wired clubs

Some concert halls are taking matters into their own hands. Instead of relying on another Web site to netcast an event, these venues do the work on their own.

Of course, tuning into a wired club means that you're not going to hear music from the place down the street. But you do get a prime seat for anything — and sometimes, everything — that plays from the home page's home stage.

Check out these sites:

Jazz Radio

Jazz From Lincoln Center in New York City has become a highlight concert series for jazz lovers around the world. Now, you can tune in online without having to make the trip to the big city.

Jazz Radio (www.jazzradio.org), as shown in Figure 13-4, carries Lincoln Center's award-winning productions, such as The Ellington Centennial — a recent tribute to Sir Duke featuring Wynton Marsalis. You can also check out other productions you may have missed in the sound archives.

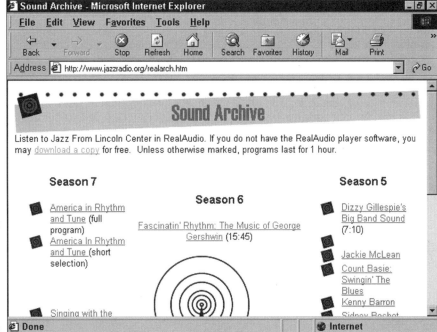

Figure 13-4:
RealAudio
shows from
Jazz From
Lincoln
Center.

House of Blues

The House of Blues (www.hob.com/internetradio), the club chain started by Blues Brothers showman Dan Ackroyd, brings its concerts online at its own HOB.com Web site.

Here, you can find a wide variety of events — from blues and jazz stars, such as Michelle Wilson, to major pop and rock stars, such as Kid Rock.

For those of you who have high-speed Internet access (cable modems, DSL, T1, and so on), the House of Blues also offers pay-per-view shows that bring video broadcasts to your computer for a one-time fee of around $8.

Knitting Factory

Live from downtown New York City, the eclectic Knitting Factory (www. knittingfactory.com/live/index.html) club lets you tune into specially selected events.

Home to everything from avant-garde klezmer music to well-known scenesters like Lou Reed, the Knitting Factory has been among the most wired clubs around, bringing concerts and festivals to people across the Net. The Knitting Factory is also one of the founding venues in the burgeoning Digital Club Network, an online organization for clubs who bring their events and schedules to the Net.

Guides for online concerts

If you want a larger view of the concerts taking place online, you can check out some *TV Guide* style sites to help you through the fray:

✔ Broadcast.com (see also Chapter 12), at `www.broadcast.com`, has a special section devoted to live events. But be warned: Apparently, the site's administrators don't actively maintain the site. Still, it has dozens of events available for you to listen to. Concerts are grouped into categories: rock, pop, jazz, classical, and so on.

✔ The Windows Media Guide (`www.windowsmedia.com/Music/events.asp`) details live music events that are available in the Windows Media format. This site includes daily listing of major concert events and even in-studio radio station performances.

✔ Real.com Guide (`http://realguide.real.com/music/?s=concert-series`), as shown in Figure 13-5, has a special subsection devoted to live concerts from sites across the Net, including the BBC, VH-1, Rolling Stone.com, SonicNet, and even the Kennedy Center in Washington D.C. The types of performers are just as varied, ranging from chamber musicians to hip-hop artists.

Figure 13-5:
Real.com Guide's special section devoted to live concerts.

Fan pages

Although fan pages may have plenty of information about a band, they're unlikely to actually netcast a concert themselves.

Still, if you're wondering when a band's going to be performing online, checking in with other fans is a great place to start.

Watching Concerts Online

These days, not only can you listen to concerts online, but you can also watch them. More and more sites are beginning to carry live video netcasts of concerts.

Because data still has to squeeze through tiny phone lines, video quality may be pretty lousy. It may skip, hop, jump, cut, and putter out in the middle of your favorite song.

To access a House of Blues cybercast, follow these steps:

1. **Go to** www.houseofblues.com.

2. **On the House of Blues home page, click All Cybercasts on the left side of the screen.**

   A schedule of upcoming cybercast events appears.

3. **Click the name of the artist whose show you want to listen to.**

   The artist's page loads, as shown in Figure 13-6.

   If you click an upcoming event, you can choose to receive an e-mail reminder to make sure you plant yourself in front of your PC at the right moment. Click Remind Me to fill out the form.

4. **When you're ready to view an event, click your appropriate connection speed.**

   The choices are 28.8K, 56K, and Broadband; 28.8K and 56K are lo-fi options and are free for viewing. Broadband access, however, requires a fee.

   If you're interested in Broadband viewing, you must purchase access ahead of time. Click Pay-Per-View from the HOB home page and then follow the links for the show you wish to see in broadband splendor. You have to provide some personal information and a credit card number (of course). Then you can proceed on your way.

   After you choose your connection speed, either RealPlayer or Windows Media Player launches and plays your concert.

   For information on downloading and installing these players, see Chapter 4.

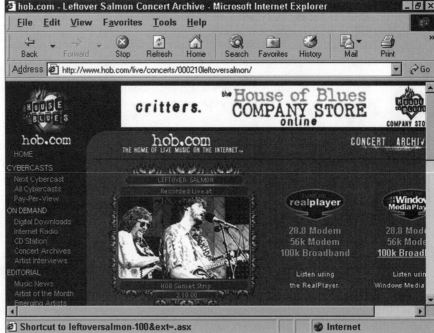

Figure 13-6:
Watch a concert at the House of Blues Web site.

Going Backstage: Chatting with Bands Online

Of course, the ultimate concert experience is going backstage to meet your favorite artist in person. The problem is that backstage passes aren't easy to come by.

Many sites that netcast concerts now offer the opportunity for fans to chat live with the bands, using chat programs that do not require a download (just following the links with your browser gets things going).

Often, these services convince a band to spend time at the keyboard before or after a show. After you log on, the artist takes your questions (which often go through a chat host first).

Some sites that offer chat include the following:

✔ SonicNet, `www.sonicnet.com`

✔ VH1, `www.vh1.com`

✔ MTV, `www.mtv.com`

- Rolling Stone.com, www.rollingstone.com
- Spin, www.spin.com
- Live Concerts, www.liveconcerts.com

Want to get your questions answered? If you're in an unmoderated chat room (without a host), try addressing the artist by name before you ask your question (for example, "SHIN FAT: What's your favorite album?"). That's a great way to get someone's attention during the flood of questions.

If a moderator is screening the questions, state your question as succinctly and eloquently as possible. The more you stand out, the better your chances of getting a response.

Finding Shows You Missed

The great thing about concerts on the Internet is that they never fade away. Long after the show hits the wires, you can surf around and listen to what you missed. All the following sites offer archives of shows for your listening pleasure:

- House of Blues, www.hob.com
- MTV, www.mtv.com
- VH1, www.vh1.com
- Virtue TV, www.virtuetv.com
- KCRW, www.kcrw.com

Just find the show you want to watch or listen to, and then follow the steps in "Watching Concerts Online" earlier in this chapter to enjoy the show.

Just because you can play back an archived show doesn't mean it's yours to save. Because these netcasts are stored in streaming format, you can listen to them while you're connected, but not after the fact. That is, unless you have your computer hooked up to your stereo and you decide to tape the show. For more information on this, see Chapter 2.

Getting Concert Information

While you're kicking back and listening to your favorite artist perform live online, you may want to find out when that band is coming to town.

A host of sites enable you to search for and get information about international tours. Of course, because you probably want to buy tickets for these events, you can also check the home pages of major ticket vendors, such as Ticketmaster (www.Ticketmaster.com).

Gigmania

Straight out of Brooklyn, New York, Gigmania (www.gigmania.com) is a lean, mean Internet machine devoted to helping you keep track of all your touring idols.

The site, as shown in Figure 13-7, also features a nifty guide to live concerts online. To find these shows, click the Live Online tab on the right side of the screen.

To find a gig near you, use the search options at the top of the screen. Here, you can do the following:

✔ **See all upcoming events in your location.** Gigmania features listings from a couple dozen major U.S. cities. Select your city and the date from the Scene drop-down menu and then click Go for the results.

✔ **Search by venue, city, or artist.** Simply select your chosen category, type in the name of what or whom you're looking for, and then click Search. A list of results appears.

Tourdates.com

This site (www.tourdates.com), as shown in Figure 13-8, features national concert tour listings, searchable by artist, city, or venue. You also find My Tourdates, a personalized service that lets you stay on top of a specific band's schedule. You can even program the service to e-mail updates to you when/if the band heads your way.

You can also find some opinions; the Critic's Corner gives you the lowdown on whether the shows are worth the admission price.

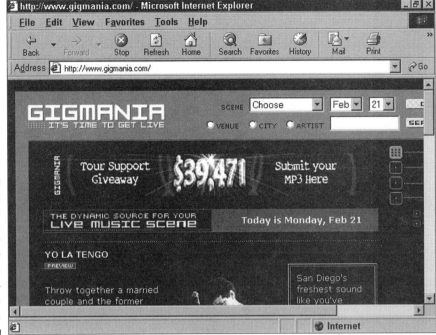

Figure 13-7:
Gigmania
helps you
find the tour
dates for
your favorite
bands —
online
and off.

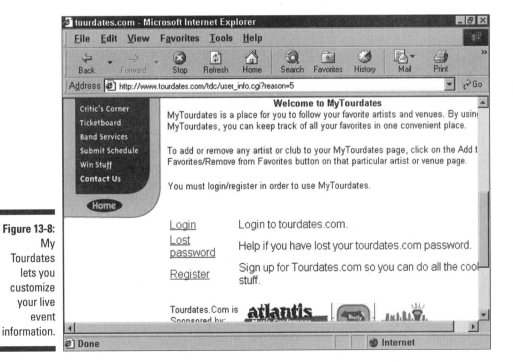

Figure 13-8:
My
Tourdates
lets you
customize
your live
event
information.

Chapter 14

Becoming a Net Radio DJ

*A*t some point, every music fan wants to be a radio DJ. There you are behind the controls, calling your own shots, playing all your favorite music.

Some people take matters into their own hands by becoming ham radio geeks. Then again, when was the last time you heard of someone dancing to ham radio?

These days, all you have to do to be a DJ is to head online. With some special software, some basic computer equipment, and a place to host your music, you can broadcast live online to millions of people around the world.

And because it's your show, the content is up to you. Here are just a few ideas:

✔ You can have full-blown, 24/7 action with music, DJs, bands, and guests.

✔ You can broadcast yourself yodeling every Thursday night at 11 o'clock.

✔ You can put up clips of your band, so that others can download your streams somewhere along the line.

In this chapter, you find out how to Webcast using RealAudio, since this is the main program used by people who want to create their own streaming media. You also discover how to pump up your show with added features, such as chat and video.

Understanding the Legalities

Just like MP3 (see Chapter 5), Webcasts are subject to certain legal restrictions.

Net radio is not, in itself, illegal. But Net radio can be used in a legal or illegal way.

If you're Webcasting your own material — your music, your voice, your ode to tuna casserole — you're covered. But if you start Webcasting someone else's intellectual property — a song, poem, whatever — you need to have a license.

If you really want to go the Webcast road musically, you need to contact the artist's record company to find out how you go about licensing the artist's music. You may find certain restrictions governing how often you can play a song, how many songs by a particular artist you can play, and how you can't use songs for advertising.

For more information, the Recording Industry Association of America (RIAA) has created its own FAQ, available at `www.riaa.com/weblic/wl_faq.htm`.

Webcasting with RealAudio

In addition to being a popular way to listen to streaming audio and watch streaming video over the Net, RealAudio (`www.real.com`) enables surfers to put their own multimedia goods online.

Getting equipped

Before you begin, download and install three different bits of free software from the RealNetworks product page, `www.realnetworks.com/products/`:

- ✔ **RealProducer Basic:** RealProducer lets you encode your audio and video before you broadcast it online.

- ✔ **RealPlayer Basic:** The standard RealAudio and RealVideo player that lets you experience the sights and sounds. (For more information about using RealPlayer Basic, see Chapter 3).

- ✔ **RealServer Basic**: This program sets you up to carry your media over the Net.

Converting audio into a RealAudio file

After you do the hard work of getting your music, whatever that may be, onto your computer (for details about how to do this, see Chapter 10), you need to turn these files into RealAudio files. Here's how:

1. **Launch RealProducer.**

   As shown in Figure 14-1, the New Session dialog box appears.

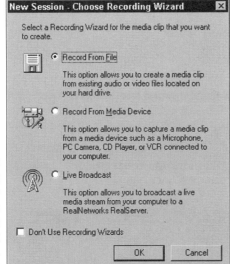

Figure 14-1: The New Session dialog box helps you get started.

2. **Click the Record From File radio button.**

   The Recording Wizard dialog box opens.

3. **Use the Browse button to locate the audio or video file you want to convert.**

4. **Click Next.**

   The RealMedia Clip Information dialog box appears.

5. **Enter the following information in the provided spaces:**

   - **Title:** The title of the audio clip

   - **Author:** Your name (or the name of whoever made the audio)

   - **Copyright:** Year and owner of the clip's copyright

   - **Description:** A brief summary of the clip's content

   - **Keywords:** Buzzwords to help people find your clip

6. **Click Next.**

   The File Type dialog box opens.

7. **Select the type of RealMedia file you want to create: SureStream or single rate.**

   SureStream is recommended for most users, because it can tailor your media for different types of listeners.

8. **Click Next.**

   The Target Audience dialog box opens.

9. **Select up to two connection speeds for the listeners you want to reach.**

   Most people surf at 28.8K or 56K.

10. **Click Next.**

    The Audio/Video Format dialog box opens, as shown in Figure 14-2.

11. **Select the option that best suits the content of the file.**

12. **Click Next.**

    The Output File dialog box appears.

13. **Accept the default location for the converted file, or use the Save As button to save the file somewhere else.**

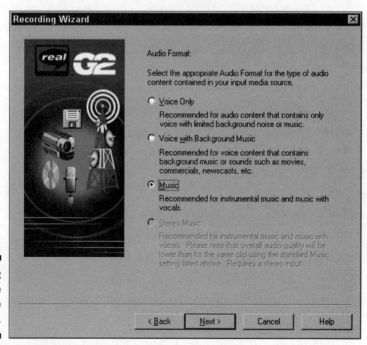

Figure 14-2: Choose your audio format.

14. **Click Next.**

    The Prepare to Record dialog box opens.

15. **Review all the information about the recording session.**

    If the information is correct, click Finish. You can use the Back button to cycle back through the wizard and change any incorrect information.

16. **Click Start to begin recording.**

    The converted file appears in the location you specified.

Putting your RealAudio online

Okay, you have your RealAudio formatted. Great. Now comes the tricky part: getting it online. Basically, you have to find a place to store or host your music.

To broadcast on-demand content over the Web, you have two choices:

✔ **Get your own Web server, which allows people to access information over the Net.** This is a pretty pricey proposition; you many want to try the next option first.

✔ **Place your information on someone else's server.** Your Internet service provider is the best place to start. Contact them to see how much space they provide for RealAudio/RealVideo files. Odds are, though, it won't be enough; ISPs tend to give only 6 to 10MB of Web space to users. However, other sites, such as Yahoo! GeoCities or Tripod, may be able to help. You can also check Real.com's own references at `http://partners.real.com`.

A way to get lots of server space is to sign up for several of the free Web-hosting services, such as Yahoo! GeoCities and Tripod. You can then connect your pages together with hyperlinks.

Here's some great news. RealProducer contains built-in programs that enable you to create and publish your own Web pages, as well as get your content online. For the easiest method (which assumes you have created your own Web page and have somewhere to put it), follow these steps:

1. **Launch RealProducer.**

2. **Choose Tools⇨Publish a Web Page.**

    The Publishing Wizard appears.

3. **Click Next.**

4. **Browse to the location of the HTML file for your Web page, double-click the filename, and click Next.**

   The Publishing Profile dialog box opens.

5. **Choose an Internet service provider from the list or select Generic-No Defaults if your provider is not listed.**

6. **Click Next.**

   The Streaming Method dialog box opens.

7. **Click Stream Media Clip from a Standard Web Server and then click Next.**

   The FTP Server Information dialog box opens.

8. **Type in the name or IP address of the FTP server to which you are uploading your files and the directory on the FTP server to which your page will be sent.**

9. **Type in your username and password and click Next.**

   The Web Page URL dialog box opens.

10. **Type in the name or IP address of the Web server and URL directory that users will use to locate your page on the Internet.**

11. **Click Next.**

    The Upload Progress dialog box appears.

12. **Click Next to begin uploading your files.**

    Your files automatically upload to your Web server.

13. **Click View Now! to view your published Web page.**

14. **Click Finish when you are done viewing your published Web page.**

SHOUTcasting

RealAudio isn't the only way to netcast your show. SHOUTcast (as described in Chapter 12) is specifically designed for creating and hearing MP3 broadcasts over the Internet. SHOUTcast relies on the Winamp MP3 player.

After you're up and running, you can modify your show by downloading and installing various SHOUTcast plug-ins available at www.shoutcast.com/download/broadcast.phtml.

To sample some SHOUTcasted shows, go directly to the SHOUTcast home page at www.shoutcast.com.

Enhancing Your Show

Soon enough, anyone will be able to plug in a microphone and start up his or her own Net radio show. And, if you think about it, that's a scary prospect.

Imagine this: All around the world, people are glued to their desktops, ranting into microphones and playing whatever music they want. Then again, maybe that wouldn't be so bad after all.

No matter how great the competition, though, you can do a lot more with Net radio than just play music. Think about your favorite radio shows offline — what do you like about them? What don't you like? What keeps you coming back?

Don't forget the *show* part of your Net radio show. Just because you're on the Net doesn't mean your listeners and viewers don't want to be entertained.

Think as if you were on the offline radio — what would you do?

- ✔ Book guests?
- ✔ Create comedy bits?
- ✔ Read the news?
- ✔ Have bands on for live performances?
- ✔ Take phone calls?
- ✔ Get a sidekick?

You can do anything online that you can imagine doing on an offline radio show. Plus, you can do a whole bunch of things that you could never possibly do offline.

Read on.

Planning a Net radio Web page

If you're going to have a Net radio show, you need some place to call home.

Creating a Web page for your Net radio show shouldn't be an afterthought. After all, this is where visitors are going to come to roost and boot up your action.

So, you want to give them the best presentation you can, letting them know what your show is about, what they can expect, and why they should stick around. For a crash course on launching your own Web site, see Chapter 11. For even more detailed information, see *Creating Web Pages For Dummies*, 4th Edition, written by Bud Smith and Arthur Bebak and published by IDG Books Worldwide, Inc.

Here are some examples of successful Net radio home pages:

- **The Womb** (`www.thewomb.com`): Electronica music from Miami. Well-made, well-produced, easy on the eyes and ears.

- **88 Hip-Hop** (`www.88hiphop.com`): Hip-hop music and culture with the energy and style of downtown New York City.

- **Beta Lounge** (`www.betalounge.com`): Techno music with a cool urban feel (see Figure 14-3).

Yes, these sites use some fancy HTML and Java tricks, but each site really reflects a certain personality. You feel that the people behind the shows take pride in what they're doing and want to give you a unique listening experience.

Figure 14-3:
The Beta Lounge is a good example of a Net radio home page.

Here are some things to let visitors know when they arrive at your Net radio page:

- ✔ What kind of show will they hear?
- ✔ What software do they need?
- ✔ How often is your show updated?
- ✔ What kind of music do you play?
- ✔ Is your show ever Webcast live? If so, when?
- ✔ Is there a program schedule? Describe the shows.
- ✔ How can listeners communicate with you?

No matter how big or small your show may be, you want to let people know what they're in for as soon as you can.

Getting interactive: E-mail, message boards, and chat

If you look at some of the more successful Net radio hubs, such as Pseudo.com (see Figure 14-4), you can see that a big part of the action is audience interaction.

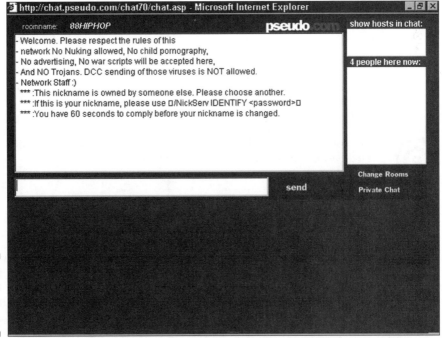

Figure 14-4:
A Pseudo
.com
chat room.

One huge advantage that the Net has over other entertainment mediums is that the Net is totally interactive. Unlike offline, audience members don't have to wait on the phone, hoping to get through to the studio. With e-mail, message boards, and chat, fans can stay in touch with you.

They can also interact with each other, swapping music recommendations or even talking about you behind your back. (Hey, what do you expect — it's human nature.)

To include e-mail on your home page, just post your e-mail address in a prominent place. You may also want to have different addresses dedicated to specific topics, such as requests@yourisp.com, feedback@yourisp.com, or opinions@yourisp.com.

Most basic HTML programs let you create your own message boards with just a few clicks of a mouse. Do it. If you want to, select the topics yourself and pop in now and then to keep the conversation going. Message boards are also a good place to take requests.

To incorporate chat into your site, the easiest way is to click over to ICQ (www.icq.com). This enormously popular chat freeware enables you to set up your own chat channel so that your audience can interact with you at any time. Other companies, such as iChat (www.ichat.com), allow you to purchase software to customize your own personal chat rooms.

Taking calls

Okay, here's one area in which the Web isn't really much like offline radio. Taking calls is not really that sensible online.

First, you're probably not going to be Webcasting live. Second, you may have listeners all around the world, so do you really want to get calls from listeners in Finland at three in the morning?

The conventional wisdom online: If you want to be contacted, post your e-mail address, not your telephone number.

Booking guests

I once had a job as a professional chat host at SonicNet (see Figure 14-5). I had to book the guests, get them online, and, somehow, try to interview them — while typing.

Figure 14-5:
The list of events on SonicNet.

These days, convincing someone to come online to chat with fans is not nearly as difficult. Up-and-coming bands may be especially open to reaching out, even if your site is just getting started. If your show looks and sounds good to them, they may want to get involved.

Be creative when arranging interviews. Post a message on your Web site telling listeners that, for example, you're going to a record signing for your favorite artist. Then, solicit questions from your listeners. Show up at the signing with a tape recorder and conduct your interview. After you get the goods, come back to your site and post the answers online.

Be sure to get the artist's permission before you post an interview with him or her.

Spreading the Word

After you get up and running, you want to let other listeners know when, where, and how to check out your show.

Here's a list of sites and newsgroups on which you can post information about your Net radio show. Often, you need to submit your "station's" information: URL, genre, shows, and so forth. Don't be intimidated; many shows are done by amateurs.

- ✔ Yahoo, www.yahoo.com
- ✔ Radio X, www.radiox.com
- ✔ VTuner, www.vtuner.com
- ✔ Radio Spy, www.radiospy.com
- ✔ SHOUTcast, www.SHOUTcast.com
- ✔ Alt.internet.radio
- ✔ Alt.radio.internet

Don't forget about your offline outlets, too. The late Bill Graham, the famous rock promoter, used to staple all his concert posters up around San Francisco. Here are some ideas for how to promote your show offline:

- ✔ Post flyers and leaflets around town.
- ✔ Drop off promotional post cards at record stores.
- ✔ Suggest a story about you and your station to a local music magazine or alternative newspaper.
- ✔ Pass out flyers at local concerts.

Creating Customized Radio Downloads

Sometimes, Webcasting is a one-way affair. If you don't feel like creating your own show, you can do the next best thing: Customize somebody else's.

At sites like Spinner, SonicNet Radio, and Radio Moi, surfers can play DJ with a selection of online tracks. Think of it as the ultimate all-request radio show: You pick the songs, the genres, and the lineup for your own listening pleasure. If you want to hear one song over and over and over and over again, you can do that, too.

After you make your selections, just click a button, kick back, and enjoy. But they're only for you to listen to; they're not meant for broadcast.

Spinner

Spinner (www.spinner.com), as shown in Figure 14-6, is one of the oldest Net radio customization sites online . . . and it was just launched in 1996.

Figure 14-6:
Spinner
lets you
customize
your own
Net radio
listening
station.

Here's how the site works: Download the Spinner Plus Player (currently available only for Windows), and then simply select songs from more than 120 channels. You can find everything from the latest Madonna single to classic rock tracks from Yes. Mac users, and those who don't want to download the software, can use the Web-based player — Spinner Lite — that lets you listen online.

SonicNet Radio

SonicNet (www.radio.sonicnet.com), the mega-music site shown in Figure 14-7, has its own custom radio section appropriately named SonicNet Radio. Visiting here is kind of like going to a Dim Sum Chinese buffet.

After registering, you can select from specific musical genres, including modern rock (Fiona Apple, Beck) and Americana (Steve Earle, Lyle Lovett). Then, you click how often you want to hear these types of songs: never, sometimes, or a lot.

SonicNet soon plans to have guest DJs cueing up their favorite tracks, too.

Figure 14-7:
SonicNet's custom radio page.

Part V

The Part of Tens

"I hope you're doing something online. An indie band like yours shouldn't just be playing street corners."

In this part . . .

This part gives you the quick dirt on how to refine your search for music online. You also find out about which issues to watch and, most importantly, how to keep up on them.

Chapter 15

Ten Questions for Music Fans (and Musicians)

. . . .

In This Chapter

▶ Zeroing in on your musical tastes

▶ Assessing your musical needs

▶ Adjusting your expectations

. . . .

*T*he more you know about yourself as a music fan and as a musician, the better your online music experience can be.

This chapter contains questions that you can ask yourself as you wind your way through the musical corridors of the Internet.

What Kind of Music Do I Like to Listen To?

Okay, this may seem like an obvious — or unnecessary — question. But when you're venturing onto the wires, you can more easily plan your journey if you know what you're looking for ahead of time.

The fact is, rock and pop fans definitely have the easiest time. Right now, an undeniable bias on the Web exists toward rock music. Why's that? Well, rock fans were among the first settlers of the Net — particularly fans of the Grateful Dead, who started the San Francisco bulletin board service called The Well.

Hip-hop, electronica, and techno music fans can also find a wealth of resources on the Net. This makes sense, of course, because these particular forms of music rely heavily on computer production.

If you're a fan of jazz, blues, country, or world music, you can find some specialized sites, but don't expect as much as, say, pop and rock. All the more reason for you to get out there and start making your own sites!

How Often Do I Listen to Music?

For some reason, you may find that the amount of time you spend listening to music decreases as you get older. Maybe this is because you have less free time or you suffer from media saturation.

Because students make up the greatest part of the record-buying public, you shouldn't be surprised to find so many young people online. And the more often people listen to music offline, the more often they surf, read, and download music online.

If you don't listen to music that often in the car, living room, or shower, odds are you won't spend a lot of time surfing online.

Okay, you're busy. That's cool. My advice for you: Sign up for some mailing lists and personalized e-mail updates that give you hard and fast information about your favorite artists. For example, check out the following:

- ✔ **CDNOW** (www.cdnow.com): Get info about new releases from your favorite bands. For more on CDNOW, see Chapter 6.

- ✔ **The House of Blues** (www.houseofblues.com): Get e-mail reminders of when the bands you like are cybercasting online. For more on the House of Blues, have a look at Chapter 13.

If you spend a lot of time listening to music, you're probably all over the Net, downloading songs, buying records, reading news, keeping tuned in, right? Maybe the next step is to start giving something back, like so:

- ✔ Create your own Web page, as explained in Chapter 11.

- ✔ Host a Net radio show, as discussed in Chapter 14.

- ✔ Post your own band's MP3s online, as discussed in Chapter 11.

- ✔ Write reviews for music e-zines such as those described in the *Music Online Directory*.

Where Do I Like to Listen to Music?

Aha! Good question!

If you're like most people, you like to listen to music just about everywhere, right? At this stage in the evolution of music online, you're going to get most of your listening pleasure when your backside is planted smack in front of your PC. That usually means at work or at home.

The excellent thing is that office workers, for example, have never had more music at their fingertips:

- ✔ Radio shows
- ✔ Online concerts
- ✔ MP3s

That is, if your boss lets you tune in. Be very careful about listening to online tunes behind your boss's back at work. Some employers have been known to monitor their employees' Internet activities.

The better news is that with the advent of portable digital music players, as described in Chapter 9, you can take your show on the road, like so:

- ✔ **Driving:** Buy an MP3 car radio player.
- ✔ **Jogging:** Use a portable MP3 player.
- ✔ **Flying:** Portable MP3 player, again, to the rescue.

How Patient Am I?

As Tom Petty once sang, "The waiting is the hardest part." For years, that was the adage for listening to music online. When Aerosmith first released a song online in the mid-1990s, the song took an hour to download.

These days, downloading is hardly such an ordeal. An MP3, if you use an average speed (56K) modem, takes about twice as long to download as the length of the song itself.

Streaming audio, though, plays within seconds of clicking the right button.

Still, while the speed of audio downloads is improving, you may undoubtedly find your patience tested in a much more human way — when you're searching for the tunes. The complaint I hear most from friends who go online is that they get frustrated when hunting for the music they want.

The bottom line is this: You need patience. Even if you read this entire book ten times, you'll still find new challenges, bugs, and blips along the way. Take a lesson from the Eastern philosophers: Think of your search for music as not just a destination, but a journey. You'll be happier along the way.

Do I Like to Discover New Artists?

If the Net affords anything, it's the opportunity to make discoveries:

- New Web sites
- New people
- New music

If you're not a music adventurer now, maybe you should reconsider. Most people, of course, have their particular musical tastes. Some like rock. Some like pop. Some like hip-hop.

Ultimately, though, genres are categories and categories are pretty limiting. Is Beck alternative or rock or pop or hip-hop? Probably all of the above.

If you're big into new music and new artists, then the Net's the perfect place for you. On sites like MP3.com and the Internet Underground Music Archive, you can find all kinds of new bands waiting to be discovered.

If you're not that psyched about exploring the unfamiliar domain of songs and sounds, you can try another alternative. Most music commerce sites, from CDNOW to Amazon.com, have recommendation services. Punch in the name of an artist, and you find a bunch of other artists who have either been recommended by the sites or, often more reliably, by other fans.

Is Analog Dead?

Not yet.

Though digital music is taking off, people are still going to be listening to tapes and even albums for many years to come.

But this may change when broadband — the big fat flow of online data — makes the online music experience even more dynamic than the offline listening experience.

Within the next ten years, you're going to see a dramatic boom in the amount of music that's available online. And you'll find more devices that allow you to play Net music anywhere you go.

Have I Ever Wanted to Be a Musician?

So maybe you play the guitar. Or the spoons. Or perhaps you're a really mean hand clapper. Everyone has some music inside in one form or another.

Even if you never considered yourself a musician, you can try thinking like one when you're surfing online. After all, surfing is an inherently creative act. You're out there, choosing your songs, selecting your information, putting it all together. With MP3, you're the ultimate producer, selecting what songs you want and discarding the rest. Online, you're the one calling the shots.

But beyond this, ask yourself another question: If you feel that you have the natural ability to be a musician, would you go for it? If so, the next few questions are for you.

Can I Make MP3 Music Even If I'm Not Musical?

Most definitely. See all those CDs on your shelf? Those albums? Those tapes? They're all waiting to be preserved in pristine digital form.

Okay, you say, that isn't right. You want to know if you can *really* make music, like from scratch, with no ability at all? I'd still say, yes. MP3 DJ software — see Chapter 14 — lets you take existing songs and mix them from scratch.

Just be careful not to infringe on any copyrights. See Chapter 5 for more info on copyright legalities.

If I'm a Musician, What Are My Goals Online?

Say you're definitely into using the Net to expand your musical reach and power. You're in a band, you're solo, or you're just getting started.

Here are some things you can do:

- ✔ Release your songs online on MP3.
- ✔ Create your own Web site.
- ✔ Create a Net radio show.
- ✔ Release your songs online in streaming audio or video.
- ✔ Set up an e-mail newsletter for fans.
- ✔ Set up a message board forum for fans.
- ✔ Post a band bio.
- ✔ Post band photos.

These are just a few ways to get started. For more ideas, see the *Music Online Directory*, where I list some sites by famous artists.

Do I Need to Deal with the Music Business to Make Music Online?

You may have to deal with the business aspects of making music (for example, marketing, promoting, or selling your music), but you don't have to deal with the traditional corporate powerhouses of the music industry.

This is a main reason why artists go online in the first place. The online universe is completely do-it-yourself, for better or worse.

- ✔ You're your own manager.
- ✔ You're your own publicist.
- ✔ You're your own techie.

Everything you do is by and for yourself. Of course, a downside exists. Without a record label's marketing power, you may have to work extra hard to get noticed. But plenty of artists, from Chuck D to Ani DeFranco, have paved the way for other indie-minded musicians to follow.

Reaching out to fans directly and having them reach right back has never been easier.

Chapter 16

Ten Music Online Issues to Watch

● ●

In This Chapter

▶ Watching the future of music online

▶ Keeping tabs on the future of the Web: shopping, news, and information

▶ Making sense of it all

● ●

*F*or the jockeys of digital culture, the future can't happen quickly enough. Not so long ago, sci-fi authors did most of the daydreaming. But now with billions of dollars at stake, just *imagining* the future isn't enough. You have to *invent* it. Or someone else will.

With this kind of pressure, you can understand why a niche industry has bloomed around technology research. While players like Microsoft and America Online duke it out on the field, research firms, such as Jupiter Communications, Forrester Research, and Cyber Dialogue, call the game.

The role of these companies is to provide the necessary objective elements — analyses, projections, statistics — that put the competition in context. If Bill Gates is the quarterback, these companies are the head coaches.

Coaches for hire, that is. After all, everyone in the business wants to diagnose the elusive biorhythms of consumer behavior. As a result, these research firms earn tens of millions of dollars annually by selling reports to companies like Disney and Federal Express.

Now, you get a taste of some informed soothsaying. Here are ten trends that may affect music online over the next decade or so.

Place your bets.

Copyright Wars

One of the biggest issues affecting the future of music online — and, specifically, MP3 — is copyright infringement. Nothing has epitomized this controversy like the circumstances around the program called Napster.

For the most part, MP3ers have to spelunk alone through the dark, occasionally underground, havens of online music. Frankly, if you weren't an intrepid explorer by nature, you probably wouldn't have the patience to hunt down a song you like, wait for the download, and pray that the connection works.

In 1999, Napster came along to change all that. Available for free download (from `www.napster.com`, as shown in Figure 16-1), Napster takes digital audio to a rather revolutionary next step: user-friendliness. Napster enables you to search for specific artists and songs on the hard drives of other Napster users and then download those songs from their hard drives to your computer. This also means that other Napster users can search your hard drive for songs and then download them from your computer. You can also chat in real-time with other Napster users.

Sounds kosher, huh? Well, it is . . . if you use Napster to distribute your own music (that is, music that *you* hold the copyright to). The controversy that surrounds Napster stems from the fact that many (if not most) users are unlawfully distributing music copyrighted by the artists and record labels. For example, heavy metal rockers Metallica and rap star Dr. Dre were the first groups to file suit against Napster because the program allows users to distribute illegal copies of their songs. In fact, Metallica, one of the most bootlegged bands short of the Grateful Dead, has every one of its songs available via Napster, plus all sorts of unsanctioned live performances. Theoretically, you could download MP3 versions of every Metallica song ever recorded without shelling out a single penny for a CD. You can understand why the group and their label are up in arms.

That's not to say that Napster isn't gaining support from some music groups. The alternative-pop band Limp Bizkit believes that Napster is good for business, creating more exposure for their music.

Whatever you think about Napster, you can't deny that it's changed the face of digital music. However, at this writing, the court cases are still pending, and a recent injunction against MP3.com (specifically, its service that enables you to download MP3 versions of CDs that you already own) could mean bad news for Napster (and MP3) proponents.

Napster and the MP3 format have raised a number of questions for the recording industry, such as the following:

- ✔ How can artists be protected from illegal distribution of their music online?

- ✔ How can artists who want to distribute their music online also be compensated?

- ✔ How will copyright protection evolve in the digital age?

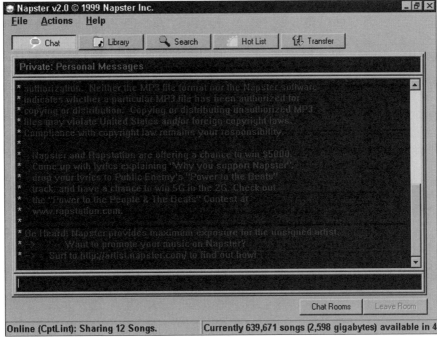

Figure 16-1:
Napster, the
controver-
sial little
program
that could.

These issues are important to you for several reasons. Mainly, they'll dictate how freely you can search for, find, and trade digital music online. They'll also have a large impact on how major recording artists decide to deal with the sticky issues that come with releasing their music over the Net.

If more artists like Metallica position themselves against freewheeling MP3 co-op sites, trading *all* kinds of music — including independent releases — on your own will become even more difficult.

For more information on how to keep abreast of stories like Napster's, see Chapter 17.

The RIAA's Battles

The Recording Industry Association of America (RIAA) is the main organization representing major recording artists and labels. Nothing has shaken this group more at the roots than music online.

Napster is just the latest company to make the RIAA's most wanted list. Here's a look at some other notable cases in the brief, tempestuous life of MP3:

✔ **June 1997:** RIAA sues three Web sites in Texas, California, and New York for hosting illegal MP3s; the court rules that the illegal MP3s must be removed from the sites.

✔ **May 1998:** RIAA sues both a Web site and the ISP that hosted it in Washington state for offering MP3s of popular artists, including Mariah Carey, Elton John, and Kenny G. The site comes down within three days of the lawsuit.

✔ **October 1998:** RIAA seeks an injunction against Diamond Multimedia Systems' release of the portable MP3 player, Rio PMP300, claiming the device could destroy a legal marketplace for digital audio. RIAA loses when an appeals court judge determines that Rio is not a recording device for digital audio.

✔ **April 2000:** RIAA wins suit against MP3.com on the grounds that MP3.com violated copyright laws by providing a service that allowed users to download MP3 versions of songs from copyright-protected CDs, if the user already owned the CD. The court ruled that the MP3s were illegal copies of the songs.

While the lawsuits continue, the RIAA is pursuing its own copyright protection mission called The Secure Digital Music Initiative (`www.sdmi.org`, as shown in Figure 16-2). This initiative ensures that digital music can be downloaded only if the artist has given permission.

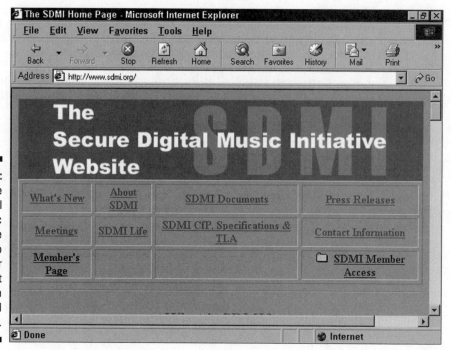

Figure 16-2:
The Secure Digital Music Initiative hopes to offer copyright protection to digital musicians.

Stay tuned.

MP4 and the World of Upgrades

MP3, despite its recent popularity, is hardly new.

MP3 is part of an evolution that began over a decade ago, when the first bits of music began appearing online.

Since that time, various digital music formats have appeared:

- ✔ Liquid Audio
- ✔ A2B
- ✔ RealAudio
- ✔ Windows Media

And more are sure to come. For digital music fans, this means — for the time being — making sure you have all the appropriate software and hardware that enables you to get the most out of all these formats.

Ironically, it's not so much the music formats that you need to watch as it is the music-playing software. As the software evolves, new versions come equipped with more and more sophisticated tools for playing the various forms of music online. Many, like MusicMatch or Winamp, can now handle several kinds of formats. Eventually, you may need only one type of player to handle everything.

In the meantime, make sure to keep abreast of updates as they occur. One of the best ways to do this is to join the newsletters or mailing lists that are being run by sites like Real.com and MusicMatch. For other ways to help stay clued about updates, see Chapter 17.

Digital Music Distribution

Few high-tech trends have captured as much ink and imagination as digital music. Over the next decade, another major issue will be digital distribution.

Over the next decade, music will be digitally distributed everywhere from airport kiosks to coffee shops. Already, some stores are experimenting with services that are something like music ATMs. You go up to the machine, punch a few buttons, select your songs, and — voilà! — the songs are instantly burned to your own custom disc. If these machines take off, you may see the shelves of CD stores thin out; instead, you'll create your CD according to your own preferences — in your own sequence, your own package, your own everything.

You may see subscription services where you can download a new monthly package of tunes for a set price. Of course, you may wonder what songs will be available? What artists? How will upcoming bands get on these services as well? The answers will affect their future . . . and yours.

Music Online Communities

Few digerati buzzwords have been as overwrought and abused as *community*.

Any site with a message board or a chat area seems to constitute a social gathering, whether or not the people involved have created a substantive bond. Nevertheless, the allure of a dedicated and impassioned set of netizens is a sure way to get marketers chomping at the bit.

According to recent reports, the communities of Yahoo!, AOL, and GeoCities attract up to 60 million unique visitors per month. You see the reason for the excitement.

Over the next decade, however, these burg-like haunts may face some heated competition. Expect niche sites to move in steadily on their territory. These niche sites, dedicated to everything from hip-hop to pro golf, have better success at generating the all-important ad revenue by offering a lucrative blend of e-commerce and community.

For music fans, this will affect how easily you can find the music you're looking for. As communities become increasingly niche-like, and as you garner tools that enable you to spawn your own hangouts (such as those offered by Yahoo! Clubs), you may find it even easier and more efficient to reach out to other fans.

The best way to stay on top of this issue? Stake out your own home on the Net in the form of a club or home page. Doing so keeps you positioned right at the front lines.

The Tube's Convergence with the Net

After years of speculation, interactive television seems on the verge of reality. Why? Advertisers are finally coming onboard. A recent report estimates that interactive TV will generate $20 billion in revenues by 2004.

The big question is this: What will interactive TV (or iTV) look like?

Most analysts agree that, by the end of the decade, the Net and the Tube will fit snuggly together into one new digital appliance. Already, you've seen examples of this with devices like WebTV (see Figure 16-3). But the broader changes will come gradually:

- ✔ Net-enhanced broadcasts, which combine interactive trivia and game show style content with regular shows, should hit about 24 million homes by 2004.

- ✔ Around this time, users in about 13 million homes will surf the Net on TV.

- ✔ Right now, only about 2 million homes have high-speed, T1 Internet access at home, but that number is expected to jump to 16 million within five years. And with cable and satellite companies getting into the action, mass deployment of high-speed access will have many permutations.

For music fans, all this means better ways to see online concerts, better power to access archives of music videos, better means to call up on-demand content from a variety of entertainment providers. And with next-generation HDTV sets, juiced with pure digital power, the images will be all the more pristine.

Figure 16-3: WebTV hopes to merge the Tube and the Net.

You may also see more expansive convergence between stations like MTV and the Net — you'll be able to interact with artists on TV, request songs live, even do spontaneous karaoke as the song plays on the Tube.

Shopping Online

How will your shopping experience for music online evolve?

- ✔ According to Jupiter Communications, consumers spent $705 million online in 1996.
- ✔ In 1999, that number rose to $12 billion. By 2002, it will hit $41 billion.

Though analysts expect the surge to level off in the middle of the next decade, e-commerce is definitely here to stay. But despite the growth, a number of untapped services still exist. You can easily buy CDs online, but what about a complete, deluxe home entertainment system?

These days, more and more offline retailers, like Tower Records and HMV, will be migrating to the Web, making it easier to purchase more than just books and CDs. While only a few electronics stores, such as Circuit City and the Wiz, currently operate online, more high-end stereo stores are sure to take their business to the Net.

In addition, expect to see a much more sophisticated array of personalization services. Instead of just being able to custom order a computer, surfers will be readily able to customize, say, a car stereo system or a home music studio.

Privacy

The good news about e-commerce is that services are likely to get more personalized. That's also the bad news.

In order to customize the kind of made-to-order experience that is already available online (such as Amazon.com's music recommendation service), surfers have to willfully and trustingly submit personal data about themselves, their interests, and their buying habits.

Despite efforts by the Federal Trade Commission, the Better Business Bureau, and special online organizations like TrustE, shoppers are not apprised. Most people still don't know the issues pertaining to the personal info they're giving away. For example:

✔ How Web sites can use personal information for direct marketing

✔ How "free" services often require — in fine print — that you allow your Web surfing to be tracked for marketing purposes

✔ How credit card information can wind up in the hands of thieves

My advice: Don't take anything for granted while surfing for music online. The good and bad thing about the world of music online is that it's always filled with new, pioneering services — from e-commerce sites to communities. Often, they'll be online before anyone's really had a chance to test them out. Don't be paranoid, but do proceed with the same caution and skepticism you exercise in your daily life.

If a deal sounds too good to be true, it probably is. Take the time to read the fine print and make sure you're not sacrificing your privacy with the click of a mouse.

Personalization of News and Information

If you're a true music fan, you're always scanning newspapers and magazines for the latest releases, news, and gossip. These days, you probably read newspapers and magazines online. Nevertheless, the publications' offline counterparts have yet to become concerned about the potential cannibalization of their readers. The reason?

In a nutshell: Buses and bathrooms. There's still nothing as portable as the morning paper.

What will change, some say, is the growth of editorial aggregators, from personalization services like My Yahoo! to special-interest sites like MediaNews (www.poynter.org/medianews), a site for publishing cronies (see Figure 16-4).

Rather than surfing around to separate news and info sites, consumers are getting accustomed to going to one-click pit stops. Although none of the analysts expect the sites to be able to charge for their services, people might pay for music information and news.

The revenues will likely come from enhanced commercial services, like financial investing information from *The Wall Street Journal*. Credibility issues, inevitably, will get stickier as a result.

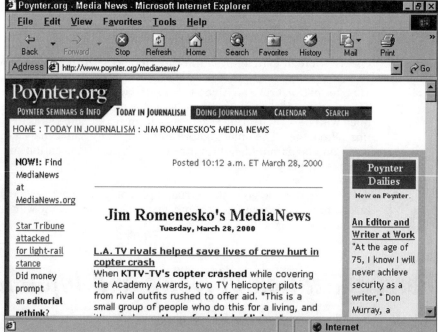

Figure 16-4:
MediaNews
gets aggre-
gated on
media
gossip.

The Web Itself

And for the $64,000 question: What about the future of the Web? After all,
without the Web, music online isn't very viable at all.

Jupiter Communications estimates that, within three years, the number of
people online will nearly double from 34 million to 62 million.

And as broadband access and Net-ready devices increase, the Net will be
pretty much impossible to escape according to the Institute for the Future.
Everything from the fridge to the phone will be hooked up online.

The future of the Net will be brighter and easier, indeed. But, of course, all
this saved time creates an entirely new challenge: What to do with it? For
you, the music fan, the growth of the Web — its speed, its population, its
ubiquity — will directly affect the growth of music online.

In other words, you're rooting for the Web. You want it to grow. You want more people out there, more bands, more labels, more stores. Never before has a music fan had so much incredible power at his or her fingertips. Imagine what it would have been like to download "Stairway to Heaven" in the 1970s? Or, in the 1980s, watch Live Aid online from anywhere in the world?

And at the heart of this new movement are the fans. Without them, there would be no music online.

Chapter 17

Ten Ways to Stay on the Cutting Edge

Knowledge, especially with music online, is power. To get it, you have to stay on top of the latest and ever-changing happenings. This chapter tells you how to stay tuned.

New Release Updates

If you want to stay on the edge, you probably want to know when new music by your favorite artists is hitting the shelves . . . or the Web sites.

You can easily stay on top of the upcoming action; bands, labels, and fans eagerly post new album information online. Here are a few sites to check out:

- ✓ **Billboard New Releases** (`www.billboard.com/releases/`): Thousands of new releases detailed by *Billboard* magazine and organized by music genre (see Figure 17-1). Also includes a search engine so that you can find information by artist or label name.

- ✓ **New Releases Video** (`www.newreleasesvideo.com`): New site dedicated to video releases.

- ✓ **Preview Tunes** (`www.previewtunes.com`): Devoted exclusively to new releases. Preview audio and video snippets of upcoming albums, songs, and videos.

- ✓ **Wall of Sound** (`http://wallofsound.go.com/releasedates/index.html`): Detailed information about upcoming releases.

Figure 17-1:
New
releases are
detailed on
Billboard's
site.

Music Charts

Music fans have become fairly obsessed with pop music charts — the top listings of bestselling albums, singles, videos, and concert ticket sales across the country.

Tuning into these charts gives you a quick snapshot of where the music world is heading — from electronica to dance, from grunge to boy bands. Check out these chart sites:

✔ **Billboard Charts** (www.billboard.com/charts/): The music industry's source publication charts albums, singles, and radio shows.

✔ **CMJ Charts** (www.cmjmusic.com/CMJCharts/): This site charts the top 200 albums, and it breaks down the albums according to genre, including hip-hop, loud rock, and jazz.

✔ **Gavin Charts** (www.gavin.com/Charts/index.html): This standard for the radio industry lists Top-40, urban, rap, country, and smooth jazz (see Figure 17-2).

Figure 17-2:
Gavin charts
the Top-40.

✔ **International Charts** (http://dir.yahoo.com/Entertainment/
Music/Charts/Countries/): This site includes lists of the top-selling
music in many countries around the world.

✔ **New Music Express Charts** (www.nme.com/charts/): NME is a highly
respected music magazine from England that covers more cutting edge
music.

Online News Magazines

With the advent of the Net, news has never been more accessible. You no
longer have to wait for the evening TV broadcast, the next day's newspaper,
or next month's magazine.

Everything's online just after it happens.

To stay on top of the best new music, the best new artists, concerts, songs, and other happenings, just plug into these sites:

- ✔ **CMJ (College Music Journal) Online News** (`www.cmj.com`): Cutting edge music and business news.

- ✔ **Country Cool News** (`www.countrycool.com/news/index.html`): Info and updates for country music fans.

- ✔ **Webnoize** (`www.webnoize.com`): Web-only news service dedicated to music business insider news (see Figure 17-3).

- ✔ **Wired News** (`www.wired.com`): Daily online news service from *Wired* magazine. Check out its MP3 Rocks the Web section for frequent updates on the MP3 movement and wars.

- ✔ **ZDNet Music News** (`http://music.zdnet.com`): Music news service from Ziff-Davis, publisher of numerous computer magazines.

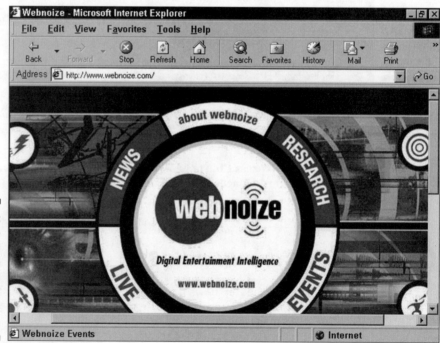

Figure 17-3: Webnoize gives you the inside scoop on the digital music business.

E-zines

For a little more perspective, analysis, and opinion, check out the sharp-witted, and sometimes sharp-fanged, e-zines. These sites cover music and popular culture and everything in between:

- ✔ **Feed** (`www.feedmag.com`): Feed is an NYC-based e-zine dedicated to digital and popular culture (see Figure 17-4).

- ✔ **Salon** (`www.salon.com`): A bit like the *New Yorker* of the Web, Salon has been active in following the online music revolution with essays on everything from Napster to MP3.

- ✔ **SonicNet** (`www.sonicnet.com`): This e-zine covers alternative music and community, offering chat, cybercasts, and radio.

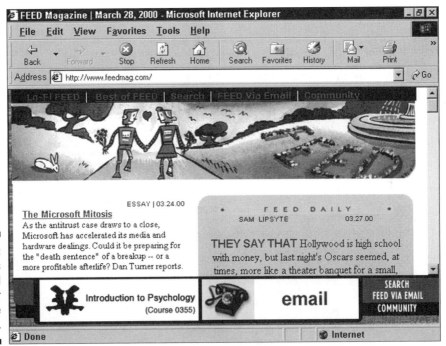

Figure 17-4:
Feed covers digital and popular culture trends.

Consumer Music Magazines

Offline music magazines are all over the digital evolution, and many magazines also publish their content online. Some of these include the following:

- ✔ **Alternative Press** (www.alternativepress.com): This edgy magazine covers alternative, hip-hop, and electronica (see Figure 17-5).

- ✔ **Billboard** (www.billboard.com): *Billboard* is the main magazine for the music business.

- ✔ **Circus** (www.circusmagazine.com): Formerly ruling the heavy metal era, *Circus* is still published — off and online.

- ✔ **Musician** (www.musicianmag.com): This magazine is geared toward working and amateur musicians.

- ✔ **Q** (www.qonline.co.uk): *Q* covers pop music culture from England.

- ✔ **Relix** (www.relix.com): *Relix* covers acid rock from San Francisco.

- ✔ **Rolling Stone** (www.rollingstone.com): *Rolling Stone* magazine's site has a limited number of articles from the magazine.

- ✔ **Spin** (www.spin.com): Like its competitor, *Rolling Stone*, *Spin* offers a few excerpts from its print version.

- ✔ **Vibe** (www.vibe.com): *Vibe* covers urban and hip-hop music and culture.

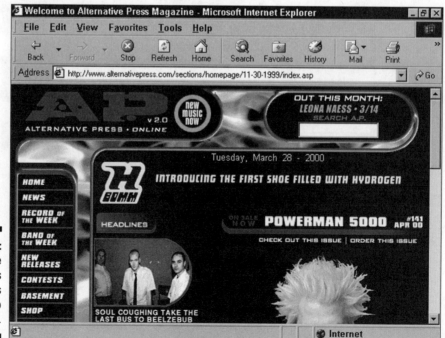

Figure 17-5:
Alternative
Press brings
music news
and info
online.

Insider Chats and Forums

Of course, one of the best sources for news and information is other fans and industry insiders. Drop by these hangouts to find out the latest buzz from people in the know:

- ✔ **Get Signed (**`www.getsigned.com`**):** A site where you can get direct tips from music industry pros. Label execs, managers, and promoters drop by to answer questions from aspiring music stars.

- ✔ **The Velvet Rope (**`www.velvetrope.com`**):** This site started out as a music insider's list on America Online and recently moved to the Web. Here, you can find the skinny straight from people who work in the business (see Figure 17-6).

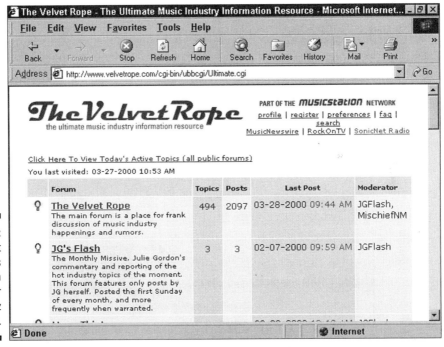

Figure 17-6:
The Velvet
Rope is
filled with
insider
music biz
gossip.

Digital Music Reports

Many online news services have created hubs in which fans, artists, and music business insiders can stay tuned into the constantly changing world of digital music. Check out these sites:

- **MP3 Newswire** (www.mp3newswire.net): Regular feed covering MP3 developments (see Figure 17-7).

- **The New York Times — Online Music** (www.nytimes.com/library/ tech/reference/index-music.html): Collected reports from "the paper of record" about online music.

- **Time — MP3 Central** (www.time.com/time/digital/reports/mp3/index.html): *Time* magazine's ongoing coverage of MP3.

- **Yahoo! Full Coverage — Digital Copyright Law (http://headlines. yahoo.com/Full_Coverage/Tech/Digital_Copyright_Law/):** Yahoo!'s comprehensive coverage of copyright issues related to digital music and otherwise.

- **Yahoo! Full Coverage — MP3 and Digital Music** (http://fullcoverage .yahoo.com/Full_Coverage/Tech/Online_Music/): Daily news and information about digital music online.

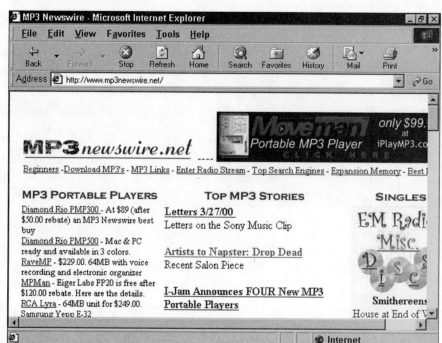

Figure 17-7:
MP3
Newswire.

Mailing Lists and Usenet

Music biz experts like to take discussions into their own hands. One of the easiest, most direct ways to do so is to launch a mailing list or Usenet discussion. Check out these resources:

- ✔ Alt.music.independent: Usenet forum for indie-minded artists and producers.
- ✔ **Head Space** (www.head-space.com/iworld/supersonic/lists.html): Resource for mailing lists related to the British music biz.
- ✔ **Musinc** (www.ilist.net/musinc/): Mailing list for music industry insiders (see Figure 17-8).
- ✔ Rec.music.makers: Usenet forum for musicians and performers.
- ✔ Rec.music.marketplace: Usenet discussion for people looking to make it in the music business.
- ✔ Rec.music.promotional: Usenet group devoted to promotional information for bands and artists.

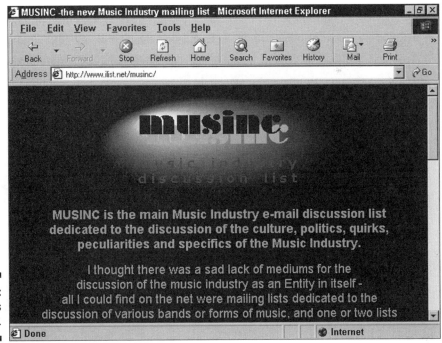

Figure 17-8: Musinc's mailing list.

Music Channels

Video didn't kill the radio stars completely; it just helped them sell a lot more records. Now MTV, VH1, BET (Black Entertainment Television), TNN (The Nashville Network), and other channels offer views on the evolving, ever-unpredictable music industry.

MTV and VH1

Watching these sister networks for 30 minutes a day will probably keep you fairly plugged into the zeitgeist. Here are different online resources from the big guns that you may want to follow:

- **MTV Headline News (**www.mtv.com/nav/intro_news.html**):** Daily updates about music industry and pop culture news and events, as shown in Figure 17-9.

- **MTV News 1515 (**www.mtv.com/sendme.tin?page=/mtv/news/1515/**):** Music news week-in-review, broadcasted every weekend on MTV.

- **The Wire (**www.vh1.com/thewire**):** News and information from VH1 online.

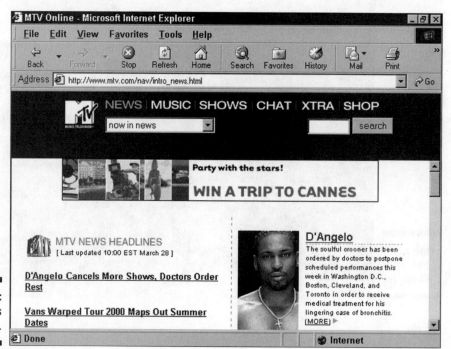

Figure 17-9:
MTV's news
headlines.

Much Music

Got that burning yen to know what's hot in Canada? If you're hoping to catch the next Alanis (or, better yet, Triumph!) video, boot up the Web site for Much Music (`www.muchmusic.com`), the Great White North's national music video network.

In addition to the playlists you find on MTV, this site spotlights up-and-coming Canadian artists, such as Chantal Kreviazuk. Unfortunately, a lot of the stuff you really want to view, such as obscure tracks by Nine Inch Nails, are available only in brief snippets.

Black Entertainment Television

BET (`www.bet.com`) covers lifestyle issues as well as all things related to music: urban, hip-hop, and rap. This is the place to hear about Da Brat's latest look or the Artist's latest D-I-Y distribution plans.

Online, you can also stay on top of all the new releases, checking out on-demand music videos or previewing audio tracks by new and unsigned artists. BET also brings you daily headlines from around the black entertainment industries, as well as special features created specifically for the Web.

The Nashville Network

Straight from Nashville, TNN (`www.thenashvillenetwork`) brings you daily coverage of all things country: big stars, big shows, big hair, and big hats.

Online, you can read the latest news of, say, how Alan Jackson made a guest appearance with George Strait during the Nashville leg of Strait's tour. Or you can get the latest expert picks for events such as the American Country Music awards — my money's on Garth. For up-to-the-minute news, the site has links to Country.com, the sprawling country music online resource.

Music and Internet Conventions

If you have the time, motivation, and social graces, you can attend any of these music and Internet conventions that deal with the digital frontier:

- ✔ **CMJ Marathon** (`http://206.215.141.2/Marathon/`): Annual convention in New York City sponsored by the College Music Journal.

- ✔ **Comdex** (`www.zdevents.com/comdex/`): International electronics shows held all over the world.

✔ **Consumer Electronics Show** (`www.cesweb.org`): Gadget and gizmo mania every January in Las Vegas.

✔ **South by Southwest** (`www.sxsw.com`): Massive music biz gathering in Austin, Texas (see Figure 17-10).

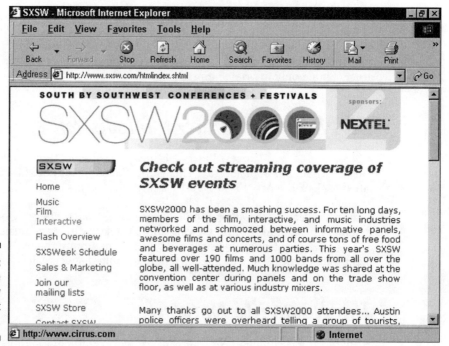

Figure 17-10:
The
South by
Southwest
home page.

Appendix

About the CD

*H*ere's some of the stuff available on the *Music Online For Dummies* CD-ROM:

- ✔ RealPlayer Basic, shareware version, for listening and watching Real media
- ✔ Internet Explorer, commercial version, for browsing the Web
- ✔ Netscape Communicator, commercial version, for browsing the Web
- ✔ WinZip, evaluation version, for unzipping files ending in the letters *ZIP*
- ✔ Windows MP3 players, for playing MP3 songs
- ✔ Macintosh MP3 players, for playing MP3 songs
- ✔ Windows Media Player, freeware version, for playing Windows Media files

System Requirements

Make sure that your computer meets the minimum system requirements listed below. If your computer doesn't match up to most of these requirements, you may have problems using the contents of the CD.

- ✔ A PC with a 486 or faster processor, or a Mac OS computer with a Power PC processor.
- ✔ At least 200MB of hard drive space available to install all the software from this CD. (You need less space if you don't install every program.)
- ✔ Microsoft Windows 95 or later, or Mac OS system software 7.5.5 or later.
- ✔ At least 16MB of total RAM installed on your computer. For best performance, we recommend at least 32MB of RAM installed.
- ✔ A CD-ROM drive — double-speed (2x) or faster.
- ✔ A sound card for PCs. (Mac OS computers have built-in sound support.)
- ✔ A monitor capable of displaying at least 256 colors or grayscale.
- ✔ A modem with a speed of at least 14,400 bps.

If you need more information on the basics, check out *PCs For Dummies,* 7th Edition, by Dan Gookin; *Macs For Dummies,* 6th Edition, by David Pogue; *Windows 98 For Dummies* and *Windows 95 For Dummies,* 2nd Edition, both by Andy Rathbone. (All published by IDG Books Worldwide, Inc.)

Using the CD with Microsoft Windows

To install the items from the CD to your hard drive, follow these steps:

1. **Insert the CD into your computer's CD-ROM drive.**

2. **Open your browser.**

   If you do not have a browser, you can find Microsoft Internet Explorer and Netscape Communicator in the Programs folders at the root of the CD.

3. **Choose Start⇨Run.**

4. **In the dialog box that appears, type D:\START.HTM**

   Replace D with the proper drive letter if your CD-ROM drive uses a different letter. (If you don't know the letter, see how your CD-ROM drive is listed under My Computer.)

5. **Read through the license agreement, nod your head, and then click the Accept button if you want to use the CD.**

   After you click Accept, you jump to the Main Menu, which walks you through the content of the CD.

6. **To navigate within the interface, simply click any topic of interest to take you to an explanation of the files on the CD and how to use or install them.**

7. **To install the software from the CD, simply click the software name.**

   You see two options — the option to run or open the file from the current location or the option to save the file to your hard drive. Choose to run or open the file from its current location and the installation procedure continues. After you finish with the interface, simply close your browser as usual.

Using the CD with the Mac OS

To install the items from the CD to your hard drive, follow these steps:

1. **Insert the CD into your computer's CD-ROM drive.**

   In a moment, an icon representing the CD you just inserted appears on your Mac desktop. Chances are, the icon looks like a CD-ROM.

2. **Double-click the CD icon to show the CD's contents.**

3. **Double-click the License Agreement icon.**

   This is the license that you are agreeing to by using the CD. You can close this window once you've looked over the agreement.

4. **Double-click the Read Me First icon.**

   The Read Me First text file contains information about the CD's programs and any last-minute instructions you may need in order to correctly install them.

5. **To install most programs, open the program folder and double-click the icon called "Install" or "Installer."**

   Sometimes the installers are actually self extracting archives, which just means that the program files have been bundled up into an archive, and this self extractor unbundles the files and places them on your hard drive. This kind of program is often called an .sea. Double-click anything with .sea in the title, and it will run just like an installer.

6. **Some programs don't come with installers. For those, just drag the program's folder from the CD window and drop it on your hard drive icon.**

After you have installed the programs you want, you can eject the CD. Carefully place it back in the plastic jacket of the book for safekeeping.

What You'll Find

Here's a summary of the software on this CD arranged by category. If you use Windows, the CD interface helps you install software easily. (If you have no idea what I'm talking about when I say "CD interface," flip back a page or two to find the section, "Using the CD with Microsoft Windows.")

If you use a Mac OS computer, you can take advantage of the easy Mac interface to quickly install the programs.

Shareware programs are fully functional, free trial versions of copyrighted programs. If you like particular programs, register the software with its authors for a nominal fee and receive licenses, enhanced versions, and technical support. *Freeware programs* are free, copyrighted games, applications, and utilities. You can freely copy them to as many PCs as you want but they have no technical support. GNU software is governed by its own license, which is included inside the folder of the GNU software. No restrictions exist on the distribution of this software. See the GNU license for more details. Trial, demo, or evaluation versions are usually limited either by time or functionality (such as being unable to save projects).

Web browsers

Microsoft Internet Explorer

For Windows and Mac. Commercial Version.

Microsoft Internet Explorer enables you to browse the World Wide Web. You can find updates and more information about Internet Explorer on the Microsoft Support Site at `www.microsoft.com/ie`.

Netscape Communicator

For Windows and Mac. Commercial Version.

Like Internet Explorer, Netscape Communicator lets you browse the Web. Deciding which browser to use is a matter of your own taste. Check them both out and see what you like. For updates and information about Communicator, see Netscape's support site at `www.netscape.com/browsers/index.html`.

An Internet service provider for Windows and Mac OS

MindSpring Internet Access
Commercial Version.

If you already have access to the Internet, then don't install this software. But in case you don't have an Internet connection, the CD-ROM includes sign-on software for MindSpring, an Internet service provider (ISP). An ISP lets you connect to the Net for a fee on a monthly basis.

Also, when you install MindSpring on the Mac, the installation program asks you for a key code. Enter **DUMY8579** into the dialog box. Be sure to use all capital letters, just as it's shown here.

If you already have an Internet service provider, installing MindSpring may replace your current settings. You may no longer be able to access the Internet through your original provider. You also need a credit card to join. For more information and updates, see the MindSpring Web site at www. mindspring.com.

WinZip — for compressing and decompressing zip files

WinZip, from Nico Mak Computing, is an evaluation version of a utility that lets you compress and decompress Windows files. To save time, people like to compress files before they send them across the Net.

WinZip does the compressing and decompressing with pretty much just one click. If you see a file ending in the letters with the extension .zip, then you need this program to open it. For more information, see www.winzip.com.

Digital music players and tools

This CD-ROM includes the following digital music players for Windows and Macintosh computers.

Real Player Basic

For Windows and Mac. Plug-in.

RealPlayer from RealNetworks enables you to play audio and video files in the RealMedia format. Unlike MP3 files, RealMedia files play instantaneously, or *stream*, directly to your desktop. You don't save these files; you just point, click, and listen (or watch).

Numerous Web sites use RealMedia files for everything from songs to interviews and concert broadcasts. RealPlayer also plays most other media formats.

For more information and updates, see the RealNetworks site at www.real.com.

Windows Media Player

For Windows. Freeware Version.

The Microsoft Windows Media Player is an alternative to RealPlayer. Like RealPlayer, Windows Media Player plays streaming media files, both in the Windows Media format and the RealMedia format.

These days, sites tend to offer both Windows Media and RealMedia versions of streaming media files. So you may want to install both programs so that you're equipped to handle whatever files you may come across on your journeys.

For more information, see www.windowsmediaplayer.com.

SoundJam MP

For Mac. Shareware Version.

SoundJam MP from Casady and Greene is an all-in-one MP3 player for Macintosh systems. SoundJam lets you create, play, and record MP3s. For example, pop a CD into your CD-ROM, select a few songs, and SoundJam automatically compresses them into MP3 format. You can also use the program to organize your MP3 songs.

This copy is a seven-day trial; for more information on how to update to the full version, see www.soundjam.com.

Liquid Audio Player

For Windows and Mac. Shareware Version.

Liquid Audio is an alternative digital music format, similar to MP3. To play Liquid Audio songs, you need to download the Liquid Audio Player. Popular artists, including the Smashing Pumpkins, have released songs specifically in Liquid Audio format. Like other digital music players, Liquid Audio Player lets you customize your playlist; it also plays other formats, including MP3s, as well.

For more information and updates, see www.liquidaudio.com.

Xaudio Player

For Windows and Mac. Shareware Version.

If you think that Mac users have a tough time finding software, how about Linux and UNIX fans? Xaudio, from MpegTV/Xaudio, is music to the ears of MP3 fans who use the Linux and UNIX operating systems. The player gives you all the essential track controls, and it's available for a host of other operating systems.

For more information and updates, see www.xaudio.com.

MP3 songs

To get you started with listening to digital music, this CD-ROM includes the following MP3 songs that you can play in your MP3 player:

- ✔ "Lonely Satellite" by The Common
- ✔ "Looks like Rain" by Josh Schachterle
- ✔ "Believe" by Josh Schachterle
- ✔ "Tonight's Inspiration" by Harbor Lights
- ✔ "Never Looking Back" by Harbor Lights
- ✔ "Forever" by Harbor Lights
- ✔ "Squeeze" by Joe Kiempisty
- ✔ "Eyeball Eclipse" by Joe Kiempisty
- ✔ "Paid Off, Baby" by Joe Kiempisty

If You Have Problems (Of the CD Kind)

I tried my best to compile programs that work on most computers with the minimum system requirements. Alas, your computer may differ, and some programs may not work properly for some reason.

The two likeliest problems are that you don't have enough memory (RAM) for the programs you want to use, or you have other programs running that are affecting installation or running of a program. If you get error messages like `Not enough memory` or `Setup cannot continue`, try one or more of these methods and then try using the software again:

- ✔ **Turn off any anti-virus software that you have on your computer.** Installers sometimes mimic virus activity and may make your computer incorrectly believe that it is being infected by a virus.

- ✔ **Close all running programs.** The more programs you're running, the less memory is available to other programs. Installers also typically update files and programs; if you keep other programs running, installation may not work properly.

- ✔ **In Windows, close the CD interface and run demos or installations directly from Windows Explorer.** The interface itself can tie up system memory, or even conflict with certain kinds of interactive demos. Use Windows Explorer to browse the files on the CD and launch installers or demos.

✔ **Have your local computer store add more RAM to your computer.** This is, admittedly, a drastic and somewhat expensive step. However, if you have a Windows 95 PC or a Mac OS computer with a PowerPC chip, adding more memory can really help the speed of your computer and enable more programs to run at the same time.

If you still have trouble installing the items from the CD, please call the IDG Books Worldwide Customer Service phone number: 800-762-2974 (outside the U.S.: 317-572-3343).

The Music Online Directory

The 5th Wave — By Rich Tennant

"It's a site devoted to the 'Limp Korn Chilies' rock group. It has videos of all their performances in concert halls, hotel rooms, and airport terminals."

In this directory . . .

Music online means everything from Net radio to MP3s and buying CDs. In this directory, I cover all the basics. I discuss some of these sites in greater detail elsewhere in the book.

Sites are always changing, of course, especially as the world of music online evolves. Keep this in mind while surfing.

In these pages, you can get sites for:

- ✔ Finding music
- ✔ Buying music
- ✔ Getting information about music
- ✔ Finding info on your favorite bands

About This Directory

To use the directory, all you need to do is browse through it, read the descriptions that appeal to you, and then visit those sites.

To help you judge at a glance whether a site may be useful to you, this directory includes some handy miniature icons (otherwise known as *micons*). Here's an explanation of what each micon means:

$ You have to pay a fee to access some services at this site.

     This site gives you a chance to talk to fellow music fans, musicians, and even pop stars.

     You can download software or other files at this site.

     Information about electronic commerce or shopping-cart software is available at this site.

     This site has particularly good hyperlinks, which can be very useful for music online research.

     Turn up the volume; this site contains audio files.

★★
★★   This site is truly worthy of a four-star rating. It's a particularly valuable resource due to its content, links, free software, or all of these.

Artists

Many bands are Webheads, but some are using the Internet for a more ambitious purpose: to reach their fans directly. No label. No publicist. No middleman. It's cheap, grass roots, and, in the textbook spirit of rock, totally D-I-Y. For now, most record companies don't mind letting their bands handle the Web work – as long as no one's uploading new releases for the download.

Man or Astro-man?

www.astroman.com

Spacey indie band site: Like Devo, their spiritual forefathers, Man or Astro-man? carries the geek rock torch. They dress up in spacesuits, purport to come from another planet, and, of course, are fluent in HTML Web programming.

The result is an exhaustive resource for such a relatively unknown group, complete with rampant band postings, tour diaries, and an Astro-store selling asteroid fragments. The band's strong Web presence just goes to show how a band on an indie label, Touch and Go, can tweak a more impressive site than the majors.

Prince

www.npgonlineltd.com

Everything about Prince: Since emancipating himself from Warner Bros. Records, Prince has become the king of D-I-Y marketing. Consider his Web site: the clearinghouse for his music and musings.

Billing itself as "a collective conscience of unity, love and truth," the site flexes his usual style (new-agey floating globes, purple font), plus info on Prince's charitable clothing drives. It's a royal love-in . . . with preorders of new albums thrown in for good measure.

Radiohead

www.radiohead.com

Official site for Radiohead: Word has it that Radiohead originally wanted to release *O.K. Computer* on their Web site, but their label balked. Too bad. The CD's Orwellian space rock would provide perfect accompaniment. Radiohead ditches the usual band site fare (bio, photos, discography, and so on) for a minimalist satire of online bombast. Links are spelled out generically, "link." Merchandise are W.A.S.T.E. products. And to get through the site, you're forced to check off different "reasons for temporary lulls in productive thinking." Moshing is no excuse.

Squirrel Nut Zippers

www.snzippers.com

Southern comfort at this band's home page: Looking for a baritone saxophone with deep A key, late 1970s/early 1980s model? Well, the Squirrel Nut Zippers have got one for you, all for the low, low price of $1,700! The Carolina swingers' homespun Web site is like a neighborhood garage sale. Everything's on discount or display, from the band's used instruments to banjo player Katharine Whalen's still-life paintings. Oh yeah, you can also find weekly updates on the band's road life, too.

Ween

http://chocodog.tradenet.net/ween

Ween's wacky Web hub: Guitarist Dean Ween tweaks his warped chameleon duo's site from a tape-strewn room in his New Hope abode. You see every-once-and-a-while updates complete with concert dates, plus – for intrepid fans – info on how to help get the band to come to your town. Best of all, Dean is his own best bootlegger; he regularly digitizes live shows and old four tracks for online consumption. Until you've heard the "Grab Bag of 4 Track 'Doody,'" you haven't lived.

Other Sites to Check Out

Beastie Boys
   www.beastieboys.com

David Bowie
   www.davidbowie.com

R.E.M.
   www.remhq.com

Classical Music Sites

Bach and Beethoven have found their place online alongside Korn and Puff Daddy. Classical music sites are still a bit few and far between, especially relative to rock and pop sites, but you can still find plenty of good information available. And music, too.

Classical Net

www.classical.net

Classical composers galore: For a crash course on classical composers – their work, their lives, and their legacies – this site has it all. This site also provides a link to discussion areas where you can take up the conversation on whether, for example, current conductors can truly interpret the classics as they were meant to be heard.

Classical Music on the Web

www.musicweb.uk.net

Classical chat: Run out of England, this site offers its own bulletin boards and forums dedicated to classical music. Fans can find CD Reviews and composer profiles, as well as news and links to other classical resources around the Web.

Other Sites to Check Out

ClassicWeb
www.classicweb.com

Essentials Of Music
www.essentialsofmusic.com

Collectibles

Hankering for a Yellow Submarine lunchbox or a Dolly Parton oven mitt (okay, maybe that doesn't really exist)? The Net offers all kinds of pit stops to pick up the sublime and mundane of music collectibles.

ArtRock

www.artrock.com

Vintage posters for sale: This site has all the groovy concert posters from your – or your parents' – forgotten youth. May as well pick up a Woodstock backstage pass while you're here.

The Jazz Store

www.thejazzstore.com

Jazz goods: Miles Davis. John Coltrane. Ella Fitzgerald. If those names bring music to your ears, boot up the Jazz Store for all kinds of bebop merchandise: calendars, music stands, even a swinging Santa Christmas tree ornament.

Jukeboxes Etc.

www.jukeboxesetc.com

Jukeboxes to go: If you're hankering to have a vintage Wurlitzer jukebox in your basement, visit this site, which specializes in jukeboxes from the 1940s – today. Average price? Roughly $3,000 to $5,000. But you never have to waste anymore quarters again.

123 Posters

www.123posters.com

Contemporary posters central: This poster depot offers hundreds of artists to choose from, from classics like the Grateful Dead to the latest pop bands like the Backstreet Boys. The perfect place to shop for posters – whether you're lining your dorm room or your high school locker.

Rockabilia

www.rockabilia.com

Rock 'n' roll memorabilia: Looking for a backstage pass from the original Woodstock or a Grateful Dead mousepad? Rockabilia handles all these classic rock collectibles online. Choose from buttons and pins to shot glasses and lighters (just the things you need to wave during that next encore).

Other Sites to Check Out

Hollywood U.S.A.
www.hollywood-usa1.com

Peace Rock
www.peacerock.com

Vroom
www.vroom.com

Country

Country music fans gather at these rodeos. As with classical music sites, you won't find nearly as many country hangouts as rock and pop hangouts. But you can find a lot of useful information, generally not limited to the music, but covering the culture as well.

Country.com

www.country.com

Country living: Hank Williams, Jr., Dolly Parton, monster trucks: Whatever flavor of country life you crave can be found at Country.com. Run by The Nashville Network, this site gives you all the latest news and info on your favorite country stars and events.

The Roughstock Network

www.roughstock.com

Country music sound files: This site, heavy on the Garth Brooks stuff, is aimed at contemporary country music fans. The COWPIE archives feature chords and sheet music for those who want to try their hand at picking, while the Country Countdown brings you sound clips and weekly charts.

Other Sites to Check Out

CountryCool.com
www.countrycool.com

CountryNow.com
www.countrynow.com

2Steppin.com
www.2steppin.com

Custom CDs

Miss the old days of making the ultimate mix tape? Custom CD sites let you pick and choose songs for your own personal CD. You pay per song, as well as for shipping and packaging. But for those looking for a quick hit of favorite tunes, customized CDs is a speedy way to go.

CustomDisc

www.customdisc.com

Easy to make CDs: CustomDisc offers one of the best interfaces around for CD compilation. All the songs you click are viewable in a handy little window, so you can play around with the order to set just the right mood.

MusicMaker

www.musicmaker.com

Massive CD song choices: MusicMaker burns your own D-I-Y CD based on choices you make from over 150,000 songs. In the United States, a minimum order of $9.95 per disc gets you about five songs; each additional song after that costs $1. A handy drop-down menu keeps tabs on how much time you have left on your disc.

Other Sites to Check Out

Amplified.com
    www.amplified.com

EZCD
    www.ezcd.com

Orbit Music
    www.orbitmusic.com

Digital Downloads

It hasn't taken long for people to get the bright idea that not only can you download digital music, you can sell it, too. The idea works similarly to other pay-to-download deals for software: Pay a price on your credit card and then suck down the goods.

It's certainly a great idea, not only saving you trips to the record store, but also the postage on ordinary online purchases. For more information on how to listen to digital music on your computer, see Chapter 9.

EMusic

www.emusic.com

Digital download superstore: EMusic is firmly entrenched in the future of music distribution. The Web site deals exclusively in selling downloadable MP3 songs. Selections, as is usually the case, run along the lines of electronica, hip-hop, and indie rock.

To get the music, you must have your own MP3 player and a credit card. Pick the song you want and EMusic charges about 99 cents. An entire album is around $8.99; an EP, $4.99.

Liquid Music Network

www.liquidmusicnetwork.com

Alternative to RealAudio: Liquid Audio supports the MP3 format and all the leading file formats for music online. The artists who release their music in Liquid Audio format range from indie bands to major artists, such as Queen and Beck.

Mjuice

www.mjuice.com

Legal MP3s for purchase: One of the biggest concerns about MP3 distribution is copyright infringement (see Chapter 5 for more information about legalities). Mjuice is a digital music retailer online that's taken a few extra steps to protect artists.

All of its songs are formatted in a special Mjuice way that ensures that only the person who downloads the music can listen to it. After registering for free, you purchase Mjuice dollars to get the music; songs cost about $1 each.

Other Sites to Check Out

A2B music
www.a2bmusic.com

Direct Audio
www.directaudio.com

Play Hear.com
www.playhear.com

Electronica

Electronica, dance, techno: Whatever you want to call it, this computer-friendly back-drop for rave culture was tailor-made for the Net. Fans of this genre have helped spearhead the MP3 revolution, using digital music at house parties around the world.

Beatseek

www.beatseek.com

Electronica news and views: This site is an excellent place for finding electronic music, news, information, and techno fans. If you're an aspiring DJ, you can surf the directory of DJ resources or the links to Internet audio files and wares.

Hyperreal

www.hyperreal.org

Techno commune online: Since the dawn of the Web in 1994, Hyperreal has been the sprawling source for all things techno: music, culture, lifestyle, and raves. The site started when the founder mooched bandwidth from his employers to launch SFRaves, a rave mailing list.

Today, Hyperreal is a thriving community made up of hundreds of volunteers. They provide info on everything from national weekly raves to the best new wares for the DJ sect.

Other Sites to Check Out

Beatflow.com
www.beatflow.com

DJ Rhythms
www.djrhythms.com

Fan Sites

No matter what kind of music you listen to, you can find like-minded fans on the Internet. And just where do they hangout? Most of the time, they're surfing each other's sites. Here's a look at some of the major sandbars for different kinds of music fans available out on the waves.

iMusic

www.imusic.com

Humongous fan haven: Run by ARTISTdirect, the company behind the Ultimate Band List (see Chapter 7 for more information about the UBL), iMusic is home to over 1.5 million music fans of all shapes and sizes.

You can search for message boards by typing in the band name in the artist search section. Or you can join in on discussion topics ranging from Beck's latest release to Lil' Kim's latest garb. You can also find featured long-term discussions on such erstwhile topics as rock versus rap or misheard lyrics.

Yahoo! Clubs

http://clubs.yahoo.com/music

Do-it-yourself music clubs: Lately, search engines have been getting into the community game with their own special interest, D-I-Y clubs. Yahoo! has capitalized on its formidable traffic of surfers with its own active communities. Basically anyone can start their own club – complete with chat, message boards, Web pages, and multimedia files. Club topics range from car audio to songwriter.

Other Sites to Check Out

Excite People & Chat: Music
www.excite.com/communities/entertainment/music

Go Music Message Boards
http://boards.go.com/cgi/entertainment/request.dll?LIST&room=Music&topics=1

Hip-Hop

Hip-hop artists were into computer sampling long before digital music came into vogue. It's no wonder that hip-hop and rhythm and blues communities have been growing online at such a rapid pace. Here's a listen.

aka.com

www.aka.com

Links to hip-hop: Sort of like a Web ring, aka.com is a network of over 125 hip-hop oriented sites. The main page is a great launch pad for reviews of hip-hop songs and countless digital music files. The site features its own bulletin board where aspiring DJs can do battle with their latest rhymes or just shoot the breeze.

Support Online Hip-Hop

www.sohh.com

Hip-Hop community: Since 1996, Support Online Hip-Hop has been doing just that. Rap fans from around the world have been hanging out here, discussing the latest MCs, swapping thoughts on East Coast versus West Coast battles, and rallying together around the music they love. SOHH hosts an annual awards show for the best hip-hop sites online.

Vibe

www.vibe.com

Vibe's homepage: The Web site for *Vibe* magazine is a good place to stay informed about and connected to the hip-hop, R&B, and funk music scene. In addition to reading features and reviews from the magazine, you can chat with other fans.

Other Sites to Check Out

HipHopSite.com
www.hiphopsite.com

The Source
www.thesource.com

Independent, Imports, and Hard-to-Find Music

The expression *hard-to-find* was obviously invented long before the Internet. Nothing, it seems, is hard to find anymore, now that so many people have taken to selling online.

For fans of independent, import, or other niche music, there's no better place to start searching than the Web.

MusicFile

www.musicfile.com

Rare music goods: Can't find what you're looking for at the usual suspects' sites? This is your place! Recently acquired by Amazon.com, MusicFile has all kinds of obscure vinyl and plastic (that's tapes and CDs).

You can even post your needs in the accompanying message boards and hope that another fan, with the magic music, surfs on by. Then, you have to make a deal.

Independent Distribution Network

www.idnmusic.com

Indie store central: The IDN site is basically a hub for independent record dealers who specialize in categories from children's music to electronica. This is where heavy metal fans can find obscure, new music from the band Neptune or a self-titled vinyl album by The Creeps.

Dr. Wax

www.drwax.com

Vinyl fever: The good Dr. Wax specializes in vinyl records, new and old. Based in Illinois, Dr. Wax serves up plenty of new independent releases, especially in the areas of indie rock and hip-hop. Posters, videos, and CDs are also on the menu.

Other Sites to Check Out

Backtrack Records
www.backtrackrecords.com

Vinyl 4 Ever
www.vinyl4ever.com

Instruments and Equipment

Crank up that guitar or bang your drum. Whether you're in a band or just always wanted to be, you can find plenty of places online to buy up instruments and equipment.

Sam Ash

www.samash.com

Band equipment: The Web site for this national retailer has all the goods: guitars, drums, synthesizers, and even those little plastic eggs you can shake for percussion. Some holiday seasons, the site even offers free shipping – just the thing you need if you're buying a new pair of monster congas.

The DJ Store

www.thedjstore.com

DJ stuff: Wedding DJs and electronica ravers can stock up at the DJ Store, an online retailer specializing in dance party wares. Pick up some vintage turntables or even your own Magnum Pro Smoke Machine. Just the thing for your next house party.

Other Sites to Check Out

eBopp
www.ebopp.com

Pulse Music
www.pulseonline.com

Roxy's Music Store
www.roxys.com

Jazz and Blues

Fans of Miles Davis or John Lee Hooker can find community on these sites. Jazz sites can be as thorough and encyclopedic as jazz music fans are themselves. Cool sunglasses, optional.

The Blue Highway

www.thebluehighway.com

Homespun blues info: This homemade site chronicles the lowdown blues world of Muddy Waters, John Lee Hooker, and the rest. You find regular news and essays on the site, plus an active topic board where you can swap blues MP3s and discuss big stars like Koko Taylor and lesser-known acts, such as Delaware Joey.

Blue Note Records

www.bluenote.com

Major label home page: The famous Blue Note Records has defined jazz since 1939. Recently, the label launched an accompanying Web site. In addition to information about the company's artists and culture, an active message board lets fans discuss new releases and recommend albums.

Jazz Online

www.jazzonline.com

Everything jazz: Jazz Online is a massive resource and community dedicated to all things jazz. You can find discussion boards on dozens of different artists, plus reviews, feature articles, Liquid Audio music downloads, and a Jazz 101 educational series covering styles from hard bop to fusion.

Other Sites to Check Out

Jazz Stuff
www.jazzstuff.com

JazzWorld.Com
www.jazzworld.com

Warner Bros. JazzSpace
www.wbjazz.com

MP3 Sites

Yes, the Web contains thousands of sites out there that collect MP3 songs. But a few hubs are emerging from the buzz. Here's a look at some of the bigger sites offering free digital music.

MP3.com

www.mp3.com

MP3's main hub: The mother ship of all MP3 sites, MP3.com is the place to start your journey for new MP3 music. And I emphasize the word *new*. What you won't find here are songs by bands that already line your record shelves. MP3.com, instead, mainly features music by independent and unsigned artists.

Yes, there is definitely a reason why some of these bands don't have record deals – they're just not very good. But there are always the prospects of a future star in the making – or just someone who's worth a listen, but maybe outside the radar of the popular music machine.

A recently revamped interface makes it easy to browse through the most picayune categories: from East Coast Hip-Hop to Rock en Español. You can also search by artist, region, musical genre, or according to MP3.com's own weekly charts – based on the most frequently downloaded songs on the service.

Musicmatch

www.musicmatch.com

The MP3 player's pit stop: The homepage for the popular MP3 software player is competing with MP3.com as a hub for free MP3 music. MusicMatch features many of its own artists – searchable by artist name, genre, or hometown.

RioPort

www.rioport.com

MP3 links: Diamond Rio, the most popular MP3 portable player, has launched this accompanying Web site. Similar to Winamp, the site has amassed its own formidable collection of MP3 audio – including a fair share of spoken word, such as old time radio shows and poetry.

Winamp

www.winamp.com

Winamp mania: Like MusicMatch, Winamp offers its own selection of potentially awesome or terrible MP3 artists. This time around, though, you can blame or thank the employees at Nullsoft, Winamp's developer.

They've gathered their own favorite MP3 files and put them up on their homepage, along with others by various e-friendly artists. Even better, Winamp – by virtue of being one of the more ubiquitous MP3 players on the planet – attracts a lot of cool extras, such as a recent package from Beck; this one included a groovy Beck skin along with an MP3 track from his new album.

Other Sites to Check Out

Dimension Music
www.dimensionmusic.com

DailyMP3.com
www.dailymp3.com

Sonique
www.sonique.com

MP3 Search Sites

Outside of the main MP3 music hubs, you can have a go at search engines tailored specifically for finding digital audio. Like any search engine, finding good search results means being a good searcher – using appropriate keywords and combinations to unearth the songs you're craving.

Listen

www.listen.com

Legal song search: This professionally run site is a clean and fresh spot for finding legal MP3s; the site edits its picks, so you find only copyright-protected artists here. One nice feature is that the site suggests bands that are similar to popular artists. Type in **Madonna** and you get links to up-and-coming wannabes, such as Holly or Aura & Diva.

Lycos

www.mp3.lycos.com

For combing MP3s on the Web: Of all the major search engines, Lycos has committed itself most to the MP3 revolution. The good news is that it's got one of the fastest MP3 search engines around.

Just type in the name of your favorite band and artist, press Enter, and boom! You get pages of files based on a search of more than 1,000 MP3 computer servers. The bad news is that using this site is a lot like tossing a real fishing net into a murky lake; it's up to you to pull out the weeds. (In this case, that means the illegal or faulty MP3 files.)

MP3now.com

www.mp3now.com

More MP3 links: This ever-expanding site lets you search for your favorite MP3 songs or artists. It also packs in its own formidable library of MP3 resource information about hardware, software, news, and other important up-to-date information.

2Look4

www.2look4.com

Search for MP3s: Another search site specializing in MP3s. This stripped-down site is similar to Lycos, except that it enables you to scale down the reliability levels so that you can search for unreliable stuff as well (if you're really a serious collector). It also has a neat feature in that it lets you see the last 20 MP3 items that were searched for on the site. You may be surprised what people really want.

Other Sites to Check Out

FileQuest
www.filequest.com

MP123
www.mp123.com

Oth
www.oth.net

Music Clubs

At some point or another, almost everyone has signed up by filling out one of the ubiquitous magazine postcards to join a record and tape club. For just a penny (or something like that), you get several CDs as long as you promise to buy a certain number of CDs somewhere down the line.

BMG Music Service

www.bmgmusicservice.com

Music club's home: BMG offers 12 CDs for the price of 1, if you sign up for its membership plan. And don't worry about getting hooked, if you run out of cash you can even pick up your very own BMG credit card. Ouch.

Columbia House

www.columbiahouse.com

Columbia House's hangout: The gargantuan music club Columbia House brings all its services to its equally gargantuan Web site. You can browse through all the latest hits and specials, or read up on special artists in editorial features.

While you're here, you can also sign up for DVD and computer game clubs if you've got the extra pennies.

Other Sites to Check Out

The CD Club Web Server
    www.cd-clubs.com

EveryCD
    www.everycd.com

Music Videos

With streaming media players (see Chapter 3 for more information), surfers can now tune in to music videos online. Now, you don't have to wait for MTV or VH1 to show your favorite video; you can just boot it up on the Net.

That's the good news.

The bad news: bandwidth. Because music videos are fat with data, they have a little trouble squeezing through an average modem. The result is choppy viewing. Just as a video gets started, you may see the singer suddenly freeze. No, he's not break dancing; he's just stuck in transfer. Those with broadband connections, such as a T1 or cable modem, however, can view a fairly nice, consistent image.

LAUNCH

www.launch.com

Music videos on demand: After scoring a deal to host every video from every artist associated with Warner Music Group, LAUNCH has become a formidable competitor to MTV online. Madonna, R.E.M. – they're all here. Stay tuned for more.

MTV

www.mtv.com

MTV's massive site: MTV has – no surprise – a massive collection of videos available on its Web site. On the main page, you can search for your specific favorite band or use the drop-down menus to scroll to an artist by name.

Surfing on this site is like being in a music video library. In addition to all the popular videos you see on TV, you get all kinds of arcane clips from MTV's well – including live in-studio gigs.

Video SonicNet

www.sonicnet.com/videos/

Eclectic music videos: Run by SonicNet, a popular music news and entertainment site, this video haven is like having your own multimedia jukebox. Browse through hundreds of songs arranged in categories including rock or urban. You can search by band name as well.

VH1

www.vh1.com

VH1's online home: MTV's sister network, VH1, offers its own library of videos geared toward music fans in their 20s and 30s. Click Sounds and Visions on the main menu and you can find archives of streaming audio and video.

Bonuses include previously unreleased footage from VH1 live performances like the *Storytellers* series – a show-and-tell review featuring artists like Elvis Costello and Tom Waits talking about and playing their music. You can search by artist name as well.

Other Sites to Check Out

The Box
www.thebox.com

MuchMusic
www.muchmusic.com

Vidnet
www.vidnetusa.com

Net Radio

With so much power to do your own thing with Internet radio, many intrepid DJs have been creating shows that only appear online. Sometimes, these shows are like traditional radio broadcasts: playing songs interspersed with chatty banter. Other times, they are full-blown multimedia Webcasts, mixing everything from chat to message boards, gaming, and video.

Green Witch

www.greenwitch.com

D-I-Y radio: There are good witches. There are bad witches. And there is Green Witch, a Net radio production company in San Francisco that aims to be a little of both – helping out grass-roots music lovers while scrambling the digital music machine.

Hard Radio

www.hardradio.com

Hard rock Net radio: Today, the Hard Radio database includes about 1,500 songs. Though fans are likely to hear whiplash faves like Megadeth and Whitesnake, they can also get a heavy dose of indie tough guys like Union and In Flames.

KCRW — Morning Becomes Electric

www.kcrw.com

 ★★ ★★

Awesome performances and interviews: KCRW, an eclectic station in Santa Monica, has attracted an online cult following for its show, *Morning Becomes Eclectic:* an interview program that has featured rare appearances and performances by artists like Tom Waits and P.J. Harvey.

Pseudo

www.pseudo.com

Internet TV: For the past half-decade, the company located in the heart of New York's Silicon Alley has been using a Batbelt of wares to create a new school of radio broadcasting that combines audio, video, chat, message boards, and, well, basically, you name it.

When booting up any one of Pseudo's shows, surfers get to choose from real-time audio and/or video streams. Rather than having to dial a studio line and pray to get through, surfers can directly e-mail questions or participate in chat.

The Womb

www.thewomb.com

Miami-based techno: Home to more than 60 amateur DJs, producers, artists, and writers from around the world, The Womb is something of a perpetual electronica recital – and you don't even have to endure "Chopsticks."

Since July 1998, The Womb has parlayed its worldwide reach into worldwide content. DJs from the States to Japan take turns spinning their own two-hour shows. In Miami, local spinners regularly drop by Graziadei's studio to have a go. Every show is archived for future listening pleasures and, in all, the tunes add up to 'round-the-clock online radio.

WRTO — Latin Music

www.wrto.com

Latin radio: Craving those Latin beats, check out this site, which broadcasts live from Miami – the center of this pop music explosion. Listen live, take surveys, chat with fans, and keep up on the latest, greatest Latino rhythms.

WWOZ — New Orleans Jazz

www.wwoz.org

Nawlins radio: Live from "Nawlins," WWOZ 90.7 is the place to tune in for your dose of jazz, blues, zydeco, and Cajun rhythms.

Tune in to the latest live broadcast or even browse through the MP3 store to purchase some southern fried music of your own. And, during Mardi Gras, this is the best place to shake your booty, without getting crushed by the crowds.

Other Sites to Check Out

Broadcast Music
www.broadcastmusic.com

Real Guide
www.real.com

Spinner
www.spinner.com

Online Retailers

Amazon.com

www.amazon.com

Amazon.com's superstore: Remember when Amazon.com just sold books? Neither do I. These days, you can find just about everything that's entertainment-oriented on this massive superstore site. Music lovers get the same recommendation services they find when buying books. Plus, you can find plenty of easy gift services, so you can buy a present, get it wrapped, and be on your way.

ARTISTdirect Superstore

www.ubl.com

Band-specific goods: Run by the makers of the sprawling music resource site, the Ultimate Band List (see Chapter 7 for more information on the UBL), this site is basically a music superstore, like it says. You can find deals on everything from CDs to tour jackets, T-shirts, and even stuff like an autographed guitar from the rock band Green Day.

Barnes and Noble

www.bn.com

BN's online store: The Barnes and Noble Web site has crept up on its main competitor, Amazon.com, as one of the premier places to buy books and music online. You find all the usual services – swift searches, gift shopping, audio clips. Plus, you can take advantage of some helpful cross-referencing materials so that when you click one album by a particular artist, you are linked to other related products.

Borders

www.borders.com

Books and more: Borders joins the superstore march online with its own expansive Web site. You can find specials based on the Billboard 100, the top-selling charts from the music industry's main tome. You can also get more than just sound clips of your favorite artists; you can get free bonuses, such as, for Grateful Dead fans, an entire download of the Jerry Garcia song "Deal."

buy.com

www.buy.com

Electronics market: At buy.com you can pick up everything from computers to video games and music. Not only does buy.com sell compact discs, but that old analog format called cassettes, too. And you may even pick up some cheap electronics, like CD players and receivers. For even better deals, buy.com offers a low-price guarantee – if you've got the time to hunt down a cheaper price, this site matches it.

DVD EXPRESS

www.dvdexpress.com

DVD deluxe shopping: This site carries everything and anything that's in DVD – including a great selection of concert films, music video compilations, and music-related documentaries. The bonus of DVD music video is that they often come packed with groovy little extras.

For $22, a copy of Pink Floyd's quintessential midnight movie, *The Wall,* comes with previously unreleased footage and interviews with the band.

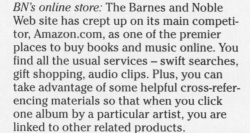

HMV

www.hmv.com

HMV's Web shop: HMV is another offline mega-retailer that's offering its goods and services online. Because it's based in Canada, many of the prices are in Canadian currency. When translated to other denominations, though, they're still good deals.

Tower Records

www.towerrecords.com

Tower's e-commerce site: Tower Records, the well-known entertainment retailer, has a sprawling Web site. Here, you're almost sure to find anything by Top-40 artists, plus plenty of obscure stuff along the way.

Tunes.com

www.tunes.com

CDs and MP3s for sale: Tunes.com sells all kinds of CDs and MP3s. It also does a good job resurrecting the grand old shopping ally: the listening booth. Tunes.com features RealAudio clips of many of the records it sells; just click the highlighted song and see how you like it (or hate it).

Virgin Megastore

www.virginmega.com

Virgin's superstore online: Like Tower Records, Virgin Megastore has helped pioneer the superstore approach to shopping. Their Web site offers a similarly expansive selection of popular CDs. They've also sweetened the deal with juicy sales and promotions, with savings up to 40 percent off what you may find in a store. The site offers videos and other music-related merchandise.

Other Sites to Check Out

Camelot Music
www.camelotmusic.com

CD Warehouse
www.cdwarehouse.com

Music.com
www.music.com

Yes, rock 'n' roll is a massive category — so massive that it defies categorization. If you're looking for sites that let you sample the variety of rock's many colors, read on.

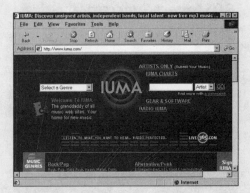

Internet Underground Music Archive

www.iuma.com

Unknown bands: If you're looking to stay on the cutting edge of new and unsigned artists, IUMA is the place. Several years before MP3.com, this site offered space to artists who wanted to spread their word online.

Now you can surf at leisure, download new songs, and check out artists that tend to run along the alternative and indie rock lines.

Rolling Stone

www.rollingstone.com

Rolling Stone's Web site: Run by the popular rock magazine, the *Rolling Stone* Web site features daily news, reviews, and e-commerce specials. The site also offers a lively message board area with topics ranging from your last record store purchase to individual artists like Britney Spears.

SonicNet

www.sonicnet.com

Multimedia music site: This site (which, incidentally, I used to work for) has been around since its early days as a bulletin board service in 1994. These days, it's a massive music network, offering everything from streaming music videos (see Chapter 7 for information about their site, SonicNet) to celebrity chat, news, and reviews.

Spin

www.spin.com

Spin's online home: Spin magazine's online home, with interviews, news, downloads, and excerpts from the print magazine.

Other Sites to Check Out

GoGirlsMusic.com
www.gogirlsmusic.com

Rock Online
www.rockonline.com

Sheet Music

To play along with your favorite bands, you've either got to have a good ear, a convincing air guitar, or a nice, fat sheath of sheet music. Online, sheet music dealers have taken the obvious step by delivering sheet music in digital form. Just fill out your credit card info, select the desired sheet music, and download the notes.

Sheet Music Direct

www.sheetmusicdirect.com

Sheet music to go: This international sheet music dealer has put the whole transaction online. First, you download the special MusicPage software that lets you view the sheet music on your PC. You can search by song title, artist, or notation style. Simply order the song you want and then download it for future reference. Pick not included.

Sheet Music Plus

www.sheetmusicplus.com

More sheet music: This site features a wide selection of popular, classical, and instructional sheet music. There's also frequent specials on artists ranging from the Beatles to Jimmy Buffett.

Other Sites to Check Out

Free Sheet Music
www.freesheetmusic.com

Music Students
www.musicstudents.com

Score Online
www.score-on-line.com

Stereo Equipment

You probably wouldn't be searching for music online unless you had some kind of stereo system at home. Though there's nothing that quite captures the experience of listening to a potential piece of stereo equipment first hand, there's a great opportunity to find discounts and specials online.

My advice: Shop with your ears offline and then move online to find the best deals.

Circuit City

www.circuitcity.com

Stereo stuff: The offline retail electronics chain has a wide selection of audio equipment available through its Web site. You can find Net-only specials and even contests for free stereos. A wide selection of home and car stereo products is also available.

Stereo Liquidators

www.stereoliquidators.com

Stereo deals: For 30 years offline, Stereo Liquidators has been offering rock bottom prices on rocking stereo equipment. They have everything from CD players to sub-woofers, speakers, and, for those on the go, portables.

Other Sites to Check Out

Adcom
   www.adcom.com
The Sound Professionals
   www.soundpros.com

Tickets

Wouldn't it be nice to buy concert tickets without having to listen to busy signals or wait in long lines? These days, you can cut to the chase and shop for seats online.

Sold Out

www.soldout.com

Sold out tickets: The show's sold out? Don't cry. Surf to this site. They have plenty of available tickets for the hottest shows in town. And be prepared to pay. A pair of seats for a Bruce Springsteen show might run as much as $1,000. But if you're a fan, it's well worth the price. Right?

Ticketmaster

www.Ticketmaster.com

Ticketmaster's domain: Everything starts here. Ticketmaster has more tickets than any other site. And it has all the services you need, from a personalized My Ticketmaster tool that updates you when your favorite band comes to town, to electronic tickets you can print from your own PC.

Ticket Web

www.ticketweb.com

Low-fee tickets: Worried about high service fees? This site has fewer tickets than Ticketmaster, but it's set on only charging you a buck per seat. The venues tend to be smaller, but if you look hard, you might actually find tickets for shows you gave up on at other sites.

WebTix

www.webtix.com

Want ads for tickets: Launched four years ago, this classifieds-only ticket haven claims to be the first to provide such a service online. Sure, you might find just as many deals on eBay, but WebTix is unique in that it lets you post want ads, something unavailable at other ticket sites.

A word of caution: Many of the ads are simply fronts for brokers (surprise, surprise), but because the classifieds are updated hourly, you can occasionally get lucky and find something golden before it gets snatched.

Other Sites to Check Out

Bass Tickets
www.basstickets.com

Culture Finder
www.culturefinder.com

T-Shirts

What's a music fan without a commemorative T-shirt? Now you don't have to schlep to a concert to get one. Though, actually, that's probably more fun than clicking your mouse.

Kung Fu Nation

www.kungfunation.com

Hip tees: This ultra-indie T-shirt company out of Raleigh, North Carolina makes shirts for iconoclastic rockers like Beck, Pavement, and Cibo Matto. Sorry, no iron-ons.

Star 500

www.star500.com

Band shirts: This is the place to find shirts from artists ranging from the Doors to Alice in Chains. Fortunately, the shirts are better looking than this Web site.

Other Sites to Check Out

CountryTees.com
www.countrytees.com

Future Primitive
www.futureprimitive.com

Gear Ink
www.gearink.com

World Music

Where better than the World Wide Web to enjoy and explore some world music?

Roots World

www.rootsworld.com

World tunes: Bagpipes? Accordions? Indonesian guitars? Whatever your world music fancy, Roots World has something for you. This site is truly global in its scope, offering links and information on folk artists from the U.S. to India.

Folk Roots

www.froots.demon.co.uk

Folk Roots magazine's homepage: This world music site, based in England, is the offshoot of a magazine of the same name. You get news and reviews, plus updates on world music events like WOMAD.

Other Sites to Check Out

Luaka Bop
www.luakabop.com

New Native
www.wcpworld.com

Index

• X •

Xaudio Player, 284

• Y •

Yahoo! Clubs
  creating, 134, 135
  naming, 135
  overview of, 134
  Web site, D-14
Yahoo! Digital Web site, 119
Yahoo! Full Coverage — Digital Copyright
     Law, 274
Yahoo! Full Coverage — MP3 and Digital
     Music, 274
Yahoo! Geocities Web site, 186, 187
Yahoo! search engine, 12, 188

• Z •

ZDNet Music News Web site, 270
zines. *See* e-zines
Zip drive (Iomega), 39

Notes

Notes

Notes

Notes

IDG Books Worldwide, Inc., End-User License Agreement

READ THIS. You should carefully read these terms and conditions before opening the software packet(s) included with this book ("Book"). This is a license agreement ("Agreement") between you and IDG Books Worldwide, Inc. ("IDGB"). By opening the accompanying software packet(s), you acknowledge that you have read and accept the following terms and conditions. If you do not agree and do not want to be bound by such terms and conditions, promptly return the Book and the unopened software packet(s) to the place you obtained them for a full refund.

1. **License Grant.** IDGB grants to you (either an individual or entity) a nonexclusive license to use one copy of the enclosed software program(s) (collectively, the "Software") solely for your own personal or business purposes on a single computer (whether a standard computer or a workstation component of a multiuser network). The Software is in use on a computer when it is loaded into temporary memory (RAM) or installed into permanent memory (hard disk, CD-ROM, or other storage device). IDGB reserves all rights not expressly granted herein.

2. **Ownership.** IDGB is the owner of all right, title, and interest, including copyright, in and to the compilation of the Software recorded on the disk(s) or CD-ROM ("Software Media"). Copyright to the individual programs recorded on the Software Media is owned by the author or other authorized copyright owner of each program. Ownership of the Software and all proprietary rights relating thereto remain with IDGB and its licensers.

3. **Restrictions on Use and Transfer.**

   (a) You may only (i) make one copy of the Software for backup or archival purposes, or (ii) transfer the Software to a single hard disk, provided that you keep the original for backup or archival purposes. You may not (i) rent or lease the Software, (ii) copy or reproduce the Software through a LAN or other network system or through any computer subscriber system or bulletin-board system, or (iii) modify, adapt, or create derivative works based on the Software.

   (b) You may not reverse engineer, decompile, or disassemble the Software. You may transfer the Software and user documentation on a permanent basis, provided that the transferee agrees to accept the terms and conditions of this Agreement and you retain no copies. If the Software is an update or has been updated, any transfer must include the most recent update and all prior versions.

4. **Restrictions on Use of Individual Programs.** You must follow the individual requirements and restrictions detailed for each individual program in the "About the CD" section of this Book. These limitations are also contained in the individual license agreements recorded on the Software Media. These limitations may include a requirement that after using the program for a specified period of time, the user must pay a registration fee or discontinue use. By opening the Software packet(s), you will be agreeing to abide by the licenses and restrictions for these individual programs that are detailed in the "About the CD" section and on the Software Media. None of the material on this Software Media or listed in this Book may ever be redistributed, in original or modified form, for commercial purposes.

5. **Limited Warranty.**

   (a) IDGB warrants that the Software and Software Media are free from defects in materials and workmanship under normal use for a period of sixty (60) days from the date of purchase of this Book. If IDGB receives notification within the warranty period of defects in materials or workmanship, IDGB will replace the defective Software Media.

   (b) IDGB AND THE AUTHOR OF THE BOOK DISCLAIM ALL OTHER WARRANTIES, EXPRESS OR IMPLIED, INCLUDING WITHOUT LIMITATION IMPLIED WARRANTIES OF MERCHANTABILITY AND FITNESS FOR A PARTICULAR PURPOSE, WITH RESPECT TO THE SOFTWARE, THE PROGRAMS, THE SOURCE CODE CONTAINED THEREIN, AND/OR THE TECHNIQUES DESCRIBED IN THIS BOOK. IDGB DOES NOT WARRANT THAT THE FUNCTIONS CONTAINED IN THE SOFTWARE WILL MEET YOUR REQUIRE-MENTS OR THAT THE OPERATION OF THE SOFTWARE WILL BE ERROR FREE.

   (c) This limited warranty gives you specific legal rights, and you may have other rights that vary from jurisdiction to jurisdiction.

6. **Remedies.**

   (a) IDGB's entire liability and your exclusive remedy for defects in materials and workman-ship shall be limited to replacement of the Software Media, which may be returned to IDGB with a copy of your receipt at the following address: Software Media Fulfillment Department, Attn.: *Music Online For Dummies*, IDG Books Worldwide, Inc., 10475 Crosspoint Blvd., Indianapolis, IN 46256, or call 800-762-2974. Please allow three to four weeks for delivery. This Limited Warranty is void if failure of the Software Media has resulted from accident, abuse, or misapplication. Any replacement Software Media will be warranted for the remainder of the original warranty period or thirty (30) days, whichever is longer.

   (b) In no event shall IDGB or the author be liable for any damages whatsoever (including without limitation damages for loss of business profits, business interruption, loss of business information, or any other pecuniary loss) arising from the use of or inability to use the Book or the Software, even if IDGB has been advised of the possibility of such damages.

   (c) Because some jurisdictions do not allow the exclusion or limitation of liability for conse-quential or incidental damages, the above limitation or exclusion may not apply to you.

7. **U.S. Government Restricted Rights.** Use, duplication, or disclosure of the Software by the U.S. Government is subject to restrictions stated in paragraph (c)(1)(ii) of the Rights in Technical Data and Computer Software clause of DFARS 252.227-7013, and in subparagraphs (a) through (d) of the Commercial Computer–Restricted Rights clause at FAR 52.227-19, and in similar clauses in the NASA FAR supplement, when applicable.

8. **General.** This Agreement constitutes the entire understanding of the parties and revokes and supersedes all prior agreements, oral or written, between them and may not be modified or amended except in a writing signed by both parties hereto that specifically refers to this Agreement. This Agreement shall take precedence over any other documents that may be in conflict herewith. If any one or more provisions contained in this Agreement are held by any court or tribunal to be invalid, illegal, or otherwise unenforceable, each and every other pro-vision shall remain in full force and effect.

Installation Instructions

The *Music Online For Dummies* CD offers valuable information that you won't want to miss. To install the items from the CD to your hard drive, follow these steps.

1. **Insert the CD into your computer's CD-ROM drive.**

   In a moment, an icon representing the CD you just inserted appears on your Mac desktop. Chances are, the icon looks like a CD-ROM.

2. **Double-click the CD icon to show the CD's contents.**

3. **Double-click the Read Me First icon.**

   The Read Me First text file contains information about the CD's programs and any last-minute instructions you may need in order to correctly install them.

4. **To install most programs, just drag the program's folder from the CD window and drop it on your hard drive icon.**

5. **Other programs come with installer programs — with these, you simply open the program's folder on the CD and then double-click the icon with the words "Install" or "Installer."**

   Sometimes the installers are actually self-extracting archives, which just means that the program files have been bundled up into an archive, and this self-extractor unbundles the files and places them on your hard drive. This kind of program is often called an .sea program. Double-click anything with .sea in the title, and it runs just like an installer.

   After you have installed the programs you want, you can eject the CD. Carefully place it back in the plastic jacket of the book for safekeeping.

For more information, see the "About the CD" appendix.

IDG BOOKS WORLDWIDE
BOOK REGISTRATION

We want to hear from you!

Visit **http://my2cents.dummies.com** to register this book and tell us how you liked it!

✔ Get entered in our monthly prize giveaway.

✔ Give us feedback about this book — tell us what you like best, what you like least, or maybe what you'd like to ask the author and us to change!

✔ Let us know any other *For Dummies*® topics that interest you.

Your feedback helps us determine what books to publish, tells us what coverage to add as we revise our books, and lets us know whether we're meeting your needs as a *For Dummies* reader. You're our most valuable resource, and what you have to say is important to us!

Not on the Web yet? It's easy to get started with *Dummies 101*®: *The Internet For Windows*® *98* or *The Internet For Dummies*® at local retailers everywhere.

Or let us know what you think by sending us a letter at the following address:

For Dummies Book Registration
Dummies Press
10475 Crosspoint Blvd.
Indianapolis, IN 46256

BESTSELLING
BOOK SERIES